STUDENT'S BOOK 5

C1

Herbert Puchta, Jeff Stranks & Peter Lewis-Jones

CONTENTS

Welcome p 4 **A** Saying *yes* and adding conditions; *get used to* …; Secrets of love; Love and relationships **B** The bucket list; Verbs with *-ing* or infinitive; Issuing and accepting a challenge; Our greatest challenge; Phrases for talking about the future

	FUNCTIONS & SPEAKING	GRAMMAR	VOCABULARY
Unit 1 Brothers and sisters p 12	Using emotive language Discussing problems with siblings Talking about personal conflict	Talking about habits Adverbs to express attitude	Personality (1) Personal conflict
Unit 2 Sleep on it p 20	Giving advice Talking about dreams Discussing sleeping habits in your country	Past tense with hypothetical meaning Adverbs for modifying comparatives	Sleep Idioms with *sleep* and *dream*
Review Units 1 & 2	pages 28–29		
Unit 3 Lucky breaks p 30	Giving encouragement to someone who's feeling nervous Talking about luck	Mixed conditionals (review) Alternatives to *if*	Phrasal verbs Expressions with *luck* **Wordwise:** Expressions with *over*
Unit 4 Laughter is the best medicine p 38	Responding to jokes Talking about famous comedians	Emphatic structures Boosting	Laughter Idioms with *laugh* and *joke*
Review Units 3 & 4	pages 46–47		
Unit 5 Thrill seekers p 48	Giving and reacting to an opinion Discussion about thrill seeking	Participle clauses Verbs of perception with infinitive or gerund	Thrill seeking Idioms related to noise
Unit 6 Followers p 56	Complaining Discussing sports teams	Modals 1: *may, might, can, could, will, won't* Modals 2: *should, shouldn't, must, mustn't, can't*	Admiration Fame **WordWise:** Expressions with *take*
Review Units 5 & 6	pages 64–65		
Unit 7 Beauty is in the eye of the beholder p 66	Language of persuasion Discussing reactions to the blog	Substitution Ellipsis	Fads Emotional responses
Unit 8 It's all Greek to me! p 74	Saying that you don't understand or didn't fully hear Talking about language	Relative clauses with determiners and prepositions *however, wherever, whatever*, etc.	Language and communication Personality (2)
Review Units 7 & 8	pages 82–83		
Unit 9 Is it fair? p 84	Talking imprecisely about numbers Discussing money	Negative inversion Spoken discourse markers	Court cases Fairness and honesty **Wordwise:** Expressions with *on*
Unit 10 You live and learn p 92	Reacting to news Talking about higher education and you	Reported verb patterns (review) Passive report structures	Higher education Life after school
Review Units 9 & 10	pages 100–101		
Unit 11 21st century living p 102	Telling someone to keep calm Talking about 21st century problems	More on the passive Causative *have* (review) Modal passives (review)	(not) Getting angry Verbs with prefixes *up* and *down*
Unit 12 Unsung heroes p 110	Expressing anticipation Planning a class award Talking about things you'd intended to do but didn't	Future perfect; future continuous (review) Future in the past	Awards Success and failure **WordWise:** Expressions with *in*
Review Units 11 & 12	pages 118–119		

Pronunciation pages 120–121   **Get it right!** pages 122–126   **Speaking activities** pages 127–128

C Cheering someone up and sympathising about past situations; Life's up and downs; A helping hand; Adjectives to describe uncomfortable feelings; Talking about past ability   D Introducing news; Ways of speaking; News mad?; Verb + noun collocations with *make, take, play, do, give*; Cause and effect linkers; Sharing news

PRONUNCIATION	THINK	SKILLS	
Intonation: showing emotions	**Train to Think:** Questioning widely accepted theories **Values:** Relationships	Reading Writing Listening	Article: The pecking order Web page: People power to help you with your problems Literature: *Pride and Prejudice* by Jane Austen An email A scene from a soap opera – *The Street*
Different ways of pronouncing *c* and *g*	**Train to Think:** The rule of threes **Self-esteem:** Getting enough rest	Reading Writing Listening	Magazine article: The great teen sleeping crisis? Article: Ten facts about dreams Culture: Sleep in different cultures A proposal Interview with a sleep expert
Unstressed words in connected speech	**Train to Think:** Behaviour based on myths rather than facts **Values:** How do we feel about luck?	Reading Writing Listening	Magazine article: My lucky break Blog: Serendipity Photo story: The talisman A story Conversation about lucky objects and routines
Telling jokes: pacing, pausing and punchlines	**Train to Think:** Divergent thinking **Self-esteem:** Laughter	Reading Writing Listening	Article: The science of laughter Article: The world of comedy: Shappi Khorsandi Literature: *Three Men in a Boat* by Jerome K. Jerome A review Jokes
Connected speech feature: elision	**Train to Think:** Red herrings **Self-esteem:** Feeling alive	Reading Writing Listening	Article: Daredevil great-great-granny; Gary Connery Article: Can you stand the silence? Report: I've been to the quietest place on Earth. Culture: Top worldwide locations for extreme sports A newspaper article Interview with a psychologist about thrill seekers
Modal stress and meaning	**Train to Think:** Making logical conclusions (syllogisms) **Values:** Teamwork	Reading Writing Listening	Article: What's up with our celebrity obsession? Article: How to avoid the limelight Photostory: A new interest An essay Radio programme: Manchester United fans around the world
Connected speech feature: assimilation	**Train to Think:** Understanding irony **Values:** Valuing the beauty around us	Reading Writing Listening	Article: A history of fitness fads Blog: How would you define beauty? Literature: *Romeo and Juliet* by William Shakespeare; *When you are old* by William Butler Yeats; *Sonnet 18* by William Shakespeare A formal letter Radio programme about beauty fads
Stress in multi-syllable words:	**Train to Think:** Making connections **Values:** Learning another language	Reading Writing Listening	Article: The code-talkers Article: Multilinguals have multiple personalities Culture: multilingual communities around the world A report from a graph Radio programme about accents
Unstressed syllables and words: the /l/ phoneme	**Train to Think:** The *ad hominem* fallacy **Self-esteem:** Does the punishment fit the crime?	Reading Writing Listening	Article: Miscarriages of justice Book review: *What Money Can't Buy* by Michael J. Sandel Photostory: Saving Ms Hampton An essay Radio programme about Halden Prison, Norway
Lexical and non-lexical fillers	**Train to Think:** Doing something for the 'right' reasons **Self-esteem:** The relative importance of higher education	Reading Writing Listening	Review: whatwewatched.com – your guide to last night's television Article: Moosic, and what you probably don't know about it! Literature: *The Daydreamer* by Ian McEwan An essay Life after school
Intonation: mean what you say	**Train to Think:** Do as I say, not as I do **Values:** Modern Life	Reading Writing Listening	Article: Road rage? Pavement rage? Who's to blame, then? Blog: A modern trend: upcycling Culture: The world's last uncontacted tribes A blog post Radio phone-in: Stresses and strains of modern life
Shifting word stress	**Train to Think:** Appropriate sampling **Self-esteem:** Helping others	Reading Writing Listening	Online posts: Wanted: real-life heroes Article: I just wrote to say … thank you! Photostory: Lost and found A newspaper article Presentation about an inspirational man

WELCOME

A LESSONS IN LIFE
Saying yes and adding conditions

1 🔊 1.02 Read the dialogue and complete each space with one word. Listen and check.

LIAM This is hopeless. I give ¹_____.
KAT   What's the problem?
LIAM This new smart TV. I'll never ²_____ used to it.
KAT   Why not?
LIAM It's just so complicated. It's nothing like the old one.
KAT   Have you read the manual?
LIAM Are you joking? Have you seen the size of it? I haven't got time.
KAT   Well, you'll never know how to use it ³_____ you read it.
LIAM No one reads manuals these days. Anyway, things are just ⁴_____ to work when you switch them on, aren't they?
KAT   Didn't the man at the shop show you how to use it?
LIAM He ran ⁵_____ a few things with me and pointed out the most important features, but …
KAT   But what?
LIAM I don't think I was really listening.
KAT   You never learn, do you?
LIAM Can you ⁶_____ a look at it for me? You're good at things like this.
KAT   OK, I'll look into it ⁷_____ you promise me one thing.
LIAM What's that?
KAT   I'll get it to work for you as ⁸_____ as you …

2 Complete Kat's last line. Compare with the rest of the class.

3 SPEAKING Work in pairs and discuss.
   1 When was the last time you had a problem with technology? What happened? Did you manage to solve it?
   2 How often do people ask you to help them with technology problems?
   3 How easy do you find it to explain such things to other people?

4 WRITING Complete the sentences with your own ideas and then compare with a partner.
   1 I'll help you with your homework provided …
   2 You can borrow my laptop as long as …
   3 I'll tell Mum what you did unless …
   4 Help me clear up this mess. Otherwise …

get used to

1 Complete with the missing verbs then add some ideas of your own.

What people said about the first mobile phones:

People will never get used to
0 *texting* rather than speaking to others.
1 _____ videos on such a small screen.
2 _____ photos on a phone.
3 _____ to music through headphones.
4 _____ such a small keyboard.
5 _____
6 _____
7 _____

2 SPEAKING Work in pairs. Discuss the latest item of technology that you have. Talk about features:
   • you've already got used to.
   • you're not used to yet.
   • you think you'll never get used to.

4

WELCOME

Secrets of love

1. Read the essay quickly. What are the writer's grandfather's secrets to a successful marriage?

2. Read the essay again and answer the questions.
   1. What did other people think about how quickly the writer's grandparents got married?
   2. Why does the writer's granddad say respect is important?
   3. Why does he say patience is important?
   4. What does he say about having children?

3. **SPEAKING** Work in pairs and decide what you think the secrets of a good friendship are.

My grandparents have been together for 50 years. It's amazing, isn't it? My granddad asked my grandma out when they were 18. He asked her to marry him two weeks later, she said 'yes' and they got engaged. They were married nine months after that, although everyone else thought they were mad. His parents warned him that it wouldn't last and predicted that they'd split up before they turned 20. Well, they didn't. They proved everyone wrong and half a century on they're more in love than ever.

I'm thinking of asking my girlfriend to marry me so I asked my granddad what the secret to a long and happy marriage is and if he had any advice. He had loads. One of the most important things, he said, was respect. Without respect, there's no chance of a relationship surviving. You both have to be able to accept the other person for who they are and give them room to do the things they need to do. He also highly recommended patience. He said that it was impossible to live with someone day in, day out for 50 years without falling out occasionally. But, with patience, he said that he and my grandma have always been able to work things out. He said that having children had been a really important part of their marriage. However, he said he believed it was something that shouldn't be rushed into. They'd waited ten years before starting a family. He felt it had given them plenty of time to really get to know each other. He also said that he knew many happy couples who hadn't had children.

But the most important secret of all, he said, was something he couldn't really put into words. It was the feeling he had when he first saw my grandma. He said that from that moment on he knew they'd be together forever. And he wasn't wrong.

Love and relationships

1. **Complete the rules with the missing words.**

   start | out | over | fall | engaged | date

   1. Never _____ in love with the same person twice.
   2. Never introduce your new boy/girlfriend to your family on your first _____.
   3. Don't _____ a family with someone you're not in love with.
   4. Always get _____ before you get married.
   5. Never go _____ with your best friend's ex.
   6. Never ask someone out if you're not completely _____ your ex.

2. Do you agree with these rules? Give each rule a score from 0–5 (0 = completely disagree; 5 = completely agree).

3. **SPEAKING** Work in pairs and discuss the rules. How similar or different are your scores? Where you have different scores, try to convince your partner of your opinion.

4. **Put the words in order to make questions.**

   Things not to say on a first date.

   1. to / you / Do / marry / want / me / ?
   2. want / How / you / children / many / do / ?
   3. the / you / pay / Can / meal / for / ?
   4. and / you / to / want / mum / meet / Do / my / dad / ?
   5. don't / weight / lose / Why / a / of / bit / you / ?

5. **ROLE PLAY** Work in pairs.

   Student A: you went on a date with someone who asked you questions 2 and 3.
   Student B: you went on a date with someone who asked you questions 4 and 5.

   Write your questions in reported question form. Then tell your partner about your date, expanding on your reported questions. Whose date was worse?

   He asked me if I wanted to marry him.

B CHALLENGES
The bucket list

1 🔊 1.03 Listen to the dialogue and answer the questions.

1. What is a bucket list?
2. Which of the things in the photos has Dharma already put on her bucket list?

2 🔊 1.03 Read the dialogue and complete it with the words in the list. There are two extra words. Then listen and check.

coming | having | chance | problem | right | it online
bet | to come | manage | reckon

CONNOR What are you writing, Dharma?
DHARMA I'm just compiling a bucket list.
CONNOR A what?
DHARMA A bucket list. A list of things you need to do before a certain age. I'll be 20 in a few years' time so I thought I'd try ¹_____ up with 20 things to do before I'm 20.
CONNOR Isn't that the sort of thing people do when they think they're getting old?
DHARMA Maybe, but I don't want to get to 20 and regret not ²_____ made the most of my teenage years.
CONNOR So what's on it?
DHARMA So far, not a lot. Let's see. Get a poem published in a national magazine. Do you ³_____ I could do that?
CONNOR No ⁴_____. Your poems are easily good enough.
DHARMA Thanks. Then I've got to do a parachute jump.
CONNOR Cool. You could wear a helmet camera, record it all and then post ⁵_____.
DHARMA That's not a bad idea. I'll add it to my list.
CONNOR So what else have you got on your list?
DHARMA The only other thing is to get more than 500 friends on Facebook.
CONNOR That's too easy. Anyone can do that.
DHARMA I'm talking about real friends. 500 real friends.
CONNOR Then you've got no ⁶_____ at all. You'll never ⁷_____ that. No one can have 500 real friends in their life.
DHARMA Yeah, I think you're probably ⁸_____. But I need something on my list. I'm running out of ideas. Maybe you could help.

3 Work in pairs. Help Dharma with her list. Think of five more things she could put on it.

Verbs with -ing or infinitive

Here are some of the things that Dharma's parachute instructor said to her. Complete them with the correct form of the verb in brackets.

1. Don't forget _____ (count) to three before you jump out of the plane.
2. This is something you'll remember _____ (do) for the rest of your life.
3. Stop _____ (worry). It's perfectly safe.
4. Try _____ (take) a deep breath and see if that helps calm you down.
5. I regret _____ (say) that it's too cloudy to make a jump today.

Issuing and accepting a challenge

1 Match the sentences 1–4 with possible replies a–f. There may be more than one possibility.

1. I challenge you to sing a song in English.
2. Do you reckon you could spend a day without going online?
3. I bet you can't think of four countries that begin with 'M'.
4. I bet I can hold my breath for more than a minute.

a. I think you're (probably) right.
b. That's too easy.
c. I bet I can.
d. You'll never manage to do it.
e. Of course I can.
f. I'm sure I could.

2 Write down five challenges that your partner could do in class.

3 SPEAKING Work in pairs and challenge each other.

WELCOME

Our greatest challenge

1 Read the blog quickly. What does the writer believe is our greatest challenge?

I'm only 20 years old and I've got a really bad feeling about the future of our world. I know that sounds very dramatic, but sometimes I just can't see that there's really that much to look forward to. The way things are going, it's very likely there'll be nothing left of the natural world for our grandchildren to enjoy. I keep hoping that we'll finally come to our senses and start fiercely protecting all that we have left, but every time I see the news, there are even more stories about the destruction of our planet. It's got to the point now where I dread opening the newspaper. The latest story that got me worked up was about a golf course that they're about to start building up the coast from where I live. They've been trying to get permission for years, but it had always been denied on the grounds that the area they want to develop is a protected breeding site for thousands of seabirds. I always imagined that 'protected' meant the land could never be touched. Apparently, it doesn't. The developers must have found the right amount of money needed to get that so-called protection lifted.

I believe that more than ever our greatest challenge is to defend the natural world from man's greed. This world doesn't just belong to a powerful few. It isn't theirs to exploit. This world belongs to all of us – every man, woman and child; every animal, bird and insect. This is a challenge that we must meet now if there's any hope for the future of our world.

2 Read the blog again and answer the questions.
1 What story did the writer read about recently that has got her so concerned about the world?
2 Why is she so upset about it?
3 Who does she believe the world belongs to?
4 Which of the things she says do you agree with? Which do you disagree with? Why?

3 Complete the sentences so that they're true for you.

What's wrong in the world
1 I'm feeling quite apprehensive about …
2 I'm also a bit unsure about …
3 I'm really worried about …

The hope I have for the world
4 I've got a really good feeling about …
5 I feel quite positive about …
6 I believe our greatest challenge is …

4 **SPEAKING** Work in pairs. Compare your ideas.

Phrases for talking about the future

1 **SPEAKING** Work in pairs. Read these imaginary news headlines and discuss them. Do they refer to good or bad news? Why? Can you agree on a ranking of the stories from 1 to 5 (1 = the worst news; 5 = the best news)?
1 Manchester United *are about to* sign Neymar.
2 The prime minister *is off to* Egypt for peace talks.
3 The ice caps *are on the point of* disappearing forever.
4 University fees *are likely to* increase by 20% next year.
5 This winter *is certain to* be the coldest in 20 years.

2 Match the words in italics in Exercise 1 with their meaning.

will definitely ☐   will happen very soon ☐
will probably ☐   is going somewhere to do something ☐

3 Think of three current news stories about the near future and complete the sentences.
1 _____ about to _____
2 _____ off to _____
3 _____ on the point of _____
4 _____ likely to _____
5 _____ certain to _____

4 **SPEAKING** Work in pairs. Compare your sentences and decide who has the best news story and who has the worst.

7

C EMPATHISING
Cheering someone up and sympathising about past situations

1 🔊 1.04 **Listen to the dialogue and answer the questions.**
  1 Why is Jim miserable?
  2 What does Ella promise him for the next time?

2 🔊 1.04 **Read the dialogue and complete it. Listen again and check.**

ELLA ¹_____ _____, Jim. You look miserable.
JIM   I am miserable.
ELLA Poor you. What's up?
JIM   My driving test.
ELLA Oh ²_____. So it didn't go well then?
JIM   Well, I thought I did fine, but it ³_____ _____ that I drove too slowly and that's enough to fail, apparently.
ELLA What a shame. I'm so sorry, Jim. I know how much you want to pass.
JIM   And now I've got to ⁴_____ _____ the whole process again. The lessons, booking the exam, doing the exam … Just the thought of it ⁵_____ me _____.
ELLA I know, but try not to let it ⁶_____ you _____.
JIM   I just feel like I've ⁷_____ my friends _____.
ELLA Why?
JIM   Well, everyone was relying on me to be the first to pass so that I could drive us all to parties and things at the weekend.
ELLA Look, don't ⁸_____ yourself. You did your best and that's all you can do. Sometimes things just don't ⁹_____ _____ the way we hope.
JIM   I know. You're right. I just wish I'd been a bit less confident and a bit more careful.
ELLA Don't ¹⁰_____ on it. What's done is done. You're going to pass next time for sure.
JIM   Thanks, Ella. You're a really good friend. I hope you know that.

3 **SPEAKING** Work in pairs. What would you say to Jim to cheer him up?

4 Match 1–8 with a–h to form expressions for cheering someone up or expressing sympathy.

1	Oh	a	you
2	What a	b	terrible
3	Poor	c	get you down
4	How	d	there
5	Cheer	e	the bright side
6	Hang in	f	dear
7	Don't let it	g	up
8	Look on	h	shame

5 **WRITING** Work in pairs. Choose one of the situations below and write a dialogue of 8–10 lines between the person who's upset and the person who's trying to make them feel better.

  1 You really thought you had a chance of getting into the school football team, but the coach didn't seem to agree and you haven't been picked.
  2 You were off on holiday, but on the way to the airport you got stuck in traffic and you missed your flight. You've had to return home as there isn't another flight for a week.
  3 You got a bike for your birthday, but the first time you went on it, you fell off, broke your leg and completely ruined the bike.

Life's ups and downs

1 **Complete the questions with the words in the list. There are two extra words.**

get | taken | let | wants | blamed | hardest | way | expectations

  1 When was the last time you felt nothing was going your _____?
  2 Have you ever _____ someone for something and then found out that they didn't do it? What was it? Did you apologise?
  3 Can you think of a time when you _____ someone down?
  4 Have you ever tried your _____ to do something and still not succeeded? What was it? Did you give up or keep on trying?
  5 Can you think of something that didn't live up to your _____? What was it?
  6 What things tend to _____ in your way when you're trying to study?

2 **SPEAKING** Work in pairs and discuss the questions. Give details.

WELCOME

A helping hand

1 Read the article quickly and put the suggested titles in order from most to least suitable for you.

☐ The kindness of strangers ☐ A nightmare flight ☐ Life with an autistic child

Life with my five-year-old autistic son is a constant adventure. There are times when it's more fun than you can possibly imagine and then there are times when you get desperate, knowing there's very little you can do to bring him out of one of his frequent tantrums. You can't help feeling a little guilty when other parents look at you as if to suggest you should be doing more to keep your child under control.

So it was with a certain amount of trepidation that I boarded an aeroplane with him for the first time recently, knowing that there would be someone who knew nothing about our daily challenges sitting beside us for the next eight hours. Sure enough, our problems started before the plane had even taken off, as I tried to fasten my son's seat belt and he started screaming. But far from feeling awkward, the smartly dressed businessman sitting on the other side leant over with a smile and helped me with the task. The effect on my son was nothing short of a miracle. He stopped crying immediately. He'd made a new best friend. I never got to know this man's name or anything about him, but for the duration of the flight his charm worked wonders. Every time my son threatened to kick off, the man was able to calm him down before things got too out of hand. He even succeeded in getting my son to eat a meal.

Thanks to the compassion, patience and understanding of a man I'd never met before, we managed to get through the flight without major incident and, for once, I didn't feel like a complete failure as a mum.

2 Read the article again and answer the questions.
1 How does the writer describe life with an autistic child?
2 How was she feeling about the flight and why?
3 How did the stranger help her child?
4 How do you think you'd have reacted if you'd been sitting next to the child? How would you have felt?

Adjectives to describe uncomfortable feelings

1 Complete the sentences with the words in the list.

stuck | guilty | ashamed | awkward | puzzled | desperate

1 It was quite an embarrassing situation and I felt a bit _____.
2 Even though I'd done nothing wrong, I still felt _____ for some reason.
3 The situation was serious. I had absolutely no idea what to do. I was _____ and started to panic.
4 It was a really strange situation. How could it have happened? I was _____.
5 I had no idea how to solve the problem. I was _____.
6 Why did I do it? I've no idea. It wasn't like me at all and I felt _____ of myself.

2 **SPEAKING** Work in pairs. Think of specific situations (real or imaginary) for each of the adjectives in Exercise 1.

> *I once called my teacher by the wrong name. I felt quite awkward.*

Talking about past ability

1 Which of these things might the stranger have said to his wife when he got home after the flight? Tick all that apply. Then compare with a partner.

1 I managed to watch three films. ☐
2 I got a good night's sleep. ☐
3 Between us, we were able to get his seat belt on. ☐
4 I succeeded in finishing my book. ☐
5 I managed to keep the little boy happy. ☐
6 I succeeded in finding that perfume you like at the duty-free shop. ☐

2 Work in pairs. Imagine you've just been on a terrible flight. Agree together on all of the things that went wrong. Complete the sentences.

1 I only managed …
2 I didn't succeed …
3 I wasn't able …
4 I was able …
5 I didn't manage …

9

D BUT IS IT NEWS?
Introducing news

1 Does your school have a school newspaper? If so, what kind of stories does it feature? Do you read it?

2 Read the dialogue and complete it with the words in the list. There are four extra words.

make | time | made | run | out | done | told
certainly | about | keep | exactly | up

ABI Have you heard ¹_____ Mr Bowden?
NICK No, what's he done?
ABI He's finally announced that he's getting married to Miss Millington.
NICK So the school's most scandalous secret is finally ²_____.
ABI I guess it is.
NICK Well, I suppose it's ³_____ we put him in the school paper.
ABI What?
NICK I think we should ⁴_____ a story on them in this month's edition.
ABI It's hardly news, is it?
NICK Well, they're both teachers here. I think we could do a really funny piece on them about how they've tried to ⁵_____ their romance quiet when all along we all knew.
ABI There's no way that's a news story.
NICK It is. This is ⁶_____ the kind of news story we want. Do you know how many complaints were ⁷_____ about last month's edition? Students are bored with reading about exam results and whether or not we're going to get a swimming pool. They want a bit of gossip about their teachers.
ABI Well, I'd just like to say that I'm really against running this story.
NICK Well, I'm not and as editor of the magazine, I get the final say. This story is going in. My mind's made ⁸_____.

3 Who do you agree with most, Abi or Nick? Why?

4 Match the sentence halves.
1 Have you ☐
2 Have you heard about ☐
3 Did you ☐
4 Guess ☐
5 You'll never believe ☐

a Mr Errington?
b what?
c what I heard.
d heard?
e know … ?

5 Put the lines in order to make the dialogue.
☐ A Absolutely. Let's organise one from the whole class.
☐ A Have you heard about Mr Errington?
☐ A Yes, it was. He's in hospital.
☐ A He's broken his leg and has cuts and bruises.
☐ A Apparently, he's been in a car crash.
☐ B That's awful. How is he?
☐ B No, what happened?
☐ B No way! Was it serious?
☐ B Good idea.
☐ B We have to send him a card.

6 **SPEAKING** Work in pairs. Choose one of the expressions from Exercise 4 and use it to start a short dialogue (8–10 lines).

Ways of speaking

1 Complete the school news story headlines with the missing verbs in the correct form. There are three extra words.

introduce | apologise | recommend | warn
confess | complain | regret | announce

1 Local residents _____ about students' behaviour walking to school
2 Miss Green _____ six books that all Year 8 students should read over the summer holidays
3 Headmaster _____ new Maths teacher
4 Mr Williams _____ his retirement at the end of the year
5 Student _____ to painting graffiti on school walls

2 **SPEAKING** Work in pairs. Decide which of the stories in Exercise 1 you'd put in the school newspaper. Give your reasons.

WELCOME

News mad?

1 Read the blog entry quickly. What does the writer suggest 👍 means?

Is it just me or has the world gone news mad? It's so easy to get word out these days that every time you turn on a screen there's news waiting to be read or heard. There's no escaping it. Just turn on the TV. There are so many 24-hour news channels all competing with each other to see who can get to a story first. I could swear sometimes they break the news before it's even happened. And when there's no breaking news I find myself panicking. What's happened? Is the world still out there?

In fact, I'm beginning to fear that I may have become addicted to news. I spend far too much time checking every news feed that appears on my internet browser when I should be working, and as a result I find myself working way past midnight in order to meet my deadlines. And then, of course, it's a new day with new news to catch up on.

But it's not just world news which invades our every waking moment; people's personal news is equally omnipresent. With social media it's so easy to keep in touch with every friend you've ever made in your life. Just post what you've been up to on your wall and with one click of a button, everyone who knows you, knows what you've been up to, whether or not they even really care. And it's just as easy for them to comment immediately on your news – anything from a simple 👍 (which means they can't really be bothered) to a 140-character summary of what they really think. Be careful, though; say something stupid and before you know it, it's been retweeted halfway around the world. Consequently, *you've* become news, and not in a good way.

2 Read the blog again and answer the questions.

1. How does the writer feel when there's no breaking news?
2. How is his addiction to news affecting his working life?
3. What warning does the writer give about tweeting?
4. Which, if any, of the writer's opinions do you agree with? Explain your reasons.

Verb + noun collocations with *make, take, play, do, give*

1 Complete the news headlines with the present simple form of *make, take, play, do,* or *give*.

1. Prime Minister _____ a speech to Parliament
2. Overseas visitors to the USA _____ advantage of weak dollar
3. FIFA _____ a decision on next World Cup
4. Britain _____ a deal with Europe over immigration
5. Government _____ advice from Green Party on environment
6. Bill Gates _____ a part in peace talks
7. Record number of people _____ complaints to BBC about programme

2 **SPEAKING** Work in pairs. Make news headlines using these four verb / noun pairs.

make progress | give money | do research
take revenge

Cause and effect linkers

Rewrite the sentences using the words in brackets.

1. The weather was so bad that the president's plane was diverted to another airport. (due to)
2. There will be another election as no single party won enough votes. (consequently)
3. The Queen has cancelled the dinner as she is not well. (because)
4. So many people protested that the government have cancelled their plans. (as a result of)

Sharing news

1 Complete the sentences with the words in the list. There are three extra words.

keep | break | find | get | give | pass
let | show

1. You're going to be late home. How do you _____ your parents know?
2. How do you _____ in touch with old friends?
3. Your mum asks you to _____ on a message to your brother. How do you do it?
4. You need to _____ in touch with your best friend immediately. How do you do it?
5. You've done really badly in your school tests. How do you _____ the news to your parents?

2 **SPEAKING** Work in pairs and discuss the questions.

11

1 BROTHERS AND SISTERS

OBJECTIVES

FUNCTIONS: using emotive language
GRAMMAR: talking about habits; adverbs to express attitude
VOCABULARY: personality (1); personal conflict

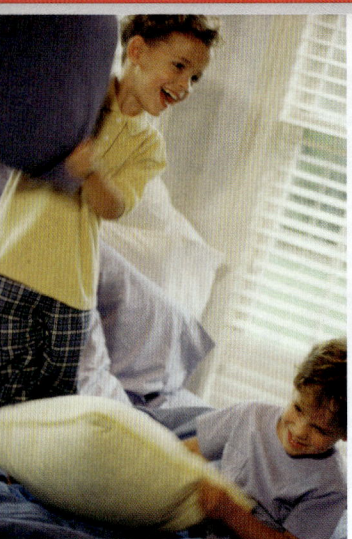  

READING

1 **SPEAKING** Read what these children say. Who do you think is speaking: the oldest or the youngest child? Discuss in pairs and give reasons.

1 He's always telling on me.
2 She can be really mean to me.
3 They used to give me all their attention.
4 Mum and Dad spoil her.
5 Mum and Dad don't seem to care about how I do at school.
6 He's always messing about.

2 Work in pairs. Think of more complaints that oldest and youngest children might have about their brothers and sisters.

3 How might things change for the boys in photo 1 if they suddenly find they have a younger sister? Read the article on page 13 quickly and check your ideas.

4 ◆)) 1.05 Read the article again. Where do these sentences come from? Match with A–E in the article. There are three you won't use. Then listen and check.

1 The science of how birth order affects personality is relatively new and still surrounded in controversy.
2 They'll have their parents' sole attention forever and equally all of their parents' energies are channelled towards them exclusively.
3 It's a very long list, because, of course, there are so many variables that can be taken into consideration.
4 There'll be no more opportunities to 'get it right' and by virtue of being the youngest, their newest offspring may well be more demanding, relatively speaking.
5 They'll always be lonely and their self-esteem may suffer as a result.
6 However, this is usually accompanied by high expectations as new parents are keen to see their child do well and the eldest child, for their part, is generally keen to meet these expectations.
7 And parents often get angry if they don't feel that their child is doing as well as they believe they should be.
8 One of the most common ways to achieve this is by making people laugh and second children are frequently the jokers of the family.

5 **SPEAKING** Work in pairs. Discuss the following questions.

1 Where do you come in your family? Which parts of the description, if any, fit you? What about your brothers and sisters?
2 How important do you think birth order is compared to other factors in determining personality? Give examples.

12

1 BROTHERS AND SISTERS

The Pecking Order

Have you ever thought about why you are the way you are? To what extent has your personality been determined by social, genetic and geographical factors; by the era you were born into, or just by pure luck? **[A]** There is, however, one simple yet compelling factor that is often overlooked: birth order. Research has indicated that the position in which we are born in our family plays a major role in forming personality.

The eldest child

For as long as they remain the only child, the eldest enjoys their parents' undivided attention. **[B]** As a result, eldest children tend to be respectful and traditional, following the examples set by their parents.

The problems arise with the arrival of another child. Suddenly, the attention they're used to receiving diminishes. As a consequence, the first-born feels insecure and will try to resolve this by doing all they can to make their parents happy. Research suggests that this might lead them to achieve great things, but regardless of what they've actually accomplished, they might also feel that they're never good enough.

The second child

The second child has no experience of life without a sibling so they never know how it feels to suddenly have to share the attention. They'll typically look at their well-behaved elder brother or sister and decide one of two things: they'll either strive to be better – which can spur them on to succeed in life – or more commonly, they'll choose to be the complete opposite. If they decide to adopt the latter approach, then they'll tend to be more unconventional and rebellious, with less concern for the way things 'should' be done. They're also often more outgoing and constantly looking for ways to attract attention. **[C]**

Again, problems can emerge when another baby arrives. Suddenly, the second child becomes the middle child and may lose a clear sense of where they fit in. They tend not to be the subject of their parents' high expectations – the burden of many eldest children – but, equally, they no longer enjoy the extra attention that comes from being the youngest.

The youngest child

With the birth of their final baby, parents will often feel this is their last chance to bring up a child. **[D]** This means the youngest child, more often than not, is spoilt with attention and affection. This can lead them to be rather self-centred, believing that the world revolves around them. Always being treated as the 'baby' of the family can also result in the youngest child lacking motivation and underachieving. But in an effort to break new ground in the battle for their parents' attention, youngest children also tend to be outgoing, charming and creative.

The only child

Only children are similar to eldest children in that they're eager to please their parents and tend to copy their parents' behaviour. The difference lies in the fact that they never have to experience the arrival of another child. **[E]** This makes their bond with their parents even stronger and only children tend to be very confident in social situations, even around adults. However, as they grow older they may feel that this relationship is too intense and can therefore be quite keen to leave home as soon as possible.

TRAIN TO THiNK

Questioning widely accepted theories

Although we often draw conclusions based on what we've read, heard or observed, it does not mean these conclusions are always 100% correct. The article talks about personality traits that relate to a person's position in the family. There will always be plenty of exceptions.

1 Which of these examples contradict claims made in the article?

1 My youngest child Tom is so thoughtful. If he knows his elder brother Jack is revising for exams, he'll always put on his headphones.
2 Oliver's our eldest. He wants to be a doctor, just like his dad.
3 Mum and Dad weren't too bothered by my low grades at school and as I'm an only child there was no brother or sister to be compared to.

2 **SPEAKING** Work in pairs. Think of people you know who contradict the claims made in the article.

3 **SPEAKING** Work in pairs. What other theories about personality have you heard or read about? Can you think of people you know who contradict these theories?

GRAMMAR
Talking about habits

1 **Match the example sentences with the descriptions. Then complete the rule.**

1 They'll typically look at their well-behaved elder brother or sister and decide one of two things.
2 He's always telling on me.
3 They used to give me all their attention.
4 Eldest children tend to be respectful and traditional.

a ☐ Talks about a habit in the past.
b ☐ Expresses irritation about the habit of another person.
c ☐ Uses a future construction to talk about what we might expect from someone's behaviour.
d ☐ Talks about something that is often (but not always) true.

> **RULE:** There are a number of ways we can talk about habits:
> - *used* + [1]_____ or *would* + infinitive to talk about habits in the past.
> - *always* + [2]_____ tense to refer to behaviour which irritates us.
> - [3]_____ + infinitive to refer to habits in general (not future).
> - [4]_____ (not) to + infinitive to refer to the way a person is likely to behave.

2 **Complete each space in the text with one word.**

My little brother really used [1]_____ annoy me – and I mean *really annoy* me! Every little thing he did, every little noise he made with his mouth and every little thing he said [2]_____ drive me crazy. We [3]_____ to fight all the time and get in big trouble with our parents. It always ended up with both of us being grounded. It was terrible. These days things have improved and we tend [4]_____ get on a lot better. I'm not sure what changed, but I probably worked out that life would be a lot less stressful if I could try and find him less irritating. It's not always easy. I mean, he still [5]_____ to say silly stuff and I find myself getting annoyed, but I [6]_____ just get up and walk away now. There is one thing that does get me really angry, though. He's [7]_____ walking into my bedroom without knocking, despite the big 'Keep Out' sign on the door. When he does that, I tell him to 'get lost'. He knows I mean it and tends [8]_____ to hang about. It's important to make sure that he still knows who's boss!

3 **WRITING** Look at the cartoon. What are the dog and the cat thinking? Write three sentences for each. Use the structures for talking about habits from Exercise 1.

Workbook page 10

VOCABULARY
Personality (1)

1 **According to the article on page 13, which child (eldest, second, youngest or only) tends to be:**

1 traditional?   5 rebellious?
2 insecure?   6 respectful?
3 unconventional?   7 outgoing?
4 demanding?   8 self-centred?

2 **Which adjective describes someone who:**

1 shows admiration and consideration for someone?
2 doesn't do things in the usual or expected way?
3 only thinks about themselves?
4 likes to cause trouble by not doing as they're told?
5 doesn't like change very much?
6 is very sociable?
7 expects a lot of time and attention from others?
8 often feels very unsure of themselves?

3 **WRITING** Write five sentences about the habits of people you know. Use personality adjectives.

My sister is really outgoing. She loves talking to people and she knows everyone at school.

4 **SPEAKING** Read your sentences to your partner but don't say the personality adjective! Can your partner guess the adjective?

Workbook page 12

1 BROTHERS AND SISTERS

LISTENING

1 **SPEAKING** Look at the photo and read the magazine listing. Discuss in pairs and make notes.

  1 How do you think the people in the photo are related?
  2 What do you think they're talking about?
  3 How are they feeling? Why?

2 ◁)) 1.06 Listen to a scene from *The Street*. Check your predictions from Exercise 1.

3 ◁)) 1.06 Listen again and mark the statements T (true) or F (false).

  1 Shreya is surprised when Rahul returns home.
  2 Shreya wants to go and live with her brother.
  3 Maya and Shreya haven't been in touch for over a year.
  4 Maya and Shreya fell out over a boy.
  5 Shreya says her brother, Samir, isn't happy about her decision.
  6 Shreya wants to leave because of a boy.
  7 Shreya's dad doesn't understand why Shreya needs to go.
  8 We discover something terrible about Shreya's brother, Samir, at the end.

7.30 – 8 pm The Street

Rahul finally finds out why Shreya's been acting so strangely and he's not happy. But how will she react when she finds out his news? More shocks and drama from our favourite soap opera.

FUNCTIONS
Using emotive language

1 Look at the sentences from the listening. Who says each one, Rahul or Shreya?

  a I'm sick of this place. I'm sick of my dead-end job.
  b But what about your job? You can't just walk out on that.
  c I don't understand, Shreya. Why didn't you tell me?
  d And I do need to move out, Dad. I really do.
  e Tell me you haven't done that.
  f It's that boy, isn't it?

2 Match each of the sentences with the emotive technique it uses.

  1 ☐ question tags
  2 ☐ repetition of a word (or phrase)
  3 ☐ rhetorical questions (questions for which you don't expect an answer)
  4 ☐ emphatic use of the auxiliary verb in positive statements
  5 ☐ phrases such as *tell me, I don't understand, you can't be serious* or *you must be joking*

3 **WRITING** Work in pairs. Remind yourselves how the scene ended and then write the next eight lines of dialogue. Use emotive language.

Pronunciation
Intonation: showing emotions
Go to page 120.

THiNK VALUES
Relationships

1 Think about your family and your friends. Giving examples to support your choices, write about someone who:

  1 you can tell anything to.
  2 you find it difficult to talk to.
  3 is really fun to be with.
  4 is quite boring to be with.
  5 you have the most in common with.
  6 you have the least in common with.
  7 knows you the best.
  8 doesn't know you at all.

2 **SPEAKING** Work in pairs. What could you do to improve your relationship with one of the people you wrote about in questions 2, 4, 6 or 8? Take turns to suggest some ideas to your partner. Would you be interested in trying any of these ideas? Why (not)?

READING

1. Make a list of problems you might have if you were at the same school as your brother or sister. Compare with a partner.

2. Read the web page quickly. What two problems does it describe?

3. Read the web page again. Put the advice for each problem in order of usefulness. Compare with a partner. What extra advice would you give?

SPEAKING

Work in groups of four. Take turns to talk about a problem you have with a brother or sister. This can be real or imaginary. Give each other advice on how to deal with the problem.

Think about:
- what exactly it is they do.
- how to describe their behaviour.
- how this makes you feel.
- what you've done to try and improve the situation.
- how they've reacted to this.
- what tactics you might try in the future.

People power to help you with your problems

I've always got on well with my little brother. He's five years younger than me so I've always felt really protective towards him. Well, that was until a few weeks ago. The problem is that he now goes to the same secondary school as me and annoyingly he doesn't seem to get that school is different from home. He and his friends seem to think it's funny to follow me around and try to embarrass me. At first, my friends thought it was quite funny, but now he's really starting to get on their nerves too. I've spoken to my parents and they had a word with him, but it's made no difference. If anything, it's made things worse. Honestly, I don't know what to do next and I'm scared I'll say something to him that I might regret. **Darren93**

Ignore him – that's the key. Obviously, you'd like him to stop right away, but I reckon the more he sees how much his behaviour annoys you, the more he'll keep on doing it. Pay no attention. He'll soon get bored and realise it's much more fun to hang out with people in his own year than to pester his older brother. **JennyJ**

Turn the tables on him. Follow him around and see how he likes it. Surely you know enough embarrassing things about him that you could share with his friends to make his life miserable! **Cheeseman**

Have another chat with him. Explain to him why it upsets you and ask him how he'd feel if you did the same to him. Hopefully, he's mature enough to understand. **Sandybob**

My little sister's always been a bit of a tomboy. She's always liked hanging out with boys and always worn jeans and T-shirts. I've never seen it as a problem, but now she's 13 and showing no signs of changing, I'm starting to worry a little. All her friends are boys and I can see that she's getting left out of things – the other girls are excluding her. Admittedly, she doesn't seem to be bothered, but I know how mean girls can get. I've tried suggesting she might want to try some of my make-up but she just laughed and told me to stop being silly. Should I just let her be or do I need to be more direct? **Lauren92**

Wow, she's lucky to have a sister like you. You've certainly got your eye on her. Understandably you're concerned, but I don't think you can really force her to be a certain way. All I can suggest is that you continue to make sure she's OK and be there for her if and when she really needs you. **JB95**

Let her be. She's still only 13. Regrettably, these days there's enormous pressure on girls to grow up too quickly. Let your sister enjoy her childhood while she still can. **JoKenny**

Are you serious?! I think you're the one with the problem. Surely, we should be encouraging our younger siblings to be whoever they want to be. We shouldn't be forcing them to conform to old-fashioned stereotypes! **Sassygirl**

1 BROTHERS AND SISTERS

GRAMMAR
Adverbs to express attitude

1 **Complete the sentences with the words in the list. Check your answers in the web page.**

annoyingly | regrettably | admittedly | hopefully

1 _____, she doesn't seem to be bothered.
2 _____, he doesn't seem to get that school is different from home.
3 _____, he's mature enough to understand.
4 _____, these days there's enormous pressure on girls to grow up too quickly.

2 **Find five more examples of adverbs to express attitude in the web page and use them to complete the rule.**

> **RULE:** Words like *annoyingly, regrettably, admittedly, hopefully*, ¹_____, ²_____, ³_____, ⁴_____ and ⁵_____ are used to express how we feel about what we're saying. We usually put them at the start of the clause.

3 **Change the underlined word into an adverb and use it to make one sentence.**

1 My sister's always using my hair straighteners. I find this quite <u>annoying</u>.
2 My brother might lend me his jacket. I live in <u>hope</u>.
3 I didn't learn a musical instrument when I was younger. I <u>regret</u> this now.
4 I'm good at languages, but my sister is better than me at Maths. This is something I have to <u>admit</u>.
5 My brother says he's too busy to help me with my homework. I'm <u>sure</u> he could spare half an hour if he really wanted to.
6 I would never hurt my sister. I'm being <u>honest</u> about this.
7 My brother is jealous of me. It's <u>obvious</u>.
8 You're angry with me for being mean to my sister. I <u>understand</u> that.

> Workbook page 11

VOCABULARY
Personal conflict

1 **Match the sentence halves. Use the web page to help you.**

1 My little brother really *gets on*
2 Mum said she wants to *have a*
3 Please don't say anything. You'll only *make*
4 Stop doing that before I *say something*
5 Why don't you *turn the*
6 My elder brother *made*
7 Why don't you just *let*
8 I've got my

a *word* with me. What could it be?!
b I might regret.
c *my life miserable* when I was a child.
d *him be* and get on with your own life?
e *eye on* you, so don't try and do anything silly.
f *tables on* her and see how she likes it.
g *my nerves* when he keeps asking me questions.
h *things worse* for me.

2 **Circle the correct words to complete the expressions.**

1 Mr Thomas is making my *life / time / days* miserable. He's always picking on me.
2 The teacher had words *with / to / on* Tim about his behaviour in class.
3 Never reply to an angry email immediately in case you *say / reply / tell* something you might regret.
4 I hate the way she's always interrupting me. It really *gets / goes / puts* on my nerves.
5 She's got her eye *on / at / for* you, so be careful.
6 I was only trying to help, but judging by her reaction, I think I've just *done / made / caused* things worse.
7 If Ian wants to spend all his money, just let him *alone / be / do*. It's his money, not yours.
8 I was tired of Jim always borrowing my phone, so I *turned / switched / placed* the tables on him by leaving mine at home and borrowing his all day.

3 **SPEAKING Complete the questions with the missing words and then discuss them with a partner.**

1 What sort of things really get on your _____?
2 Have you ever said anything you later _____? What was it and what was the consequence?
3 Have you ever had to have a _____ with someone? Why? What happened next?
4 Can you think of a time when you tried to help someone but only made things _____? What happened?
5 What sort of things would make your life _____?

> Workbook page 12

17

Literature

1. What do you think might be the pleasures and the difficulties of being part of a family with either five sisters or five brothers?

2. 🔊 1.08 Read and listen to the extract. What do you learn about the relationship between Jane and Elizabeth, and about their individual characters?

Pride and Prejudice *by Jane Austen*

Mr and Mrs Bennet, who live in Longbourn, are not very rich. They have five daughters – Jane, Elizabeth, Mary, Lydia and Kitty – and hope to see them all married. Lydia had run away with a soldier but then married him. Elizabeth has a love-hate relationship with the rich but (in her opinion) arrogant Mr Darcy. Mr Darcy's wealthy friend, Mr Bingley, loves Jane but Mr Bingley's sisters do not like her very much. Darcy has just helped Bingley to propose to Jane and she has happily accepted him.

Bingley, from this time, was of course a daily visitor at Longbourn, coming frequently before breakfast, and always remaining till after supper […].

Elizabeth had now but little time for conversation with her sister; for while he was present, Jane had no attention to bestow on anyone else; but she found herself considerably useful to both of them in those hours of separation that must sometimes occur. In the absence of Jane, he always attached himself to Elizabeth, for the pleasure of talking of her; and when Bingley was gone, Jane constantly sought the same means of relief.

'He has made me so happy,' said she, one evening, 'by telling me that he was totally ignorant of my being in London last spring! I had not believed it possible.'

'I suspected as much,' replied Elizabeth. 'But how did he account for it?'

'It must have been his sister's doing. They were certainly not very pleased about his acquaintance with me, which I cannot wonder at, since he might have chosen so much more advantageously in many respects. But when they see, as I trust they will, that their brother is happy with me, they will learn to be contented, and we shall be on good terms again; though we can never be what we once were to each other.'

'That is the most unforgiving speech,' said Elizabeth, 'that I ever heard you speak. Good girl! It would upset me, indeed, to see you again being misled by Miss Bingley's pretended good opinion.'

'Would you believe it, Lizzy, that when he went to town last November, he really loved me, and nothing but a persuasion of my being indifferent would have prevented his coming down again!'

'He made a little mistake to be sure; but it is to the credit of his modesty.' […]

Elizabeth was pleased to find that Bingley had not said anything about the interference of Mr Darcy; for, though Jane had the most generous and forgiving heart in the world, she knew it was a circumstance which would make her think badly of him.

'I am certainly the most fortunate creature that ever existed!' cried Jane. 'Oh! Lizzy, why am I singled out like this from my family, and blessed above them all! If I could only see you as happy! If there were only such another man for you!'

'If you were to give me forty such men, I never could be so happy as you. Till I have your disposition, your goodness, I never can have your happiness. No, no, let me look after myself; and, perhaps, if I have very good luck, I may meet with another Mr Collins in time.'

The situation of affairs in the Longbourn family could not be long a secret. Mrs Bennet was privileged to whisper it to Mrs Phillips, and she took the opportunity, without any permission, to do the same to all her neighbours in Meryton.

The Bennets were speedily pronounced to be the luckiest family in the world, though only a few weeks before, when Lydia had first run away, they had been generally believed to be marked out for misfortune.

3. Read the extract again and answer the questions.
   1. In what way was Elizabeth useful to both her sister and to Mr Bingley?
   2. How did Bingley's sister feel about his relationship with Jane?
   3. What does Jane hope will happen in the future with Bingley's sister?
   4. What does Elizabeth think about Jane's attitude towards Miss Bingley?
   5. Why is Elizabeth happy that Jane does not know of Darcy's involvement in her relationship with Bingley?
   6. What does Jane wish for Elizabeth?
   7. What changes in the way other people see the Bennet family, and why?

1 BROTHERS AND SISTERS

4 **VOCABULARY** Match the highlighted words or phrases in the extract with the definitions.

1 explain
2 chose someone (or something) for special attention or privilege
3 knowing (or meeting) another person (n.)
4 someone's natural personality
5 tried to find; looked for
6 not caring; apathetic
7 get on well; have a good relationship
8 knew absolutely nothing

5 **SPEAKING** Work in pairs. Discuss the questions.

1 Which of the two – Jane or Elizabeth – do you think is older? Why?
2 Imagine you are Jane and someone asks you about Elizabeth's personality. How would you describe her?
3 What evidence is there in the extract that Jane and Elizabeth have a very close relationship?

WRITING
An email

1 Read the email and answer the questions.

1 How is the writer related to Sam?
2 How was Sam's relationship with his siblings when he was young? What reason is given for this?
3 How did Sam fall out of favour with his family?
4 What things happened in Sam's life that his parents never knew about?
5 What is the writer now determined to do?

2 Read the email again. In what order is the following information mentioned in the email?

- [ ] what she plans to do with this information
- [ ] what the scandal was
- [ ] how she made the discovery about her great-uncle
- [ ] the consequence of the scandal
- [ ] the little she already knew about her great-uncle
- [ ] the evidence she found about his life

3 Complete with the missing words. Then check in the email. What effect do the missing words and expressions have on the sentences?

1 _____ _____ I told you my great-aunt May died recently.
2 She was very old – over a hundred, _____ _____.
3 Anyway, _____ _____ _____ _____ that he'd done something terrible.
4 My mother had _____ _____ known what it was _____ _____.
5 It turns out that _____, he was a conscientious objector.
6 Sadly, _____ _____ he never made up with his parents.

4 Use the words and expressions from Exercise 3 to make these sentences less certain.

1 He wasn't very well liked by other members of the family.
2 He was a hero in the First World War.
3 I met my great-aunt when I was very young, but I don't really remember it.
4 He'd spent some years in prison.
5 I never found out if it was true.
6 It turns out that he never knew he had a twin brother.

5 Do the task.

You have recently found out about an interesting relative of yours. Write an email to a friend (220–260 words) about the relative. Write about:

- how the person is related to you.
- how they got on with other members of the family.
- what they did that was interesting.

Dear Diana,

I think I told you my great-aunt May died recently. She was very old – over a hundred, I believe. I was helping my mother clear out some of her things when we came across some really interesting papers all about her brother Sam, my great-uncle. I'd heard a few things about him from my grandmother over the years, but on the whole he wasn't talked about much in the family. He was the youngest of five children and generally considered to be the favourite of my great-grandparents. I think the others felt he was quite spoilt.

Anyway, there was a rumour that he'd done something terrible and that's why his name was never mentioned. But my mother had never really known what it was for sure. Well, guess what – we found out everything in a small leather briefcase in my great-aunt's attic. May was the only family member that he'd kept in touch with and he'd written her dozens of letters over the years.

It turns out that, apparently, he was a conscientious objector in World War II and had refused to fight. He was 18 when the war broke out and his parents obviously felt that he'd brought great shame on the family. They sent him away to live with a distant relative in the Scottish Highlands. He eventually became a policeman and made quite a name for himself. In the briefcase, there were loads of newspaper cuttings about things he'd done and even a medal he'd won for bravery.

Sadly, it seems he never made up with his parents and they never got to meet any of the five children he went on to have. I've now made it my mission to try and find some of my missing Scottish relatives. I'll keep you posted on what I find out! Have you ever made any interesting discoveries about people in your family?

Must run but looking forward to hearing from you soon!
Lots of love,
Helen

19

2 SLEEP ON IT

OBJECTIVES

FUNCTIONS: giving advice
GRAMMAR: past tense with hypothetical meaning; adverbs for modifying comparatives
VOCABULARY: sleep; idioms with *sleep* and *dream*

READING

1 Read the quiz at the bottom of the page and choose your answers.

2 **SPEAKING** Work in pairs. Compare your answers and decide who's the best sleeper.

3 **1.09** Read and listen to the magazine article on page 21 and mark these sentences T (true), F (false) or DS (doesn't say).

1 Approximately half of US teens are getting less than seven hours' sleep a night.
2 Girls tend to spend more time sleeping than boys.
3 One teen in every five says they fall asleep in class at least once a week.
4 Colds are more common among teens who sleep too much.
5 There are also psychological reasons why teens tend to be sleep-deprived.
6 If schools opened later, fewer teens would arrive late.
7 Afternoon naps can have health benefits for teenagers.
8 Teenagers would benefit from going to bed at the same time every night.

4 **SPEAKING** Work in pairs and discuss the following questions.

1 How many hours' sleep do you usually get? Do you feel it's too little, too much or just right?
2 How regular are your sleep patterns?
3 What time does your school day start? Would you be in favour of later / earlier starting times? Why (not)?

Are you a healthy sleeper?

1 **You wake up half an hour late for school. You think …**
 a) I should go to bed earlier.
 b) It's time I bought a new alarm clock.
 c) That's unusual. I don't usually oversleep.

2 **It's 7 am and your dad is yelling at you to get out of bed. You think …**
 a) I wish I could have another hour in bed.
 b) OK, OK! I'm getting up.
 c) Why's he shouting? I'm already up.

3 **You turned off your light half an hour ago. You think …**
 a) If only my mind wasn't on that computer game. I want to go to sleep.
 b) I'd prefer it if you didn't ask me silly quiz questions. I'm quite a light sleeper and I'm about to fall asleep.
 c) Nothing. You're fast asleep and snoring loudly.

4 **It's 11 pm and your mum suggests it's time you went to bed. You think …**
 a) No way. I'm snapchatting Rachel.
 b) OK, I'll read for half an hour before I turn my light off.
 c) I'm on my way right now.

2 SLEEP ON IT

The great teen sleeping crisis?

An age-old problem

They won't go to bed when you want them to. They hide their heads under the pillow and won't get up when you ask them to. What is it with teenagers and sleep? Well maybe it's time we revisited this topic to better understand what might be going on.

A recent study found that only around 50% of US teenagers were getting the seven hours of sleep generally considered necessary. The other half were getting on average two hours less. Interestingly, girls are more prone to skipping sleep than boys. These are worrying figures indeed, especially when you take into consideration latest recommendations from experts that seven to ten hours is optimum for teenagers.

Bad for the health

The short-term effects of not getting enough sleep are clearly evident. Just ask any secondary school teacher. 20% of teenagers admit to nodding off in class at least once a fortnight. A lack of concentration in lessons can lead to poor performance in exams, and grades often suffer as a result. It's not difficult to make the connection. Other immediate consequences include a weakening of the immune system, meaning the sleep-deprived are more likely to catch a cold or get the flu.

Even more disquieting are the long-term effects. Doctors say there are direct links between a lack of sleep and mental health issues such as depression and memory loss.

It's biological

One thing we all need to do is to stop blaming teenagers for their anti-social sleeping habits, since they do have a biological excuse for their behaviour. It's all the fault of the hormone melatonin. When melatonin surges through the body, it's telling us that it's time to go to bed. The problem is that in teenagers, melatonin is released two hours later than in adults, meaning that they get the call to go to bed much later than their parents. Then, when they're forced to wake up in the morning, their melatonin levels are still high and their bodies are urging them to stay in bed. That's why they find it such a struggle to drag themselves out from under the covers.

A change of routine

So what can be done to make life easier for everyone? Well, one simple solution would be to start the school day two hours later. In the US, 40% of all teenagers start school before 8 am, which is clearly far too early for the average teenage brain to function properly. If a 10 am start time was implemented, it would give them a much fairer chance.

In addition, teenagers themselves need to take more responsibility for their own sleeping patterns. It's been proven that people who stick to a regular routine lead far healthier lives. Going to bed and getting up at the same time each day certainly gives your body a head start. Teens can even take a nap in the afternoon if they're able to make that a regular part of their routine.

The other thing to consider is limiting their screen time, which can often run into the early hours of the morning. This is undoubtedly the main reason why many teenagers fail to get a good night's sleep. So, unfortunately for teenagers, it seems that two of their favourite pastimes – lying-in at the weekend and late-night gaming – have a role to play in the lack of sleep many of them complain about.

TRAIN TO THiNK

The rule of threes

The rule of threes states that ideas should be considered from three different perspectives.

The more perspectives you can view a problem from, the better your overall understanding. For example, imagine an aeroplane is flying through heavy turbulence.

- An experienced pilot would see it as a normal occurrence and put on the seatbelt sign.
- A nervous flier might convince themselves the plane is about to crash.
- A fan of roller coasters might enjoy the thrill of it.

1 A teenager is still asleep at 11 am on a Saturday. Who might have the following opinions of the situation?

1 What's the problem? I'm tired.
2 We need to understand that teenage sleep patterns are different to those of adults.
3 He's so lazy these days.

2 **SPEAKING** Make notes on how each of the following people might respond to the statement 'Schools should start at 10 am'. Then compare with a partner.

a teenager   a parent   a teacher   an economist   a doctor

Pronunciation

Different ways of pronouncing *c* and *g*

Go to page 120.

GRAMMAR
Past tenses with hypothetical meaning

1 **Complete the sentences from the quiz on page 20 with the verbs in brackets. Then complete the rule with *past* and *present*.**

   1 It's time I _____ a new alarm clock. (buy)
   2 I wish I _____ have another hour in bed. (can)
   3 If only my mind _____ on that computer game. I want to go to sleep. (not be)
   4 I'd prefer it if you _____ me silly quiz questions. (not ask)

   > **RULE:** With certain expressions, like *It's time*, *I'd prefer it if*, *I wish*, and *If only*, we use the ¹_____ simple tense to talk about how we would like ²_____ situations to be different. With *I'd rather* and *I'd prefer* we use the infinitive when the subject of the second verb is the same as the subject of *I'd rather* and *I'd prefer*. Also, with *I'd rather*, *I'd prefer* and *It's time*, we use the infinitive when there is no second subject.
   >
   > It's time to go.   I'd prefer to eat now.
   > It's time we left.   I'd prefer it if we ate now.

2 **Complete the dialogue with the correct forms of the verbs in the list.**

   go on | be | respect | get up | not have | show | not talk

   DAD   Come on, Ollie. It's time you ¹_____.
   OLLIE   Zzzzzzzz Zzzzzzzz
   DAD   Did you hear me, Ollie? You've got ten minutes until the school bus arrives.
   OLLIE   What?! No! If only it ²_____ the weekend. If only I ³_____ school today. If only …
   DAD   Ollie!
   OLLIE   Dad, I'd prefer it if you ⁴_____ my melatonin levels.
   DAD   And I'd prefer it if you ⁵_____ such nonsense.
   OLLIE   It's not nonsense. It's science. Melatonin. It's why I need so much sleep.
   DAD   I've never heard of it.
   OLLIE   Then maybe it's time you ⁶_____ the Internet and read about it.
   DAD   And maybe it's time you ⁷_____ your dad a bit of respect. Now get out of bed!

3 **Think about your own sleeping habits and complete the sentences so that they are true for you. Compare with a partner.**

   1 I wish I could …
   2 If only school …
   3 I'd rather … today.
   4 I wish the teachers …

Workbook page 18

VOCABULARY
Sleep

1 **Match the words on the left with those on the right to make sleep-related collocations and phrasal verbs. Then check in the magazine article and quiz on page 21.**

   1 nod   a the covers
   2 fall   b loudly
   3 lie   c off
   4 a light   d asleep
   5 fast   e a nap
   6 snore   f asleep
   7 under   g sleeper
   8 take   h in

2 **SPEAKING Work in pairs and discuss the meaning of each of the collocations and phrasal verbs in Exercise 1, using the context provided by the magazine article and quiz to help you.**

3 **Which noun collocates with all of these: *a lack of*, *over*, *skip*, *get enough*, *get seven hours*?**

4 **SPEAKING Complete the questions with collocations and phrasal verbs from Exercises 1 and 3, in the correct form, and then ask and answer in pairs.**

   1 Do you ever _____ in the afternoon or do you prefer to just sleep at night?
   2 Have you ever _____ during a lesson at school? Did anyone notice? What happened? How did you feel?
   3 Do you like to _____ at the weekend? Or do you get up early? What does it take to get you out from _____?
   4 Do you know anyone who _____ when they sleep? What's the best way to prevent this?
   5 Are you a _____ or is it difficult for you to wake up when you're _____? Is noise or light more likely to wake you up?
   6 Have you ever _____ and been late for something really important? What happened?

Workbook page 20

2 SLEEP ON IT

LISTENING

1 **SPEAKING** Work in pairs and discuss.
   1 What's the longest you've ever gone without sleep?
   2 Which of these things do you think people experience when they don't get enough sleep over an extended period of time?

   ☐ grumpiness
   ☐ headaches
   ☐ hunger
   ☐ slurred speech
   ☐ memory loss
   ☐ lethargy
   ☐ slow reactions
   ☐ impatience
   ☐ difficulty concentrating

2 🔊 1.11 Listen to an interview with a sleep expert. Which of the things in the list above does he mention?

3 🔊 1.11 Listen again and choose the correct answers.
   1 Why is sleep deprivation such a serious problem?
      a Because it's costing governments a lot of money in research.
      b Because it can cause major accidents and financial losses.
      c Because so many people suffer from it.
   2 What **doesn't** Dr Shone mention as a possible cause of the rise in sleep deprivation?
      a international travel
      b an increase in the length of the working day
      c a decrease in the average salary
   3 What are Dr Shone and his colleagues trying to do?
      a better understand the results of sleep deprivation
      b better understand the causes of sleep deprivation
      c alleviate the causes of sleep deprivation
   4 What was the first major effect Peter Tripp experienced during the sleep deprivation experiment?
      a He saw things that weren't there.
      b He found unusual things funny.
      c He became violent.
   5 What long-term effects did the experiment have on him?
      a He became confused about who he was.
      b There were significant changes in his personality.
      c He found it difficult to get work.

FUNCTIONS
Giving advice

1 🔊 1.12 Listen to the dialogue. What are Liam's problems?

2 🔊 1.12 Listen again. What advice does Sally give for each problem?

3 🔊 1.12 Complete Sally's advice with the missing words. Then listen again and check.
   1 I find that a g_____ n_____ s_____ works well for nerves.
   2 I'd recommend l_____ to m_____.
   3 You might want to consider g_____ to b_____ l_____.
   4 Try not to w_____ too much.

4 Work in pairs. Think of two pieces of advice for each of Liam's problems.

   I find that ...
   I'd recommend ...
   You might want to consider ...
   Try not to ...

THiNK SELF-ESTEEM
Getting enough rest

1 Complete the table for you.

Times when I get tired	Consequences	What can I do about this?
1 *Studying for tests*	*I get irritable with my family*	*Make a better revision timetable* *Keep clear of my little brother*
2		
3		
4		

2 **SPEAKING** Work in pairs. Compare and offer advice.

   Tests are a stressful time. I find that getting plenty of sleep during stressful periods is essential.

23

READING

1 Work in pairs. Read the questions about dreams. How many can you answer?

1 Are there any common dreams?
2 Does everyone dream?
3 Why can't I remember my dreams?
4 Why do I dream about strangers?
5 Why do I sometimes dream the phone is ringing, only to hear it ringing when I wake up?
6 Do my dreams have any special meanings?
7 Is it possible to influence what happens in our dreams?
8 Why don't I act out my dreams?
9 Do blind people dream?
10 What happens if we don't have the chance to dream?

2 Read the article quickly and match the questions with the facts, A–J. Which of the answers you came up with in Exercise 1 were correct?

Ten facts about dreams

[A] Dreams are known to have a beneficial effect on our mental well-being. A study was conducted in which people were woken just as they entered the dream phase of their sleep. They were then allowed to go back to sleep and get their normal night's sleep. However, on waking up, they displayed numerous signs of sleep deprivation.

[B] There's a state between falling asleep and entering the dream phase (known as REM) during which it is believed that we're able to control our dreams. This is also commonly experienced as we start waking up.

[C] With the exception of a very small minority of people, we all dream, even if we might not think we do. Interestingly, there's a difference between what men and women dream about. While women usually dream about both sexes, men are considerably more likely to have dreams that just feature other men.

[D] Yes, they do. The mind's need to dream is so strong that it is able to overcome any disability to ensure it does. People who lose their sight later on in life still see pictures in their dreams. However, those who were born blind dream using exaggerated sounds, smells and emotions.

[E] The simple answer is that your body is more or less paralysed when you're asleep, so you're unable to move your limbs. This is probably for our own safety and to stop us from inflicting harm on ourselves or others while we're asleep.

[F] Plenty. Falling from a great height but never reaching the ground; feeling unprepared for an exam even though you left school years ago; being chased but never caught: these are just a few types of dreams familiar to many people. Amazingly, 12% of people only ever dream in black and white.

[G] It's not really known if all dreams are significant but it's generally agreed that some dreams are far more significant than others. It's not always easy to unlock what they might be trying to tell us, but more often than not there's some sort of message. A dream psychologist could help if you're interested.

[H] No one is really sure, but the fact is that five minutes after waking up you've already forgotten half your dream. And five minutes after that, all but 10% is gone. If you want to keep a record of your dreams, your best bet is to write down all you can remember as soon as you wake up.

[I] When an external sound invades our dream, this is known as dream incorporation. And it's not nearly as mysterious as it may seem. Quite simply, this outside noise was what triggered your dream in the first place, even though it might feel that your dream had been going on for hours already.

[J] You don't. All the unfamiliar faces that you meet in your dreams belong to people that you've seen at some time in your life. Even though you've never been introduced to them, your mind stores up all these faces, meaning it has a cast of literally millions to introduce into your dreams.

SPEAKING

1 Which information in the article do you find most interesting and/or surprising? Why?

2 Do you believe our dreams are trying to tell us something? Give examples to support your opinion.

2 SLEEP ON IT

GRAMMAR
Adverbs for modifying comparatives

1 Put the words in brackets back into the example sentences. Then read and complete the rule.

1. Men are more likely to have dreams that just feature other men. (considerably)
2. Some dreams are more significant than others. (far)
3. It's not as mysterious as it may seem. (nearly)

> **RULE:** As well as using *a lot* and *much* to emphasise a comparison, we can use other adverbs, such as *considerably*, *far*, *significantly*, *extensively*, *notably*, *way* and *drastically*. By using these words, we achieve a greater level of variety in our speaking and writing.
> - *Notably* and *Significantly* are used in more [1]*formal / informal* spoken contexts and in writing. *Way* is used in more [2]*formal / informal* spoken contexts.
> - To emphasise a(n) (*not*) *as… as* construction we can use *not nearly*, *nothing like* and *nowhere near*.

2 Complete with the missing words. In some cases, more than one word is possible.

Why are other people's dreams not [1]n_____ as interesting as mine? My dreams are [2]c_____ more exciting than most other people's, but no one seems interested in hearing about them. It's strange. Anyway, the other day I had a really weird dream. It was [3]w_____ more weird than my usual dreams. I was in this house. It wasn't my house. In fact, it was nothing [4]l_____ my house at all. It was [5]n_____ bigger for a start and it was [6]s_____ more modern too, but it was really familiar and I felt like I'd been there before. Suddenly, I heard a really horrible noise. It was like a snake hissing, only it was [7]f_____ louder. It was really creepy, but it was [8]n_____ near as scary as what happened next. What did happen next? I can't remember. It was frightening though. It really was.

3 Complete the second sentence so that it has a similar meaning to the first. You must use between three and six words including the word given.

1. I feel a lot less tired than I did five minutes ago. **NOWHERE**
   I feel _____ now as I did five minutes ago.
2. My bed is nothing like as comfortable as yours. **WAY**
   Your bed _____ mine.
3. My dreams were far more exciting when I was a child. **NEARLY**
   My dreams these days are _____ when I was a child.
4. I hope tonight is much less warm than last night. **NOTHING**
   I hope tonight _____ as it was last night.

4 **WRITING** Write a short text about a dream you can remember (or make one up). Include modifying comparatives.

5 **SPEAKING** Tell your dream to a partner. Whose dream was the strangest?

Workbook page 19

VOCABULARY
Idioms with *sleep* and *dream*

1 Complete the sentences with either *sleep* or *dream* in the correct form.

1. It's a difficult decision. *Let me _____ on it* and I'll let you know in the morning.
2. It's not such a big problem – certainly nothing to *lose _____ over*.
3. I can't believe I'm getting the chance to study in Canada! That's *beyond my wildest _____*.
4. You really think I'd do that!?! *I'd never _____ of doing* something so mean. He's my best friend.
5. I'd love to be an airline pilot. It's my _____ job.
6. I can't believe I've been signed by Manchester United. It's *a _____ come true*.
7. We've got a big day tomorrow and you need to *get your beauty _____*.
8. Do you imagine I'd let you go to an all-night party? *In your _____*!

2 Which of the expressions in italics in Exercise 1 could be replaced with these words?

1. more or better than I could ever hope for
2. no way
3. the realisation of my ultimate ambition
4. give me some time to think about it
5. sleep well so that you're fresh and at your best the next day
6. worry too much about
7. It's just not in my character to do
8. perfect profession

3 **SPEAKING** Discuss in pairs.

1. What's your dream job?
2. What would be a dream come true for you?
3. What would you never dream of doing?
4. Which of the idioms in Exercise 1 can you translate directly into your language? How would you translate the other ones?

Workbook page 20

25

Culture

1 Scan the article for the answers to the following questions.
   1 What caused a change in sleeping patterns across a number of countries?
   2 How long, on average, do people sleep for?

Sleep in different cultures

It is quite apparent that there are significant differences in sleep patterns in different parts of the world, and that sleep patterns have also changed over time. Traditions, cultural values and local conditions and environments all have a bearing on sleep practices and attitudes.

One major source of these differences is the widespread availability of artificial light, which, since its introduction in the mid-nineteenth century, has led to dramatic changes in sleep patterns in the industrialised world. It is thought that today we sleep at least an hour less each night than was the custom just a century ago, and probably several hours less than before industrialisation and electricity. According to some studies, artificial lighting has encouraged people to go to bed later and to sleep in a single concentrated burst throughout the night (monophasic sleep), rather than the more segmented and broken-up sleep patterns (polyphasic or biphasic sleep) that were previously the norm.

During the long nights of the winter months, our prehistoric ancestors – and, according to some researchers, more recent ancestors up until about two hundred years ago – may have broken sleep up into two or more chunks, separated by an hour or two of quiet restfulness. In nomadic societies, even today, it is more common for people to have this kind of biphasic sleep, or sometimes even more flexible and fragmented polyphasic sleep periods, sleeping on and off throughout the day or night, depending on what is happening.

Even within the developed world, there are significant differences in sleep patterns. A study carried out in ten countries in 2002 revealed some of these regional variations. For instance, while the average time the study participants slept was about 7.5 hours a night, the results from individual countries varied from 6 hours 53 minutes in Japan to 8 hours 24 minutes in Portugal. Over 42% of Brazilians took regular afternoon naps, compared to only 12% of Japanese people. Over 32% of Belgians complained of insomnia and other sleep problems, while only 10% of Austrians claimed not to sleep well.

A daytime nap or siesta is commonplace among adults in many Mediterranean countries. Spain, in particular, has raised the siesta almost to the level of an art form, although, in the hustle and bustle of the modern world, it is less ubiquitous than it once was. Naps are also common in parts of Africa and China.

The experience of Japan is a clear example of the way a change in culture can affect sleep patterns. In the post-war years, Japan was keen to rebuild and reassert itself and, as one expression of patriotism, Japanese workers were encouraged to start work early (and often finish late as well). The *inemuri* (a nap taken at work in order to increase productivity) was encouraged as a way for an employee to demonstrate their commitment, even though it probably degraded the quality of night-time sleep even more. Today, sleep is perhaps more undervalued in Japan than anywhere else, and sleep deprivation is endemic.

It is clear, then, that there are cultural and historical differences in the amount of sleep we get and the way we get it. Yet one thing is for sure: the need for sufficient sleep, however we may define this, is universal and unchanging.

2 🔊 1.13 Read and listen to the article again and answer the questions.
   1 How has the number of hours we sleep changed over the centuries?
   2 What's the difference between monophasic and polyphasic sleep?
   3 Which country was found to sleep the least?
   4 In which countries is it usual to have a short sleep in the afternoon?
   5 Why are naps becoming less common?
   6 Why was the *inemuri* introduced in Japan?
   7 What effect did it have?

2 SLEEP ON IT

3 **SPEAKING** Work in pairs and discuss the questions.

1 What sleeping habits are typical in your country?
2 Which of the habits mentioned in the article would be unusual in your culture?
3 In what way do you think sleeping habits have changed over the last few decades?

4 **VOCABULARY** Match the highlighted words or phrases in the article to the definitions.

1 ordinary, everyday
2 not given enough importance
3 in one time rather than separated out into several short chunks
4 consisting of several separate parts
5 difficulty sleeping
6 to have an influence or effect on
7 loyalty
8 found everywhere

WRITING
A proposal

1 Read the proposal and answer the questions.
  1 What problem is the proposal trying to tackle?
  2 What recommendation does it make?

2 Read again and answer the questions.
  1 How well does the proposal answer the question?
  2 How varied is the language?
  3 How well organised is it?

3 When writing a proposal, the key things to mention are:
  - a specific problem
  - a summary of the problem and the proposed solution to it
  - an idea for a solution
  - justification of why it's a good solution

  Match each of these areas to the paragraphs A–D in the proposal.

4 Write a proposal supporting the idea that the school day should start two hours later. Use the stages outlined in Exercise 3 to help you organise your ideas.

Write a proposal supporting the idea that your place of work should introduce a nap room for employees.

[A] A recent study has shown that less than half of all Americans are getting enough sleep each night and that an overtired workforce is costing the economy millions of dollars in lost productivity each year. Clearly, anything that is losing big business so much money warrants investigation.

[B] Among several ideas that have been put forward, one of the most popular has been the introduction of nap rooms in many businesses across the USA. As the name suggests, a nap room is a place where employees can have a short rest during the working day in order to recharge their batteries. A nap room can be anything from a designated dark room with several beds to specially designed sleep pods.

[C] The idea is that rather than falling asleep at their desk, tired workers can take time out in the nap room if they need to do so. Those companies that have installed one are already reporting rises in the effectiveness of their workforce.

[D] Lack of sleep is clearly a widespread problem among the population and the introduction of a nap room in our offices would greatly benefit the well-being of the staff. If we could be offered a quiet room where we could catch up on sleep during breaks, we would see an overall improvement in our performance and efficiency, which in turn would increase the company's productivity.

CAMBRIDGE ENGLISH: ADVANCED

THiNK EXAMS

READING AND USE OF ENGLISH
Part 1: Multiple-choice cloze

Workbook page 25

1 For questions 1–8, read the text below and decide which answer (A, B, C or D) best fits each gap. There is an example at the beginning (0).

0   A over   B in   C (across)   D into

Anyone who Googles the word 'dreams' will come 0_____ thousands of sites that offer to interpret your dreams. However, there is no system of dream interpretation that is 1_____ up by scientific research. Consequently, many of these sites offer nothing more than guesswork, and, indeed, the interpretations do not 2_____ much from those that were around thousands of years ago. So, for example, if you dream that you are being chased, you are supposedly fleeing from uncomfortable 3_____. Many people dream that an authority 4_____ asks them for personal identification but they are unable to 5_____ it – this, it is suggested, indicates that you are struggling to 6_____ a feeling of social inadequacy. There is as yet no scientific data to 7_____ these ideas. However, some scientists are gathering reports from dreamers that, in the future, will 8_____ a correlation to be made between dreams and actual waking experiences.

	A		B		C		D	
1	A supported	B pushed	C backed	D grown
2	A differ	B change	C resemble	D offer
3	A remembrances	B remembers	C memories	D recalls
4	A person	B character	C officer	D figure
5	A manufacture	B discover	C search	D produce
6	A overdo	B overcome	C overreact	D oversee
7	A suppose	B discover	C support	D report
8	A allow	B make	C research	D produce

SPEAKING
Part 1: Interview

In this part of the exam, the examiner will ask you some questions about you, your life and your interests. Remember: although the questions themselves aren't difficult or complicated, your answers will be judged on, among other things, your ability to use accurate and varied grammar, and a wide and appropriate range of vocabulary.

2 In pairs, ask and answer the questions.

1 What work would you like to do in the future?
2 What do you like doing in your spare time? (Why?)
3 What do you spend most time doing – studying or relaxing? (Why?)
4 How do you usually keep in touch with friends and relatives?
5 Have you recently had a reason to celebrate something? (What?)
6 Who or what is the most important influence in your life? (Why?)

TEST YOURSELF

UNITS 1 & 2

VOCABULARY

1 Complete the sentences with the words and phrases in the list. There are four extra words / phrases.

lie-in | oversleep | sleep | dream | unconventional | insecure | sad | rebellious | miserable
asleep | traditional | take a nap | nerves | nod off

1. My aunt's very _____ . She got married in a bright red dress and dyed silver hair.
2. I'd love to be someone who designs beds. It would be my _____ job.
3. I've got nothing to do tomorrow morning, so I'm going to have a _____ .
4. Don't worry about it. It's nothing to lose _____ over.
5. He might seem very confident, but underneath he's quite _____ and worries a lot.
6. My younger sister is quite _____ and doesn't like being told what to do.
7. I often _____ when I'm watching TV. It's so annoying as I miss the end of the programme.
8. I wish he'd stop asking so many annoying questions. He's really getting on my _____ .
9. I'm going to set my alarm for 7 am because I don't want to _____ .
10. My older brother was really mean when we were younger and he made my life _____ .

/10

GRAMMAR

2 Complete the sentences with the words / phrases in the list. There are two extra words / phrases.

hopefully | got rid of | understandably | considerably | regrettably | nowhere near | get rid of | to have

1. It's time we _____ this old TV.
2. Boys tend _____ more friends than girls when they're younger.
3. _____ , we had to come home three days early from our holiday.
4. It's _____ as hot as it was yesterday.
5. _____ , no one is very happy about the fare increase on the buses.
6. It's _____ hotter today than it was yesterday.

3 Find and correct the mistake in each sentence.

1. Manchester United are nowhere nearly as good as Barcelona.
2. My younger brother always is taking my things without asking.
3. I'd prefer it if we leave half an hour earlier.
4. Not many of the birds sadly were able to survive.
5. I wish I didn't eat so much at the party last night.
6. Being the oldest in the family, my brother will be the most traditional.

/12

FUNCTIONAL LANGUAGE

4 Choose the correct options.

1. A I *find / discover* that adding eggs helps make a lighter cake.
   B *Inform / Tell* me you haven't done that. I'm allergic to eggs.
2. A Try not *worrying / to worry* too much. It's only a bike.
   B But *what / how* about work tomorrow morning? How am I going to get there?
3. A You might want to *think / consider* inviting Dan to your party.
   B I plan to invite him. I really *do / plan*. I just haven't seen him in a while.
4. A I'd recommend *to put / putting* your books away. Why don't you watch a bit of TV instead?
   B I don't *get / understand*. Are you telling me not to study?

/8

MY SCORE /30

22 – 30
10 – 21
0 – 9

29

3 LUCKY BREAKS

OBJECTIVES

FUNCTIONS: giving encouragement to someone who's feeling nervous
GRAMMAR: mixed conditionals (review); alternatives to *if*
VOCABULARY: phrasal verbs; expressions with *luck*; expressions with *over*

A

B

C

READING

1 **SPEAKING** Look at the pictures. For each one:
   1 describe what you think is happening / has happened.
   2 say what might happen next.
   3 say how each person could possibly be unlucky.
   4 say how each person could possibly be lucky.

2 Read the magazine article quickly.
   1 Match the stories to the pictures (1–3).
   2 How does each writer think they were lucky?

3 🔊 1.14 Read again and listen and mark the statements T (true), F (false) or DS (the text doesn't say).
   1 Amanda had never been in a play before.
   2 The teacher was impressed when Amanda demonstrated that she knew the main character's lines.
   3 Amanda went to drama school and then joined a local acting group.
   4 Jason's father shouted at the taxi driver when he missed his plane.
   5 None of the passengers survived the plane crash.
   6 Janine's car swerved and hit a tree.
   7 Roadside assistance arrived on the scene after 30 minutes.
   8 Janine married the man who came to fix her car.

4 **SPEAKING** Work in pairs and discuss the questions.
   1 In your opinion, who was the luckiest person: Amanda, Jason's father or Janine? Who was the least lucky?
   2 Which story do you like the most / least? Why?
   3 Can you think of any other lucky breaks that you or people you know have experienced?

TRAIN TO THiNK

Behaviour based on myths rather than facts

1 Work in pairs. Read this dictionary definition of a myth and answer the questions.

> **myth** noun (FALSE IDEA)
> a commonly believed but false idea:
> *Statistics **disprove** the myth **that** women are worse drivers than men.*

3 LUCKY BREAKS

My lucky break

We asked readers to write and tell us about a lucky break that changed their lives. Here are some of their replies.

1 Breaking into acting

At school, when I was 16, we started to rehearse the end-of-term play. The teacher gave me a small part and that was fine. As we started rehearsals, two things stood out for me. The first was that I really enjoyed this acting thing, even though it was my first go at it. I found memorising my lines really easy and I was able to remember other characters' lines, too. Secondly, I realised the girl who'd taken on the lead role couldn't act!

Anyway, about a week before the play opened, she fell over and broke her leg, poor thing. The teacher didn't know what to do. I told her I could step in. She was pleasantly surprised when I was able to recite the main character's lines off by heart at the next rehearsal and she gave me the part. The play was a huge success. Also, someone from a local theatre group came and invited me to join them. I did, and that really helped me get into drama school, which was the start of my acting career.

When that poor girl broke her leg, it was an unlucky break (ha, ha!) for her but a lucky one for me. If she hadn't broken her leg, I'd probably be in a run-of-the-mill office job or something now.

Amanda

2 A jammy escape

I know this was really my dad's lucky break, but from my perspective, it was mine too. About ten years ago, my dad had to go to a really important business meeting in another city, and he had to catch an early morning flight. He took a taxi but it got stuck in a horrendous traffic jam and by the time he got to the airport, his plane had already taken off. He was really angry because he knew he was going to be late for the meeting. They managed to get him on the next plane and off he went. When he landed and got through to arrivals, he was surprised by what he saw: there were TV cameras all over the place and crowds of people frantically waiting for news. It turned out that the plane he'd missed earlier that morning had crashed.

If it hadn't been for that traffic jam, my dad would probably no longer be here.

Jason

3 Breakdown and start-up

Just over two years ago, I was driving home fairly late one night on a quiet road when another car suddenly came hurtling towards me. I had to swerve off the road to avoid it and I almost hit a tree. I wasn't hurt, but I couldn't get my car to start. It had broken down. I felt quite anxious as it was late and there were hardly any other cars around. I phoned roadside assistance for help and they told me someone would be there in around half an hour. After about five minutes, a car pulled up and a friendly-looking man got out. He asked me if I was OK and I told him what had happened. He kindly offered to stay with me until help arrived. There was something very calm and soothing in his voice, so I took him up on his offer. We started talking and really hit it off. By the time the roadside assistance man turned up, we'd arranged to meet again. Two years on, he's now my husband and I wish I could thank the reckless driver who forced me off the road. If they were a better driver, I'd never have met the love of my life.

Janine

---

1 According to the dictionary entry, who are worse at driving, women or men?
2 If someone believes women are worse drivers than men, how might this affect their behaviour?

Sometimes we change our behaviour or make a decision because of a myth or false belief. These myths can range from culturally-shared false beliefs such as 'breaking a mirror means bad luck', to more personal ones, such as 'I wear my lucky T-shirt to every football match that my team plays in'.

Most of us are aware that such behaviour has no actual influence on the outcome of an event, but despite this, we still act as if the false belief we have is fact.

2 Which of these myths do you feel are personal beliefs and which are widely held ones?

1 I always put my left leg into the bath first.
2 If I spill salt accidentally, I throw it over my shoulder and make a wish.
3 I never walk under a ladder. It brings bad luck.
4 I never travel on Friday 13th. It's an unlucky day.
5 I tap my phone three times before I turn it on.
6 I always use the same pen to do my exams.

3 **SPEAKING** Discuss in pairs. Which myths do you or people you know have? How do these myths affect your / their behaviour?

GRAMMAR
Mixed conditionals (review)

1 **Match the beginnings and endings of these sentences from the article. Then complete the rule with *present* and *past*.**

1 If she hadn't broken her leg,
2 If it hadn't been for that traffic jam,
3 If they were a better driver,

a my dad would probably no longer be here.
b I'd never have met the love of my life.
c I'd probably be in a run-of-the-mill office job or something now.

> **RULE:** Mixed conditionals are used:
> - to connect an imaginary past (*had* + past participle) with a ¹_____ result (*would* + infinitive) as in sentences 1 and 2.
> - to connect a hypothetical present (past simple) with a ²_____ result (*would have* + past participle) as in sentence 3.

Pronunciation
Unstressed words in connected speech
Go to page 120.

2 **Choose the correct options.**

1 My cousin lived in Chicago for five years as a child. If she *didn't live / hadn't lived* there, she *wouldn't speak / wouldn't have spoken* English as well as she does.
2 Yo-Yo Ma plays the cello exceptionally well. He *wouldn't be / wouldn't have been* as famous as he is if he *didn't learn / hadn't learned* from such a young age.
3 I don't feel very well. If I *hadn't eaten / didn't eat* two bars of chocolate, *I'd be / I'd have been* OK now.
4 I'm never on time. If I *wasn't always / hadn't always been* late, I *wouldn't get / wouldn't have got* in trouble with the teacher yesterday.
5 She was really rude to me. We *would still be / would still have been* friends now if she *didn't say / hadn't said* those things.
6 I'm not very good at football. If I *was / had been* a better player, I'm sure I *would have been chosen / would be chosen* for the school team last week!

3 **Rewrite the sentences using a mixed conditional structure.**

0 I'm tired today because I didn't sleep well last night.
If I'd slept well last night, I wouldn't be tired today.
1 I know how to play the game. My friend explained it to me yesterday.
2 I haven't got any money. I didn't buy a present for my mum.
3 My sister had an accident. She's in hospital.
4 He's a very talented tennis player. He won four tournaments last year.
5 I missed the train. I'm not in Manchester yet.

4 **WRITING** Write two mixed conditional sentences about yourself or someone you know.

1 If _____, I wouldn't be here now.
2 _____ if I'd had a bit more luck.

> Workbook page 28

VOCABULARY
Phrasal verbs

1 **Replace the words in bold with phrasal verbs from the list in the correct form, then read the magazine article again and check.**

turn up | stand out | pull up | take up | break down
step in | take on | turn out

1 As we started rehearsals, two things above all else **became very clear**.
2 The girl who'd **accepted** the lead role couldn't act.
3 By the time the roadside assistance man **arrived**, we'd arranged to meet again.
4 It **finally became clear** that the plane he'd missed earlier that morning had crashed.
5 The car had **stopped working**.
6 After about five minutes, a car **approached and came to a stop**.
7 I **accepted** his offer.
8 The teacher didn't know what to do. I told her I could **help** (**in a difficult situation**).

2 **SPEAKING** Work in pairs and answer the questions.

1 What would you do if you were in a car that broke down?
2 Have you ever had to step in at the last minute? What happened?
3 Have you ever turned up far too late (or too early) for something? What happened?

3 **WRITING** Use phrasal verbs from Exercise 1 to write two more questions for your partner.

4 **SPEAKING** Work in pairs. Ask and answer your questions.

> Workbook page 30

3 LUCKY BREAKS

LISTENING

1 Can you name the people in the photos above? What's the connection between the famous people and the objects?

2 🔊 1.16 Listen and check your ideas from Exercise 1.

3 🔊 1.16 Listen again to Mark and Clare.
   1 Who believes in luck, and who doesn't?
   2 Who thinks that having lucky objects or doing things to bring luck is outdated in the 21st century?
   3 What happens to Clare at the end with the pen?

4 🔊 1.16 Listen again. Complete each sentence with between one and three words.
   1 When Mark travels anywhere, he always wears his _____.
   2 Clare thinks that whether a plane will _____ or not doesn't depend on socks.
   3 Mark's grandfather always had to put his _____ on the ship first.
   4 According to Mark, it's common to have lucky numbers, _____ and _____.
   5 Tennis player Serena Williams always bounces the ball _____ before serving.
   6 Clare needs the pen to make a list of things she needs for the _____ on Saturday.

VOCABULARY
Expressions with *luck*

1 **SPEAKING** Read the sentences. What do the underlined phrases mean? Discuss in pairs.
   1 I paid £10 for this T-shirt and then I saw the same one in another shop for £8! It's <u>just my luck</u>.
   2 He always wears those shoes when he plays. He thinks they <u>bring him luck</u>.
   3 A Does the number 21 bus stop here?
     B Yes – and <u>you're in luck</u>. Look, there's one coming now.
   4 A I missed the last train by 15 seconds!
     B Oh, <u>bad luck</u>. What did you do – walk home?
   5 A I failed my driving test.
     B Oh, sorry to hear that. <u>Better luck next time</u>.
   6 A Did you get wet on your walk?
     B No! <u>As luck would have it</u>, we got home just before the rain started.
   7 A It was my first ever go at one of those competitions, and I won!
     B Huh! <u>Beginner's luck</u>.
   8 A Dad's agreed to drive me to football practice. I think I'll ask him if he can pick me up too. I don't feel like walking home.
     B That might be <u>pushing your luck</u>. He'll be watching TV later.

➡ Workbook page 30

SPEAKING

Work in pairs and answer the questions.

1 Have you ever had beginner's luck when playing a new sport or game? When / How?
2 Do you or does anyone you know have any things that they do to bring them good luck?
3 Give an example of a time when you've pushed your luck.

READING

1. Look at the title of the blog. Have you ever seen this word before? What do you think it means?

2. Read the blog quickly to check your ideas from Exercise 1.

3. Read again and answer the questions.
   1. What was the wildlife photographer hoping to do?
   2. What was lucky about the photo he took?
   3. How do translators feel about the word 'serendipity'?
   4. What example is mentioned of serendipity in science?
   5. What example is given of serendipity in history?
   6. What example of serendipity does the writer give from her own experience?

4. Are these things examples of serendipity or not? Why (not)? Put a tick or a cross in the box. Then compare with a partner.
   1. ☐ You've lost a ring at home. You look everywhere for it. Then a family member comes in and says: 'Look! I found your ring in the car.'
   2. ☐ A footballer tries to kick the ball to score a goal. He kicks it very badly, but accidentally passes it to another player in his team, who scores.
   3. ☐ You're looking for a book in your room. You look on a shelf and see a DVD that you thought you'd lost.

5. **SPEAKING** Work in pairs. Discuss your answers to the questions.
   1. How would you translate the word 'serendipity' into your language?
   2. Do you know of any examples of serendipity from a film / book / TV show?
   3. Have you experienced serendipity in your own life (or has someone you know)?

> JANET'S 'ODD WORD' BLOG. This week: 'serendipity'.

Serendipity

A wildlife photographer was waiting, hoping to get a shot of a relatively rare bird, a particular kind of heron. He'd waited several frustrating hours with no luck at all. He needed a photo soon, otherwise it would be too dark. Suddenly, to the photographer's delight, a heron settled on a branch right in front of him. The photographer raised his camera, focused in and took the shot just before the heron flew away. Feeling particularly pleased with himself, the photographer looked at the image. To his astonishment, he saw that behind the heron, his photograph had also captured a very, very rare woodpecker flying past. He hadn't seen it, but without even trying, he'd photographed an even rarer bird than the one he was aiming for.

This is an example of serendipity – a word which, according to some translators, is among the ten most difficult English words to define and translate. It means something like 'the fact of finding interesting or valuable things by chance'. The key thing is that if you come across something fortuitous by chance, it's serendipity, provided that you weren't consciously trying to find that thing at the time.

Cases of serendipity can be found in numerous fields, such as science. Back in the 1800s, a man called Wells was at a demonstration of laughing gas (ether and nitrous oxide). After being given the gas, the patient started laughing, as expected. But then he suddenly fell over and cut his leg rather badly. To everyone's surprise, the man reported that he couldn't feel any pain. Wells hadn't been looking for it, but he'd made a medical discovery – certain gases reduce and can even almost eradicate pain. Had Wells not been there that night, anaesthesia might have taken longer to be discovered.

History offers further examples. In 1492, Columbus set out from Portugal to try to find an alternative route to India. What he found was the land we now know as America. He was looking for one thing and found another.

Most of us can probably think of at least one example of serendipity in our own lives. A friend of mine was trying to come up with an idea for an online article but got completely stuck. Frustrated, she decided to go out to a local café. She sat there and as she was sipping her coffee, she heard two people talking behind her. A man was telling a story that sounded so unbelievable that she knew it had to be true. She asked the people if she could interview them for the article – unless she got their permission, she wouldn't be able to use their story. They agreed and her article turned out to be one of the top trending articles of the week.

3 LUCKY BREAKS

GRAMMAR
Alternatives to *if*

1 **Complete the sentences from the blog on page 34 by writing one word in each space.**

   1 He needed a photo soon, _____ it would be too dark.
   2 If you come across something fortuitous by chance, it's serendipity, _____ you weren't consciously trying to find that thing at the time.
   3 _____ she got their permission, she wouldn't be able to use their story.

2 **Read these sentences. Underline the word(s) that could be replaced with *if*. Then complete the rule with *unless*, *otherwise*, *as long as* and *suppose*.**

   1 You can borrow it as long as you're very careful with it.
   2 Suppose you were on holiday – what would you be doing now?
   3 Imagine you could live anywhere in the world – where would you live?

   RULE:
   - There are many alternatives to *if*, including *provided that*, *as long as*, *unless*, *otherwise*, *suppose* and *imagine*.
   - We use *provided that* and ¹_____ in the same way as *if*, but they make the main clause even more dependent on the condition.
   - The word ²_____ is used after an order or suggestion to indicate what the result will be if the order or suggestion isn't followed.
   - When we use the word ³_____ instead of *if*, it gives the verb that follows a negative meaning.
   - *Imagine* and ⁴_____ are often followed by a second or third conditional clause.

3 **Choose the correct options.**

   1 Everything will be fine *as long as* / *suppose* / *unless* you're very careful.
   2 *Imagine* / *Provided that* / *Unless* you could meet someone famous – who would you choose?
   3 We'll arrive before eleven o'clock *provided that* / *unless* / *otherwise* the traffic is bad.
   4 Go to bed early, *unless* / *as long as* / *otherwise* you'll be tired tomorrow.
   5 *Unless* / *Suppose* / *As long as* we left now – what time would we get there?
   6 *Imagine* / *Provided that* / *Unless* you practise hard, you'll play the guitar well in a few months.

4 **Rewrite the sentences using the word in brackets.**

   0 Could you survive if you had no Internet for a day? (Suppose)
   Suppose you had no Internet for a day – could you survive?
   1 I always enjoy eating out in restaurants if the food's good. (as long as).
   2 I never work at the weekend if I don't have to. (unless)
   3 Everyone deserves some good luck. If not, it's not fair. (otherwise)
   4 I don't mind working hard if I get good exam results. (provided that)

5 **SPEAKING** Which of sentences 1–4 in Exercise 4 do you agree with? Why?

> Workbook page 29

THiNK VALUES
How do we feel about luck?

1 **Make notes on how you'd feel in each of these situations.**

   1 You know someone who, in the past, said things about you that you didn't like. You hear that they had some bad luck – they slipped and broke their right arm just before an important exam.
   2 You hear that someone you like very much has just won a competition and the prize is a week's holiday in a wonderful place.
   3 You take a multiple-choice test. You don't know many of the answers at all but you guess them. You discover that you got a score of 17 out of 20.

2 **SPEAKING** Work in pairs. Compare your answers to Exercise 1 and then discuss these questions.

   1 What would be the best response to each situation?
   2 Is this a true reflection of how you really feel?
   3 What, if anything, would be an inappropriate response?

WRITING
A story

You are going to write a story. It must begin or end with this sentence:

It was the luckiest day of my life.

1 Decide whether to base this on a true story or an invented one. But make sure that there's some luck involved.
2 It's important to plan before you begin writing. Think about and make notes on the following:
   - the background (where you were, what was happening, etc). Use a range of narrative tenses.
   - how the event proved to be lucky and changed things in your life. Try to use conditionals and some of the 'luck' vocabulary in the unit.

Write your story (250–300 words).

PHOTOSTORY: episode 1

The talisman

1 **Look at the photos and answer the questions.**
  1 Where are Jack and his mum? How do you think Jack is feeling?
  2 What is Jack's mum giving him and why?

2 🔊 1.17 **Now read and listen to the photostory. Check your ideas.**

MUM Hi, Jack. How was your final driving lesson?
JACK OK, I guess.
MUM You must be quite a good driver now, overall. Just about ready for your test, I'd say.
JACK Just about ready? I'd better be more than just about ready. After all, the test is just over a week from now!
MUM True. How do you feel about it?
JACK Honestly, I'm terrified. I just keep going over all the things that could go wrong. What if I forget to use the indicator? Or what if I get a really strict examiner, or other drivers start beeping at me? What if a dog runs out into the road or what if I go too fast …
MUM Jack, Jack, calm down. I'm sure you'll be fine. You've been practising quite a lot, and your instructor says you handle yourself and the car very well. You're going to be fine.
JACK I'm just really nervous. Passing this test is really important for me, you know? When I get my licence, well, if I get my licence, it'll mean I can be a lot more independent. Assuming you lend me the car now and again, of course.
MUM Oh, we'll sort something out. I'm sure I can let you have it sometimes at the weekend – as long as I don't need it, that is.
JACK And that's another thing. You really need your car. What if I do something to it, like, break it or damage it?
MUM Jack, stop that. You can't worry yourself sick every time you get in the driver's seat. Confidence is a big part of being a good driver.
JACK Then I'm really in trouble! I'm not feeling confident at all! Oh, Mum, I don't know. Maybe I'm not ready for this.

MUM Jack, come and sit down a minute. I think I can help you.
JACK What do you mean?
MUM I think it's time to give you the talisman.
JACK The talis– what?
MUM The talisman.
JACK What on earth is that, Mum?
MUM A talisman is like a lucky charm, or a protector. This is our family talisman. My grandmother got it when she went to Spain a long, long time ago. She never went anywhere without it. She gave it to her daughter – my mother – when she left her home and immigrated to England, to bring her good luck. And my mother gave it to me when you were born. It's always protected our family and brought us good fortune. Take this with you to the driving test, and you're bound to pass.
JACK Tell me you're not serious, Mum. Do you honestly think having that is going to affect my test? I don't believe in lucky charms.
MUM Oh, Jack. Be careful! That talisman is very powerful. Don't say anything against it. But even if you don't believe in it, carrying it can't do you any harm, can it? What have you got to lose?
JACK OK, Mum, if it makes you happy.
MUM That's the spirit. You'll thank me when you pass.

3 LUCKY BREAKS

DEVELOPING SPEAKING

3 Work in pairs. Discuss what you think happens next. Write down your ideas.

We think that Jack passes and then thanks his mum for the talisman.

4 ▶ EP1 Watch the video to find out how the story continues.

5 Answer the questions.
1. What does Amanda say about the talisman?
2. How many times has Ethan taken his driving test before today?
3. Why does Ethan think he's failed?
4. Why doesn't Mr Schultz do Jack's driving test?
5. Does Jack pass or fail the test?
6. What is Jack's view of the talisman at the end?

PHRASES FOR FLUENCY

1 Find these expressions in the story. Who says them? How do you say them in your language?
1. After all
2. now and again,
3. …, that is.
4. What have you got to lose?
5. Assuming …
6. we'll sort something out.

2 Use the expressions in Exercise 1 to complete the dialogues.
1. **A** Do you go there very often?
   B No, only _____ .
2. **A** You should ask Janine to go to the cinema with you. _____ ?
   B Well, nothing I guess, _____ I ask her and she says yes!
3. **A** Your French is amazing!
   B Not really. My mum is French, _____ .
4. **A** You've invited 50 people to the party? We can't provide food for 50 people!
   B Oh, don't worry – _____ !
5. **A** Are we going to have dinner now?
   B Yes – if it's OK with you, _____ .

WordWise
Expressions with *over*

1 Look at these sentences from the unit so far. Complete them with the words and phrases from the list.

all over | all over again | fell over
overall | just over | going over

1. She _____ and broke her leg, poor thing.
2. _____ two years ago, I was driving home fairly late one night on a quiet road.
3. I've got ink _____ my hands now! Just my luck!
4. You must be quite a good driver now, _____ .
5. I just keep _____ all the things that could go wrong.
6. So you fail, and you have to take it _____ .

2 Choose the correct options.
1. It rained a bit, but we had a good weekend *overall / all over*.
2. We weren't listening, so the teacher had to tell us *overall / all over again*.
3. It was really windy last night and a lot of trees *went over / fell over*.
4. I understand the instructions really well because we've *fallen over / gone over* them four times!
5. Look at this mess! There are books and clothes *all over / just over* the floor.
6. It took us *just over / all over* five hours to drive home.

→ Workbook page 31

FUNCTIONS
Giving encouragement to someone who's feeling nervous

1 Complete what Jack's mother says when he tells her he's feeling nervous about his test.

Mum: 'Jack calm down. I'm sure _____ _____ _____ .'

2 Which of these expressions could also be used to give someone encouragement when they're feeling nervous?
- You've got this!
- Take a deep breath.
- What a nightmare!
- I've got my fingers crossed for you.

3 ROLE PLAY Work in pairs. Student A: Tell student B something that you feel nervous about. Student B: Give encouragement to student A using and expanding on the expressions in Exercises 1 and 2. Then switch roles. Who did the best job of encouraging their partner?

Possible topics:
- you're about to sing in front of the whole school
- you're about to take a university entrance exam
- you're about to play in a crucial football or basketball match

37

4 LAUGHTER IS THE BEST MEDICINE

OBJECTIVES

FUNCTIONS: responding to jokes
GRAMMAR: emphatic structures; boosting
VOCABULARY: laughter; idioms with *laugh* and *joke*

READING

1 **SPEAKING** Rank these situations from most (1) to least (6) enjoyable for you. Compare your ideas with a partner.
   - your best friend telling a funny story at break time in school
   - your little brother or sister getting scared by a fake spider
   - your dad telling you the same joke for the tenth time
   - watching your favourite comedy show
   - being asked to tell a joke to a crowd of people
   - standing with a group of friends who are all laughing at a joke that you don't get

2 Look at the people in the photos on this page and on page 39. Why do you think the people are laughing in each one?

3 ◀) 1.18 Read and listen to the article on page 39. Number the situations in the photos in the order that they are referred to in the article.

4 Read the article again. In which paragraph (A–E) are the following points made? Some paragraphs include more than one point.
   1. Humour is often the result of events that don't unfold as we imagine they will.
   2. Scientific studies have shown the beneficial effects of laughing.
   3. Older people laugh less frequently than younger people.
   4. We sometimes laugh at people when we feel we're better than they are.
   5. Laughter can work to make us feel more relaxed in an otherwise uncomfortable moment.
   6. People are less likely to laugh when they're alone.
   7. People will often laugh in an attempt to fit in.
   8. Laughter can be seen as a sign of immaturity.

5 **SPEAKING** Work in pairs and discuss the following questions.
   1. How many times do you think you laugh in a day?
   2. How many times did you laugh yesterday? Can you remember why you laughed?
   3. Which of the three theories mentioned in the article can you relate to? Give examples.
   4. Can you think of a time when you found yourself laughing at something that wasn't really that funny?

A

B

C

D

38

4 LAUGHTER IS THE BEST MEDICINE

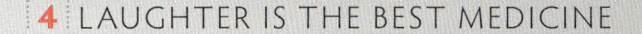

The science of *laughter*

Where does all the laughter go?

[A] It's no secret that laughter works wonders for us and much research has been carried out into the good that laughter can do for our general health and well-being. Amongst other things, it has been found to release endorphins, our bodies' natural 'feel-good' chemicals, into our blood. But as we grow older, we tend to find fewer things funny. A child will laugh on average over 300 times a day. By the time we reach adulthood, this number is more in the region of 20. But what's behind this? Why do we seemingly lose our ability [1]*to get the giggles* as we mature?

One theory suggests that it's not a case of us losing our [2]*sense of humour* but rather, as we grow older, we're socially conditioned to take things a bit more seriously. Unconsciously, we fear that by laughing, we're signalling to others that we're not taking life as seriously as we should be. As a consequence, we laugh less, which, in turn, can have a somewhat negative impact on our overall well-being.

A social occupation

[B] Laughter is very much something we do with others. Studies have shown that we are 30 times more likely to [3]*find something funny* when we're with others than when we're by ourselves. Unless we're watching comedy on TV or listening to it on the radio, we rarely laugh when we're on our own. But to laugh with others, we do need to feel a connection to them. We need to feel comfortable in their company. That's why it can be difficult to laugh in the presence of strangers. Laughter is also very contagious and one person's laugh can spread quickly throughout a group of people. But often what makes us join in is the fear of standing out and being different. We laugh, even if we don't really [4]*get the joke*. This is most evident in groups dominated by a particularly powerful person. When the head teacher tells a joke, for instance, you laugh, even though later you might wonder if the [5]*punchline* was really that funny at all.

What makes something funny?

There are many different reasons why we laugh, but these can usually be attributed to one of three widely accepted theories:

[C] **The Incongruity Theory:** It's often the unexpected that makes us laugh. When events contradict our sense of logic and familiarity, the effect is often humorous. Many jokes start out in recognisable territory where we're on familiar ground and feel that we know how things will progress. When they suddenly take a turn into the unknown, our expectations are challenged and that often results in laughter.

[D] **The Superiority Theory:** We often find the mistakes and misfortunes of others [6]*hilarious*. This would explain the popularity of online videos showing [7]*pranks*. By [8]*laughing at the stupidity of others*, we allow ourselves to feel superior, knowing that we'd never be so foolish as to be set up in the same way. Of course, all we are is just one banana skin away from being that person ourselves!

[E] **The Relief Theory:** There's nothing better to ease the tension created by an awkward situation than an outburst of laughter. Triggering laughter is a technique often used by the directors of horror films to offer their audiences some [9]*light relief*. It also explains why there are so many jokes about the darker things in life. By being able to laugh at them, we're able to face them more easily.

TRAIN TO THiNK

Divergent thinking

In the article, the incongruity theory is mentioned as one explanation of how humour works. Our brains are hard-wired to follow a logical progression of thought. If something challenges this order, the effect can often lead to some very creative ideas and this is sometimes referred to as divergent thinking. The effect can also be very humorous.

1 Look at the question and the three answers.

What can you do with a one pound coin?
a buy a bottle of water with it
b use it to make a decision (heads or tails)
c use it as a paperweight

1 Which is the most obvious?
2 Which is the funniest?
3 Which is the most creative?

2 SPEAKING Work in pairs and discuss. How many ideas can you come up with for each one?

1 What can you do with a pair of ripped jeans?
2 What's your excuse for not handing in your homework?
3 What things can money not buy?

39

GRAMMAR
Emphatic structures

1. **Complete the sentences from the article with the missing words. Then complete the rule with *it*, *what* and *all*.**

   1 _____ makes us join in _____ the fear of standing out and being different.
   2 _____ 's often the unexpected _____ makes us laugh.
   3 _____ we are _____ just one banana skin away from being that person ourselves!

   > **RULE:** To make our language more emphatic we can use cleft sentences:
   > Cleft sentences with [1]_____ shift the focus of attention to the end of the sentence.
   > Cleft sentences with [2]_____ shift the focus of the attention to the beginning of the sentence.
   > Cleft sentences with [3]_____ have the meaning of *the only thing*.

   > **LOOK!** Another way we can add emphasis is by adding *do* or *does* to a positive statement, e.g. *But to laugh with others, we **do** need to feel a connection with them.*

2. **Rewrite the sentences using the words in brackets.**

   1 Adults forget how it feels to be a child. (What …)
   2 I don't like the way he always interrupts me when I'm telling a joke. (It's … that …)
   3 I only watch comedy shows on TV. (All …)
   4 You have to remember that many people don't find those kinds of jokes very funny. (What …)
   5 Dad, he's laughing at you, not your joke. (It's … that …)
   6 You only need to say sorry and she'll forgive you. (All …)

3. **Complete the sentences so that they are true for you.**

   1 What really makes me laugh …
   2 It's … that makes me cross.
   3 All I want for my birthday this year …
   4 It's … that causes most of the problems in the world.

   → Workbook page 36

VOCABULARY
Laughter

1. **Look back at the words and phrases in italics in the article on page 39 and write the correct number (1–9) next to the definition.**

   a find the misfortune of others funny
   b very funny
   c practical jokes played on someone
   d understand a joke
   e humour in a serious situation
   f the last line of a joke
   g the ability to see the funny side of things
   h to actually see the funny side of something
   i to laugh uncontrollably

2. **Complete each space with one word, using your answers to Exercise 1 to help you.**

   I don't know anyone as bad at telling jokes as my dad. His jokes and the [1]_____ he tries to play on us are awful. The problem is no one ever really [2]_____ his jokes. The fact that he often forgets the [3]_____ clearly doesn't help. When he finishes, he bursts out laughing as if he's just told the most [4]_____ joke ever. Of course, we all start getting the [5]_____, which makes him think that we [6]_____ his joke funny. He doesn't realise it's him we're laughing [7]_____, not his joke. Luckily, Mum's usually around to tell one of her jokes (which are usually funny) and add a bit of [8]_____ relief.

3. **Answer the questions. Make notes.**

   1 What sort of things give you the giggles? What do you do to try and stop them?
   2 What kind of jokes do you find funny?
   3 Which things do you think we shouldn't laugh at?
   4 Do you prefer to tell jokes or to hear them?
   5 What do you do if you don't get a joke that someone tells you?

4. **SPEAKING** Compare your answers with other students. Can you find anyone who shares your sense of humour?

   → Workbook page 38

THiNK SELF-ESTEEM
Laughter

1. **Think about funny things that happened this week. Make notes on:**

   1 two things you did that made other people smile.
   2 two funny things that you shared or saw online.
   3 two things that made you smile.
   4 two things that you've found hilarious.

2. **SPEAKING** Work in pairs and compare your answers. Who has the funniest anecdote?

4 LAUGHTER IS THE BEST MEDICINE

LISTENING

1 ◼)) 1.19 Listen to three jokes and match each one with a picture. There is one extra picture.

A ☐ B ☐ C ☐ D ☐

2 ◼)) 1.19 Listen again and make notes on the following for each joke.
1 Who are the main characters?
2 What happens?
3 What's the punchline?
4 Why is it funny?

3 ◼)) 1.19 Listen again and rate each of the jokes from 5 (hilarious) to 0 (I didn't get it).

Joke 1 ☐   Joke 2 ☐   Joke 3 ☐

4 **SPEAKING** Work in groups of three. Choose one of the jokes and tell it to the others.

FUNCTIONS
Responding to jokes

1 ◼)) 1.20 Read and listen to four jokes. What do the people think of them?
Choose ☺ or ☹ or 😐.

1   Why is 6 afraid of 7?   Because 7 8 9.

2   What do you call a fish with no eye?   Fsh.

3   I phoned the local hospital. I said, 'Is that the local hospital?' The woman said, 'Well, it depends where you're phoning from.'

4   Knock knock!   Who's there?
    Broken pencil.   Broken pencil who?
    Never mind. It's pointless.

2 ◼)) 1.20 Complete the phrases in order to make the responses. Listen again and check.
1 That's a g_____ o_____ .
2 Ha, ha. V_____ f_____ .
3 I m_____ r_____ that one.
4 I d_____ g_____ it.

3 **SPEAKING** Work in pairs. Discuss these questions. Think about the jokes you heard in Listening Exercise 1 and Functions Exercise 1.
1 Which of the jokes, if any, did you find funny? Did you dislike any of them? Why?
2 Some people have said that the joke about the elderly couple could be considered to be in bad taste. What do you think?
3 Which of these jokes work in your language?
4 Are there any jokes that you know that wouldn't work in English?

4 **SPEAKING** Work in pairs. Think of a joke and practise telling it in English.

5 **SPEAKING** Tell your joke to another pair. Respond appropriately to each other's jokes. Whose joke was the funniest?

Pronunciation
Telling jokes: pacing, pausing and punchlines
Go to page 120.

READING

1 **SPEAKING** Work in pairs. Ask and answer the questions.

1 Which comedy shows do you enjoy watching? Why?
2 Who are the most famous comedians in your country? Are there many famous female comedians?
3 What do you understand by the term *stand-up comedy*? How popular is it in your country?

2 Read the article quickly and answer the questions.

1 What makes Shappi unusual?
2 Apart from stand-up comedy, what other things has she done?

3 Read the article again and answer the questions.

1 Why does the writer describe Shappi as 'a breath of fresh air'?
2 Why were Shappi's family forced to move from their native country?
3 Why were Shappi's early days in the UK difficult?
4 How did she survive these days?
5 Why was this a practice that 'would certainly serve her well'?
6 How does Shappi describe her early experiences of being a comedian?
7 How does she feel about her dual nationality?

The World of Comedy: Shappi Khorsandi

In a profession which has traditionally had more than its fair share of men, Shappi Khorsandi is unquestionably a breath of fresh air. She's funny. Very funny indeed.

Born in 1973 in Iran, Shappi Khorsandi moved to Britain when she was six years old. Her family left Iran because her father, Hadi, a journalist and comedian, was not at all popular with the government there. His criticism of the ruling regime meant it was no longer safe for him to stay in Iran.

However, once in the UK, the threat remained. Soon after the family's arrival, they were warned by British intelligence of a plot to assassinate Hadi. The family were forced into hiding. Trying to adapt to a new culture, coupled with the fear of this threat, meant the first few years in Britain were not always easy for Shappi. To help make light of things, Shappi and her father would always try to joke about their situation. This would certainly serve her well in her future career. Nowadays, Khorsandi tells jokes for a living and she has undoubtedly become one of the most successful female comedians in the UK. Shappi started doing stand-up comedy in 1997 at a club in London, and since then, she has gone on to make a big name for herself. She says that when she started, she was always very nervous. But, with age, she has definitely found more confidence. She says she loves being in her forties claiming that she was 'rubbish' at being young. 'I would stand up there in front of the crowd, like an open wound waiting to have salt poured onto me,' she says. Now that she's been doing this for over 20 years, it's completely different.

She is also a regular guest on several radio and TV shows, and not only as a comedian: she has appeared on a political discussion programme and on a dance show. The dance show was for charity and she enjoyed it enormously. 'It was brilliant fun – a dream come true for me,' she says. 'I've always wanted to dance on the telly, 'cos I can't dance at all.' She has also written a book, *A Beginner's Guide to Acting English*. It is about her experiences trying to become 'British' as a child and teenager. But does she feel British or Iranian now? 'I don't have to choose,' she says. 'It's like having two parents whom you love equally but in different ways.'

SPEAKING

1 Work in pairs. Make a list of the three funniest people from your country. What makes them so entertaining?

2 Work in groups. Agree together on the funniest person from your country.

4 LAUGHTER IS THE BEST MEDICINE

GRAMMAR
Boosting

1 **Rewrite the sentences from the article to include the word in brackets. Then complete the rule with *before*, *after* and *between*.**

1 Shappi Khorsandi is a breath of fresh air. (unquestionably)
2 This would serve her well in her future career. (certainly)
3 She has become one of the most successful female comedians in the UK. (undoubtedly)
4 But, with age, she has found more confidence. (definitely)

> **RULE:** When we want to make a statement stronger, we can use an adverb such as *unquestionably*, *definitely*, *undoubtedly* or *certainly*. These adverbs come:
> 1 _____ the verb *to be*
> 2 _____ other verbs
> 3 _____ auxiliary and main verbs
> Other common adverbs include *undeniably*, *clearly*, *absolutely*, *utterly*, *entirely*, *essentially*, *literally* and *totally*.

2 **Put the words in order to make sentences.**

My favourite comedian is Seth Rogen.
1 the / undeniably / he / world / of / funniest / is / actors / one / the / in / .
2 is / film / undoubtedly / best / *The Interview* / his / .
3 I've / is / seen / funniest / it / literally / the / film / ever / .
4 playing / he / losers / loves / clearly / .
5 convincing / his / was / *Steve Jobs* / performance / in / utterly / .
6 day / an / win / he / definitely / one / Oscar / will / .

3 **WRITING** Write four sentences about a comedian or actor that you really like, using adverbs to make your statements stronger. Keep their name a secret!

Read your sentences to your partner. Can he/she guess who you're describing?

Workbook page 37

VOCABULARY
Idioms with *laugh* and *joke*

1 **Match the sentence halves.**

1 The team really are *a laughing*
2 Your exam result *is no*
3 I love this programme. I *laugh my*
4 When we saw we were wearing the same dress we *burst out*
5 It was very funny to hide my shoes, but *joking*
6 He might think it's funny now, but he'll be *laughing*
7 I can't believe United paid £30 million for him. *It's a*
8 They call you a nerd because you study hard, but you'll *have*

a *laughing*. What else could we do? It was too late for either of us to change.
b *on the other side of his face* when his parents read his school report.
c *joke*. He's rubbish – not even remotely worth that amount.
d *head off* every time I watch it.
e *the last laugh* when you get into the best university in the country and they all fail their exams.
f *aside*, I need to leave. Where are they?
g *stock*. They haven't won a game for more than a year.
h *laughing matter*. 30% is just not good enough.

2 **Complete with the missing words from the idioms in Exercise 1.**

1 Have you heard Dave's new joke? I laughed my _____ _____ when he told me.
2 I got a 1% pay rise. 1%! It's a _____ !
3 I know you think I've got no talent for acting but I'll _____ the _____ when I'm rich and famous.
4 You can't wear that Superman costume to the end-of-year ball. You'll be the _____ _____ of the party.
5 Yes, I know it's funny to laugh at me in a suit, but _____ _____ , do you think it's appropriate for a job interview?
6 You'll be laughing on the _____ of your _____ when I'm your boss one day.
7 These new tax rules are no _____ _____ . Many families will find themselves a lot poorer.
8 When he bent over and split his trousers, I _____ _____ laughing. I couldn't help myself.

3 **Write a reply to each of the sentences. Use one of the idioms in each one.**

1 He thinks it's funny to drive his Porsche around town at 100 km per hour.
2 Did you think the film was funny?
3 Nigel's parents aren't going to be happy when they see what he's done to their car. I can't believe he's not more worried. He still seems to think it's funny.

Workbook page 38

43

Literature

1. How good do you think three middle-aged English men (in the 19th century) might be at cooking? How often do you imagine they cook for themselves? Under what circumstances might you expect them to cook?

2. 🔊 1.22 Read and listen to the extract and make a list of the things they put into the Irish stew.

Three Men in a Boat (to say nothing of the dog)
by Jerome K. Jerome

In this famous, late-19th century novel, a man called J and his two friends Harris and George decide to take a holiday to improve their health. They travel along the River Thames in a small boat (and they take their dog, Montmorency, with them). They are not very good sailors, or cooks, and the novel tells of their many odd adventures.

It was still early when we got settled, and George said that, as we had plenty of time, it would be a splendid opportunity to try a good, slap-up supper. He said he would show us what could be done up the river in the way of cooking, and suggested that, with the vegetables and the remains of the cold beef and general odds and ends, we should make an Irish stew.

It seemed a fascinating idea. George gathered wood and made a fire, and Harris and I started to peel the potatoes. I should never have thought that peeling potatoes was such an undertaking. The job turned out to be the biggest thing of its kind that I had ever been in. We began cheerfully, […], but our light-heartedness was gone by the time the first potato was finished. The more we peeled, the more peel there seemed to be left on; by the time we had got all the peel off and all the eyes out, there was no potato left – at least, none worth speaking of. George came and had a look at it – it was about the size of a peanut. He said:

'Oh, that won't do! You're wasting them. You must scrape them.'

So we scraped them, and that was harder work than peeling. […] We worked steadily for twenty-five minutes, and did four potatoes. […] I never saw such a thing as potato-scraping for making a fellow in a mess. It seemed difficult to believe that the potato-scrapings in which Harris and I stood, half smothered, could have come off four potatoes. […]

George said it was absurd to have only four potatoes in an Irish stew, so we washed half-a-dozen or so more, and put them in without peeling. We also put in a cabbage and a few peas. George stirred it all up, and then he said that there seemed to be a lot of room to spare, so we looked through both the baskets, and picked out all the odds and ends and the remnants, and added them to the stew. […] Then George found half a tin of salmon, and he emptied that into the pot.

He said that was the advantage of Irish stew: you got rid of such a lot of things. I fished out a couple of eggs that had got cracked, and put those in. […]

I forget the other ingredients, but I know nothing was wasted; and I remember that, towards the end, Montmorency, who had evinced great interest in the proceedings throughout, strolled away with an earnest and thoughtful air, reappearing, a few minutes afterwards, with a dead water rat in his mouth, which he evidently wished to present as his contribution to the dinner; […].

We had a discussion as to whether the rat should go in or not. Harris said that he thought it would be all right, mixed up with the other things, and that every little helped; but George stood up for precedent. He said he had never heard of water rats in Irish stew, and he would rather be on the safe side, and not try experiments.

3. Read the extract again and answer the questions.

1. Why did George think it was a good idea for them to cook supper for themselves?
2. What was the problem after the men had peeled the potatoes?
3. What was the problem when the men scraped the potatoes?
4. Why did the men start to look for other things to put in the stew?
5. What did George say was one of the positive points of making Irish stew?
6. What did the dog find, and why didn't they put it in the stew?

4 LAUGHTER IS THE BEST MEDICINE

4 VOCABULARY Match the highlighted words or phrases in the extract with the definitions.

1 left over; more of something than you need or want
2 to take off a layer of something by rubbing with a hard or sharp object
3 as far as cooking was concerned
4 not take any risks
5 almost completely covered
6 various small things of different kinds
7 everything, no matter how small, was useful
8 got something out (usually with fingers)

WRITING
A review

1 Read the review and tick the adjectives that the reviewer would agree describe the book.

☐ entertaining ☐ boring ☐ hilarious
☐ depressing ☐ exciting ☐ old-fashioned

2 Read the review again and underline:
- two examples of cleft sentences.
- four examples of boosting adverbs

3 Rewrite these sentences from the review using a cleft sentence to add emphasis.

1 The three of them decide that they are overworked and in need of a holiday.
   What the three of them decide ...
2 You get the strangest looks when you suddenly burst out laughing.
   It's when you ...
3 Some of my friends […] said it was too old-fashioned and that the plot moved far too slowly.
   What some of my friends said was ...

Note It's good to use boosting and cleft sentences in your review to give it more impact. Be careful, not to use too many. This could result in your writing sounding artificial.

4 Match each paragraph with its function. Then match the functions with advice for writing a review.

☐ a description of what the writer likes / doesn't like
☐ a brief synopsis of the story
☐ a recommendation

1 Don't give too much away.
2 Say who it might appeal to.
3 Don't forget to give reasons for your opinions.

5 Write a review of a book or film (220–260 words).
- Give a short summary
- Say how you felt about it.
- Say whether you'd recommend it and, if so, to whom.

5 SPEAKING Work in pairs. Discuss the questions.

1 How much did the men enjoy their meal when they finally ate supper, do you think?
2 Have you ever cooked (or eaten) a really badly cooked meal? What was it? Why was it so bad? Tell your partner about it.

[A] Jerome K Jerome is sitting in the living room of his house, describing an ever-growing list of illnesses from which he fears he is suffering to his sympathetic friends Harris and George. The three of them decide that they are over-worked and in need of a holiday. After deciding that a vacation in the countryside would be too dull and a voyage at sea too dangerous, they decide that a boating trip up the river Thames from London to Oxford would be perfect. So the next Saturday, accompanied by Jerome's dog Montmorency, they set off for a fortnight of amusing story-telling and mild misadventure all set in the background of the idyllic English countryside.

[B] Originally published in 1889, *Three Men in a Boat* was recently voted number 33 on the Guardian's list of The 100 Greatest Novels of all time and there's one simple reason for this: it's utterly brilliant. What I like most about it is the perfect mixture of travel guide, which is what it was originally intended to be, and comedy, two of my favourite genres. The book is laugh-out-loud funny, which can be quite embarrassing if you're reading it on a crowded underground train on your way to college! You get the strangest looks when you suddenly burst out laughing.

[C] Clearly though, it's not for everyone. Some of my friends didn't find it so humorous and said it was too old-fashioned and that the plot moved far too slowly. But it's exactly this lazy boat ride of a journey that makes it so good. If you're looking for a highly enjoyable cruise into the eccentricities of the English, with a cast of undeniably colourful characters, then this might just be the book for you.

45

CAMBRIDGE ENGLISH: ADVANCED

THiNK EXAMS

LISTENING
Part 3: Multiple choice

Workbook page 43

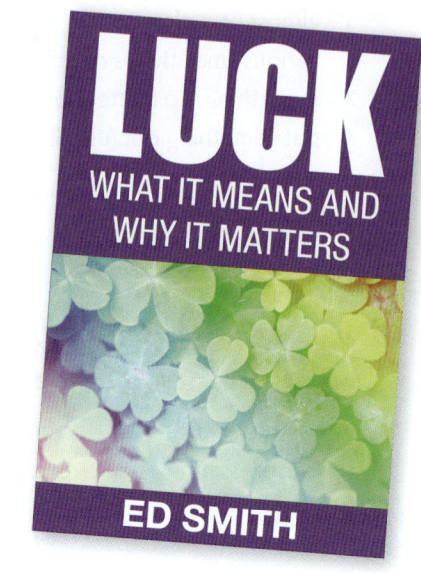

1. 🔊 1.23 You will hear a conversation on the radio about a book called *Luck: what it means and why it matters* by Ed Smith. For questions 1–6, choose the answer (A, B or C) which fits best according to what you hear.

   1. What does Ed Smith do?
      - A He's a professional sportsperson.
      - B He's a sports journalist.
      - C He's a retired professional sportsperson.
   2. According to Daniela Merchant what does Ed Smith say in his book?
      - A He believes that we have to take chances in order to be successful.
      - B He says that he didn't think much about luck in his twenties.
      - C He is only interested in events in people's professional lives.
   3. What do Daniela and the presenter agree on?
      - A Hard work and talent tend to bring success.
      - B It's more acceptable to make mistakes these days.
      - C Most people these days think success or failure depends on the individual.
   4. What does Ed Smith discuss in this book?
      - A the things that we can do to have maximum control over our lives
      - B how some factors of our birth influence our lives
      - C the relative importance of where and when we're born
   5. Why does Daniela believe that her acting career has been successful?
      - A She happened to be trained by a very good teacher.
      - B She has talent but was also lucky to get into the right acting school.
      - C She met Richard Burton at just the right time.
   6. What does Daniela think about Ed Smith?
      - A He has particularly interesting views on politics and economics.
      - B He and his wife should be very grateful that they met as they did.
      - C He is an intelligent writer, but she doesn't completely agree with all of his arguments.

WRITING
Part 2: A proposal

Workbook page 23

2. Write an answer to the following task.

   Your school has a piece of land that it wants to build on. The school has asked students to make some recommendations for what the building could be. A sports hall? A theatre? A library? A science laboratory? Something else? In preparation for a meeting to decide what the building will be, you've been asked to write a proposal to the head teacher.

   Your proposal should explain:
   - what you think should be built
   - how it could benefit the school, its pupils and (perhaps) the local community.

   Write your proposal (220–260 words).

TEST YOURSELF

UNITS 3 & 4

VOCABULARY

1 Complete the sentences with the words in the list. There are four extra words.

off | trick | giggles | through | down | punchline | stock
matter | out | beginner's | over | in | on | up

1 You need to go to the supermarket? Well, you're _____ luck. I'm just about to drive to town.
2 I loved that film. It was so funny that I laughed my head _____.
3 Don't wear that shirt. You'll be the laughing _____ of the party.
4 She really stands _____ with her bright red hair.
5 I can't believe I won. I've never played cards before. It must be _____ luck.
6 I took him _____ on his offer and went to work for him.
7 Our coach broke _____ and we had to wait two hours for a new one.
8 I'm terrible at telling jokes. I always forget the _____.
9 You've broken the window. I don't think this is a laughing _____.
10 I always get the _____ when Mr Harrison tells me off. I just can't help laughing.

/10

GRAMMAR

2 Complete the sentences with the words and phrases in the list. There are two extra.

speak | could speak | hadn't spoken | it | don't speak | didn't speak | what | all

1 Unless you _____ to the headmaster first, you won't be able to use the hall for the party.
2 _____ was Dave who suggested the idea.
3 If I _____ Spanish fluently, they wouldn't have offered me the job. I can't wait to start!
4 _____ annoyed me most was the wait.
5 Imagine you _____ another language, which language would you choose?
6 If you _____ to her so rudely yesterday, you might still be friends.

3 Find and correct the mistake in each sentence.

1 I'll do certainly all I can to help you.
2 Unless we don't leave now, we'll miss the train.
3 If I hadn't eaten so much, I wouldn't have felt so ill now.
4 It was the journey what was most fun.
5 He's made clearly a lot of enemies.
6 Provided that you could go anywhere in the world, where would you go?

/12

FUNCTIONAL LANGUAGE

4 Choose the correct options.

1 That's a great joke. I must *learn / remember* that one. Thanks.
2 Ha ha! That's a *fun / good* one.
3 Thanks for explaining the joke. I just didn't *catch / get* it at first.
4 Ha ha – very *funny / hysterical*.
5 A I can't believe I didn't win the poetry competition.
   B *Never / Don't* mind. You can always try again.
6 A Can you believe we lost the match in the last minute?
   B That really is *bad / worse* luck.
7 He'd never played football before and scored three goals. Talk about *starter's / beginner's* luck.
8 I've missed the bus by a minute. *Only / Just* my luck!

/8

MY SCORE /30

22 – 30
10 – 21
0 – 9

47

5 THRILL SEEKERS

OBJECTIVES

FUNCTIONS: giving and reacting to an opinion
GRAMMAR: participle clauses; verbs of perception with infinitive or gerund
VOCABULARY: thrill seeking; idioms related to noise

READING

1 Look at the photos. Tick the adjectives and phrases that you'd use to describe these activities.

challenging	☐	rewarding	☐
dangerous	☐	boring	☐
terrifying	☐	awesome	☐
exciting	☐	unsafe	☐
not for me	☐	awe-inspiring	☐

2 Work in pairs. Think of three reasons why people might want to do these activities and three reasons why they might not.

3 **SPEAKING** Compare your ideas with others in the class.

4 Read the newspaper articles quickly. Which of the two thrill seekers has inspired others to try the same activity?

5 **◀) 1.24** Read the newspaper articles again and listen. Answer the questions.
   1 What was it that made Mrs Hardison try paragliding?
   2 What evidence is there that she had no fear of heights?
   3 How did she reassure herself before the flight?
   4 What message does she want to send to others?
   5 What has Gary Connery become famous for?
   6 What safety precaution did Gary take?
   7 What does Gary do for a living?
   8 What is said about his emotions before he jumped?

6 **SPEAKING** Work in pairs and discuss the questions.
   1 Which of the two thrill seekers impresses you the most? Why?
   2 Give an example of a thrill seeker who went too far.
   3 Make a list of five other activities thrill seekers might enjoy. How exciting, dangerous, challenging and terrifying are they? Rank them from 1 (least) to 5 (most) for each adjective in turn.

Pronunciation
Connected speech feature: elision
Go to page 120.

TRAIN TO THINK

Red herrings

A red herring is often introduced to deliberately cause a distraction from the main issue by appearing to have some actual importance when in fact, it has none. By thinking critically, we can train ourselves to identify red herrings quickly and not be misled by them. This ultimately places us in a better position to make decisions based only on the facts that are truly important to the issue.

1 Read the text and answer the question.

Mary Ellen Hardison deserves a medal for being an inspiration to all elderly people. Not content with going on the world's most thrilling roller coasters to celebrate her 90th birthday, the great-great-grandmother has just celebrated her 101st birthday by jumping out of an aeroplane. She also has five great-grandchildren. Her motto in life seems to be, 'Be positive. Friends don't like a grumpy person.'

5 THRILL SEEKERS

Text A

Daredevil great-great-granny:
101-year-old woman soars into record books with birthday paraglide

It was confirmed today that great-great-grandmother Mary Ellen Hardison has officially broken the record for the oldest female to do a tandem paraglide. The daring old lady from the USA stole the title from a 100-year-old Cypriot woman who had previously broken the record in 2007.

Mrs Hardison flew with an instructor on 1st September last year while four generations of her family watched and cheered. The flight went smoothly and even included a few tricks, much to the delight of the fearless pensioner.

But what made her decide to try paragliding? Her 75-year-old son had taken it up and as she said, 'I didn't want him to do something I couldn't do.'

Mrs Hardison was already known for being pretty fearless. She celebrated her 90th birthday by going on all the adult roller coasters at Disneyland.

Knowing that many other people had been paragliding without any problems, she felt very confident about her own flight. 'If it's safe for them, then it's safe for me,' she said.

Motivated by her daredevil stunt, other family members and friends have already signed up for their own paragliding adventure.

While still overwhelmed and thrilled by her record, she hopes someone else will manage to break it. 'My desire is for the elderly to keep on going. Do things as long as you are physically able,' she says. 'Be positive. Friends don't like a grumpy person.'

Text B

Gary Connery: stuntman completes 2,400-foot skydive without a parachute

A British stuntman, Gary Connery, has become the first man to jump from an aircraft at 2,400 feet (over 730 metres) and land safely without using a parachute.

Having leapt from a helicopter in a death-defying stunt, the 42-year-old daredevil landed in an area containing 18,600 cardboard boxes. This afternoon, the father of two – with over 880 skydives under his belt, as well as 450 base jumps and dozens of film and television roles to boot – became the first person to survive a jump from such a height without using a parachute. He did his first parachute jump at the age of 23 and has since become a professional stuntman. He has leapt from the top of Tower Bridge, the London Eye and Nelson's Column in London and from the Eiffel Tower in Paris, all without a parachute.

In his latest stunt, Mr Connery dropped for three seconds before reaching speeds of more than 130 km per hour in a specially developed wing suit that slowed his descent. Had he not been wearing the suit, he would never have survived the jump. Landing safely on the cardboard boxes, he was cheered by thousands of people who had come to watch the stunt, among whom stood his wife, Vivienne.

Mr Connery, whose films include *Batman Begins* and *Indiana Jones*, and who, dressed as the Queen, parachuted into the Olympic stadium for the opening ceremony of the 2012 Olympics in London, said it had been an 'amazing feeling'. 'I feel absolutely wonderful. I am overwhelmed,' he told reporters afterwards.

Before the jump, Gary insisted he would survive, as performing stunts was 'his life', but he did admit to being 'a bit scared'. Mrs Connery, 45, added: 'I am just so relieved it is all over.'

---

1 Which sentence does not support the idea that Mrs Hardison deserves a medal?

A She went on the world's most thrilling roller coasters to celebrate her 90th birthday.
B She also has five great-grandchildren.
C She has just celebrated her 101st birthday by jumping out of an aeroplane.

2 **WRITING** Work in pairs. Write a multiple-choice question for Text B. Include a red herring.

3 **SPEAKING** Work with another pair. Identify each other's red herring.

GRAMMAR
Participle clauses

1 Look at the sentences from the articles. What meanings do the participle clauses (in bold) express? Decide if they mean *at the same time* (a), *after* (b), *because* (c), or *if* (d). Then complete the rule with *reasons*, *time*, *the same*, *results*, *conditions*, *present* and *past*.

☐ **Having leapt** from a helicopter in a death-defying stunt, the 42-year-old daredevil landed in an area containing 18,600 cardboard boxes.

☐ **Had he not been wearing** the suit, he would never have survived the jump.

☐ **Landing** safely on the cardboard boxes, he was cheered by thousands of people who had come to watch the stunt.

☐ **Knowing** that many other people had been paragliding without any problems, she felt very confident about her own flight.

> **RULE:**
> We form participle clauses with the present or past participle.
>
> Participle clauses are used to:
> - talk about [1]_____ relationships (things happening at the same time, or one after the other). *He was looking out of the helicopter, **feeling** slightly nervous.* (While he looked out of the helicopter, he felt …)
> - give [2]_____ to explain an action or event. ***Learning** about her son's interest in paragliding, Mrs Hardison decided to try it too.* (Because she learnt…)
> - to talk about [3]_____. ***Done** regularly, exercise can contribute a lot to an elderly person's good health.* (If an elderly person does exercise regularly, it can …)
> - to talk about [4]_____. *The elderly lady went on a lot of roller coasters, gradually **allowing** her to get **used** to extreme heights.* (…as a consequence, this allowed her to gradually get used to heights)
>
> We can introduce participle clauses with *before*, *after*, *while*, *by*, *since* and *on*.
>
> We can only use a participle clause if the subject of the two clauses is [5]_____.
>
> *While white-water rafting, **Jenny** broke her leg.*
>
> We use [6]_____ participles for active clauses and we use [7]_____ participles for passive clauses.
>
> ***Jumping** out of the plane, Emma felt exhilarated.*
> ***Carried** by the wind, she parachuted safely down to the ground.*

2 Read these sentences taken from a leaflet about the Saltwater Croc Dive in Darwin, Australia. Transform the participle clauses to make longer sentences with *after* or *if*.

A sure way to become a daredevil…

Saltwater crocodile watching

[0] Having opened its doors last year, Saltwater Croc Dive has become the best place to get a close look at the world's most dangerous reptiles. (After)

[1] Having climbed into a glass cage, the thrilled and terrified tourists are lowered into the water with the crocodiles. (After)

[2] Carried out correctly, the dive is completely safe. (If)

[3] Having returned to the safety of the beach, you can look at the amazing pictures taken by our professional photographer. (After)

[4] Sharing these photos with your friends, you will be the talk of the town. (If)

After opening its doors last year, Saltwater Croc Dive has become the best place to get a close look at the world's most dangerous reptiles.

3 Use a participle clause to shorten each of the following sentence constructions.

0 Because she'd noticed there was something wrong with her wing suit, she didn't jump out of the helicopter.
   Having noticed that something was wrong with her wing suit, she didn't jump out of the helicopter.

1 If you do these exercises regularly, they'll help you to become extremely fit.

2 After they'd watched the stunt, most people were speechless.

3 While we were watching the people in their canoes, we decided to try it too.

4 She's always been aware of the risks, and because of this she's never had any serious accidents.

5 He learnt how to climb from his father. He became passionate about climbing.

Workbook page 46

5 THRILL SEEKERS

VOCABULARY
Thrill seeking

1 **Match the sentence halves.**

1 The skydiver completed an epic *stunt* when
2 Jumping from a helicopter without
3 As Matt hung from a 76-metre crane by one hand,
4 He's a real *daredevil*. Have you ever seen
5 We need to *assess the risk* of doing this climb
6 This film explains why some people get a *real*
7 He'd never do anything extreme
8 Did you see the video of his *death-defying*

a a parachute is extremely *audacious*.
b leap from the Eiffel Tower?
c *kick out of* doing extreme sports.
d without *minimising the risk* beforehand.
e he said he wasn't scared. He was a *risk-taker* by nature.
f videos of his insane motorcycle tricks?
g he somersaulted from one glider to another at 160 km per hour.
h before making the decision to go.

2 **Complete the sentences with the correct form of the words and expressions in italics in Exercise 1.**

1 Standing on the wings of a plane, the _____ performed another terrifying feat for the crowds.
2 She often climbs without a harness. She's a _____ .
3 My brother gets a _____ skydiving from unusual landmarks. He loves it.
4 She _____ of injury by wearing a helmet.
5 It was an _____ thing to do. It showed the young motorcyclist's skill, strength and lack of fear.
6 He's performed _____ in many different films, but his most famous was in *Cliffhanger*.
7 You need to _____ before you decide whether or not to climb the building.
8 He performed his _____ jump from the top of the Shard without a parachute.

> Workbook page 48

SPEAKING

ROLE PLAY Work in pairs. Student A: Go to page 127. Student B: Go to page 128.

LISTENING

1 **SPEAKING** Work in pairs and look at the photo. In what way is this activity different from extreme sports, such as bungee jumping or base jumping? In what way is it similar?

2 ◁)) 1.26 Listen and compare your answers to what the expert says.

3 ◁)) 1.26 Listen again and complete these sentences with one or two words.

1 According to the psychologist, risk-takers need the adrenalin rush they get from doing _____ .
2 Going on a roller coaster isn't really dangerous, but it _____ real danger.
3 Some people don't seek an adrenalin rush. They have no interest in _____ their lives.
4 People who love taking risks are commonly described as _____ .
5 Some people do dangerous activities to feel adrenalin levels rise in their _____ .
6 Another theory is that they can forget their _____ by doing dangerous activities.

THiNK SELF-ESTEEM

Feeling alive

1 **Rank the activities from 1 to 6 according to how risky they are (1 = not very risky; 6 = very risky).**

- riding a motorcycle without a helmet
- base jumping
- playing tennis
- walking in the countryside
- playing ice hockey
- swimming in the sea

2 Now rank the activities from 1 to 6 according to how much they make people 'feel alive' (1 = not very alive; 6 = fully alive).

3 **SPEAKING** Work in pairs. Compare your results with your partner.

51

READING

1 Think about your answers to questions 1 and 2. Then compare with a partner.

  1 How often do you find yourself thinking that it's too noisy?

  2 Read statements a–d. Which of them do you agree with? Which do you disagree with?

  a I don't do much without music. I always have my earphones in.

  b I hate all kinds of noise. I love it when I'm in a really quiet place, for example, in nature.

  c I like music, but only if and when I get to choose it. I hate the music you're forced to listen to in shops and restaurants.

  d I love being in places that buzz with energy. Noise doesn't worry me at all – quite the opposite.

2 Read the article below quickly. What is the 'anechoic chamber' and why is it famous?

3 Read the article again and answer the questions.

  1 What happens if you stay in the anechoic chamber for too long?

  2 What's the longest someone has stayed in there?

  3 What happens to people's hearing when they're in a place that is absolutely quiet?

  4 What is the anechoic chamber used for?

4 Now read the account of a reporter who tried the experience himself. Answer the questions.

  1 Why did the reporter book a session in the anechoic chamber?

  2 Which sound did he find strange?

  3 Why did he leave the anechoic chamber?

  4 How did he feel afterwards?

Can you stand the silence?

They say silence is golden, but there's a room in the U.S. that's so quiet it becomes unbearable after a relatively short time. The Anechoic Test Chamber was deemed the quietest place on Earth in 2004 and holds the Guinness World Record. It's 99.99 percent sound absorbent, but stay there too long and you may start hallucinating. The longest that anyone has survived in the chamber is just 45 minutes.

It achieves its ultra-quietness through fibreglass acoustic wedges which are over a metre thick, double walls of insulated steel and 30 centimetre thick concrete.

The founder of the company that owns the chamber, Steven Orfield, said: 'When it's quiet, ears will adapt. The quieter the room, the more things you hear. You'll hear your heart beating. Sometimes you can hear your lungs, or your stomach gurgling loudly. In the anechoic chamber, you become the sound.'

The chamber is used by a multitude of manufacturers to test how loud their products are. Mr Orfield said: 'It's used for formal product testing, for research into the sound of different things – heart valves, the sound of the display of a cellphone, the sound of a switch on a car dashboard.'

It's also used to determine sound quality. For instance, motorbike maker Harley-Davidson used the lab to make their bikes quieter while still sounding like Harley-Davidsons.

I've been to the quietest place on Earth

My journey started when I was in the New York Subway. My children were complaining loudly, four trains came screaming into the station at once and I had to put my hands over my ears and cower – the noise was deafening.

In an attempt to recapture some peace, I went on a mission to find the quietest place on Earth; to discover whether absolute silence exists. I booked a 45-minute session in the anechoic chamber – no one had managed to stay in there for longer than that before. When I heard the door shut behind me, I strained to hear something and heard … nothing.

Then, after a minute or two, I became aware of the sound of my breathing, so I held my breath. I started to hear the blood rushing in my veins. I frowned and heard my scalp moving over my skull, which was weird. Was I hallucinating?

Then I stopped obsessing about what bodily functions I could hear and began to enjoy it. I didn't feel afraid and came out only because my time was up. Afterwards, I felt wonderfully rested and calm. My desire for silence had changed my life. I found that making space for moments of quiet in my day is the key to happiness – they give you a chance to reflect on life. The fact that I'd broken a world record was just a bonus!

5 **SPEAKING** Work in pairs and discuss the questions.

  1 Which of the bodily sounds mentioned in the articles have you ever heard? How did they make you feel?

  2 Which sounds annoy you?

  3 Which sound do you hate most?

  4 Which sounds make you happy?

5 | THRILL SEEKERS

GRAMMAR
Verbs of perception with infinitive or gerund

1 Read the sentences from the two texts on page 52. In which sentence is the sound heard from when it starts to when it ends? Circle the correct options in the rule.

1 You'll hear your heart **beating**.
2 When I heard the door **shut** behind me, I strained to hear something and heard … nothing.

> **RULE:** We use a verb of perception (*see*, *hear*, *feel*) plus a gerund to say we have experienced
> [1] *an entire action / part of an action*.
> I **saw** a man **painting** a house.
> I **felt** my heart **beating** fast.
> I **heard** someone **playing** the piano.
>
> We use a verb of perception plus an infinitive to say we have experienced
> [2] *an entire action / part of an action*.
> I **saw** a man **paint** a picture.
> I **felt** her hand **touch** my shoulder.
> I **heard** someone **close** the door.

2 Complete the sentences with the correct form of the verb in brackets.

1 We heard somebody _____ and then it was silent. (scream)
2 The noise was terrible and it went on for hours. We heard people _____ drums and _____ whistles loudly. (bang / blow)
3 When he woke up after the operation, he saw lots of people _____ around his bed. (stand)
4 When we were driving home, I suddenly saw a deer _____ across the road before it disappeared. (run)
5 I was lying in bed when I became aware of an insect _____ on my face. I switched on the light, but couldn't see anything. (crawl)
6 The rain was beating down on the roof of the car, and I suddenly felt water _____ down onto the back of my neck. (drip)

> Workbook page 47

VOCABULARY
Idioms related to noise

1 Read the sentences. Complete the idioms with *loud* (x3), *noise* (x1) or *quiet* (x2).

1 The press has been *making a lot of* _____ about the luxury skyscrapers being built in London.
2 Oh, *for crying out* _____, I've told you a million times not to leave that door open! Why don't you listen to me?
3 The teacher made his point _____ *and clear*. I need to work much harder if I'm going to pass the exam.
4 I don't think you should tell anyone what happened. You should *keep* _____ about it.
5 My grandma went home early on Saturday. She said she wanted some *peace and* _____.
6 Don't tell Joe. He'll tell everyone. He's a real _____ mouth.

2 Complete the dialogues with the idioms from Exercise 1.

1 A Oh, _____ ! I told you not to tell Stephen about the crash. He's such a _____. He'll tell everyone.
   B But Stephen's my best friend. I wanted to tell him.
   A I know he's your best friend, but you know what he's like. He can't _____ about anything.
2 A Every day, there's an article in the newspaper about the unhealthy amount of sugar we eat.
   B Yes, the press have been _____ about it.
   A I think they've made their point _____ now. People will get bored of the topic and stop listening.
3 A I hear your mum and dad are going away this weekend.
   B Yes, our next-door neighbours are doing some building work, so my parents are going away for some _____.

> Workbook page 48

FUNCTIONS
Giving and reacting to an opinion

1 🔊 1.27 Listen to the dialogues and answer the questions.

1 What opinions do the speakers express in dialogue 1?
2 What opinions do the speakers express in dialogue 2?
3 In each case, who do you agree with?

2 🔊 1.27 Listen to the dialogues again and match the phrases with functions 1–4 below.

1 giving an opinion 2 agreeing 3 disagreeing 4 conceding a point

☐ To my mind, that's …
☐ Yes, I suppose you're right.
☐ I don't accept that …
☐ The way I see it is …
☐ I hadn't thought of that.
☐ That's not how I see things.
☐ True.
☐ I'd go along with that.
☐ OK. Point taken.

3 **ROLE PLAY** Work in pairs. You're going to discuss extreme sports and try to convince your partner of your opinion. Student A: Go to page 127. Student B: Go to page 128. Use the phrases from Exercise 2 in your discussions.

53

Culture

1 Look at the photos and the article quickly and answer the questions.
  1 Where are these places?
  2 What do the activities have in common? What differences are there between them?

TOP WORLDWIDE LOCATIONS FOR EXTREME SPORTS

Extreme sports are not for the faint-hearted. They're for those people who live on adrenalin and whose idea of hell is sitting at home watching TV. If you're looking for that ultimate thrill, no matter how brief, there are places you can go to get the best experiences. Here are a few of them.

BUNGEE JUMPING

There are people who will tell you that hurling yourself off a bridge with just a cord tied around your ankles, towards a river that's not only 110 metres below you, but full of hungry crocodiles too, is complete and utter idiocy. But there are queues of people wanting to do just that over the Zambezi River in Zambia, which tops the list of places for bungee jumpers to go. In particular, it's the experienced jumpers who go there, since the length of the fall lets them do all kinds of fancy tricks as they plunge towards the river. If you're less experienced and feel like trying it – well you can. And until the moment when they put the harness on you, you can get a refund if you have last-minute doubts or panic attacks.

SKYDIVING

The beautiful city of Sydney, Australia, is a magnet for skydivers, amongst whom there is a consensus that it's one of the best places to practise this extreme sport. And make no mistake – it is extreme, and based entirely on the hope that your parachute will work when you finally decide to open it. Why Sydney though? Well, good weather, good winds, experienced pilots and trainers – plus, as you rush towards the ground at over 200 kph, there's a wonderful view of the city and the coast of New South Wales. And who knows, you might just catch a glimpse of a school of whales heading up towards the Gold Coast. Now what could be better than that?

And one for watching only (as you can't do it yourself!) …

CLIFF DIVING

La Quebrada, Acapulco, is the site of the famous cliff divers' performance. Since 1934, this has been one of Mexico's top attractions. The divers leap from cliffs 41 metres above the Pacific, landing in water just over three metres deep. There are five performances daily, including four evening shows, performed by divers carrying torches – an unforgettable display.

Anyone who's watched Acapulco's cliff divers plunge into the rough sea may wonder how daring and tricky an act this is. Ramirez Vasquez, who comes from a family of cliff divers, says that timing is key. He explains that in order to hit the water when it's at its deepest and ultimately, safest, cliff divers have a five-second window during which the wave is high. It takes three seconds to reach the water, giving them a two-second margin of error.

In preparation for his twice-daily dive, Vasquez works out from 8 to 10 am, five times a week. Meditation is also part of his routine. He still gets nervous before each and every dive, despite his vast experience. An average diver who starts their career at 17 and ends it at 45 will do 15,560 dives into the Quebrada. Many cliff divers have been involved in accidents, most caused by the impact of the water. Remarkably, no deaths have been recorded to date.

5 THRILL SEEKERS

2 ◀)) 1.28 **Read again and listen to the article. At which of the three places …**

1 will you get your money back up to a certain point?
2 might you see interesting wildlife while involved in the activity?
3 are even experienced participants always scared before the activity?
4 will you dive down towards a river full of dangerous animals?
5 will you have an amazing view of a city?
6 will you see people leap from a 41 metre cliff into the sea below?
7 could a very short delay be fatal for a participant?
8 could you see jumpers somersault through the air?

3 **VOCABULARY** Match the highlighted words in the article with the definitions.

1 (a length of) rope or string made of twisted threads
2 an agreement between all of the people in a group
3 fall or move down very quickly or with force
4 a length of time when it's possible to do something
5 not brave
6 excitement, joy
7 force or action (created by one object hitting another)
8 foolishness, madness

4 **SPEAKING** Work in pairs and discuss the questions.

1 Which of these sports would you most like to try? Put them in order of preference.
2 Which of these sports would you most like to watch? Put them in order of preference.
3 The article claims that 'one man's sport is another man's madness'. What do you understand by this?
4 What's your view on these and other extreme sports?

WRITING
A newspaper article

1 Read the newspaper article. Why did the writer choose this title?

Eight and a half seconds I'll never remember

Had anyone asked me a year ago if I'd ever be standing in a small cabin, looking out over a 134-metre drop, preparing to launch myself towards the ground below, I'd have told them they were mad. But that's exactly where I found myself yesterday morning.

I've never been much of a daredevil. I've ridden a few of the smaller roller coasters at Alton Towers, but that's about it. So why was I now about to risk life and limb for the sake of a newspaper story?

The idea to 'do' the world's highest bungee jump came from my editor. When he requested a travel article on New Zealand, naturally I leapt at the chance. It was only while I was travelling to the airport that a text came from him suggesting I check out the Nevis bungee in Queensland. OK, I thought, there's no harm in that.

36 hours later, having checked into my simple but charming hotel in the heart of the city, I spent the evening talking with locals about my imminent jump. That's when I started to wonder if I'd completely taken leave of my senses. 'It's the highest in the world,' they told me. Had any of them done it? 'No.'

The beautiful drive out to the privately owned jump is worth an article of its own, but that's not what my editor wants. He wants to know about the longest eight and a half seconds of my life as I free-fell through the air, with only a thin wire to save me from certain death. Well, I'm pretty sure it was the most frightening experience of my life – the only problem is, I don't really remember a single thing about it.

2 Read the article again and put the information below in the order in which it is mentioned.

☐ how high the jump was
☐ where the bungee jump was
☐ how long the jump lasted
☐ what the writer thought about the jump
☐ when the writer did the jump
☐ the journey to do the jump
☐ where the writer stayed
☐ when the writer realised how scary the jump might be

3 Find an example of a participle clause in the article.

4 Write a newspaper article (200–250 words) about one of the other extreme sports you've read about in this unit.
- Either imagine you did it or you saw someone else doing it.
- Think carefully about how to introduce the details of the experience. It doesn't need to be in chronological order.
- Present the facts throughout the article to maintain interest.
- Try and include at least two participle clauses.

6 FOLLOWERS

OBJECTIVES

FUNCTIONS: complaining
GRAMMAR: modals 1: *may, might, can, could, will, won't*; modals 2: *should, shouldn't, must, mustn't, can't*
VOCABULARY: admiration; fame

A

B

C

READING

1 **SPEAKING** Work in pairs and discuss.

 1 Which celebrities are currently in the news or have been recently?
 2 Why are they in the news?

2 Look at the people (A–E) in the photos. Match each one to the thoughts below.

 1 I can't believe I'm this close to him/her.
 2 Can't wait to post this on Instagram.
 3 Look at me!
 4 Leave me alone.
 5 I wonder what he's up to.

3 **SPEAKING** Compare with a partner. What other thoughts might they be having?

4 Read the article, which comes from an online magazine, quickly. What is CWS and what happens in its most extreme cases?

5 🔊 1.29 Read the article again and listen. In which paragraph are each of these points made? Write 1–4 in the boxes below and underline the words and phrases in the article which helped you choose your answers.

- [ ] The desire to learn from successful people is an inherent human characteristic.
- [ ] Most people with an interest in celebrities don't let it take over their lives.
- [ ] A few people take celebrity obsession to a dangerous level.
- [ ] TV, newspapers and the Internet have meant it's much easier to keep up to date with celebrities.
- [ ] Excessive obsession with the rich and famous now has a name.
- [ ] Throughout history, people have taken an interest in the rich and famous.
- [ ] There are many more opportunities these days to attain celebrity status.
- [ ] Many people are obsessed with celebrity culture these days and seemingly, more so than in the past.

6 **SPEAKING** Work in pairs and discuss the questions.

 1 Name the three most popular celebrities among people of your age. Why are they popular? Do you like them? Why (not)?
 2 Which famous people, if any, do you follow on Twitter or in the media?
 3 Why do you think that some people find the lives of celebrities so interesting?
 4 Would you like to be famous? Why (not)?

6 FOLLOWERS

What's up with our *celebrity obsession?*

[1] You might forgive a casual visitor to Earth for thinking that the leaders here all wear beautiful clothes, have gleaming white teeth and wave continually while they walk down red carpets into luxurious buildings. Judging by the never-ending TV coverage of award ceremonies and the stacks of glossy magazines piled up by supermarket checkouts, it's easy to see why this mistake might be made. Our [1]*fixation* on celebrities has never been more evident. But according to psychologists, this obsession may be nothing new. Our [2]*fascination* with the rich and famous goes way back, with people looking to kings and queens for examples of how to dress and behave. For instance, the popularity of the traditional white wedding dress can be traced back to the one worn by Queen Victoria at her wedding in 1840. Before this, brides traditionally wore dresses in all sorts of colours. Going back even further, our earliest ancestors lived in tribes, where leaders were watched carefully for clues on how best to survive. We still live in a society dominated by hierarchies and our modern-day obsession with celebrities could simply be an extension of a basic instinct to pay close attention to those at the top.

[2] What has changed, of course, is the rise of the media, and with it, easier access to these glamorous lifestyles – something celebrities are all too aware of. They know that by constantly appearing in online news feeds and reaching out to their fans on Twitter, they can raise their profile and make sure they're not forgotten. The growth of the media has also meant that there are now many more ways to become famous. Consequently, we're no longer simply celebrity-watchers but, celebrities-in-waiting, waiting for our chance to shine on the world stage. Many of us believe that we'll be famous one day and the idea of becoming the [3]*centre of attention* is very real in many of our minds. But until then, we're happy just watching. One theory suggests that with the decline in large families and close-knit communities, celebrities have, for some people, taken the place of these social groups. Just as we'd once been eager to find out what the neighbours were up to, we're now keen to know everything about our new 'family' members.

[3] But is there really anything wrong with caring about what our [4]*idol* is doing? Well, like most [5]*addictions*, you can suffer from it to varying degrees. Most psychologists agree that there's little harm in a casual interest, but when things escalate out of control, then it becomes more serious. So widespread is this phenomenon – albeit to varying degrees – that the term Celebrity [6]*Worship* Syndrome (CWS) has been coined to describe it. Various stages of this syndrome have been identified. The most common form of CWS is, thankfully, its mildest. 'Sufferers' at this stage tend to be extroverts who enjoy socialising in large groups. At their worst, this group of people risk boring their friends to death with details about the [7]*object of their affection*. Their obsession might even be considered no bad thing if they're taking on the healthy habits of a positive role model.

[4] At the other end of the scale there are the severe sufferers, but fortunately, these are in a very small minority. For these people, the obsession is out of control and can even lead to illegal practices such as [8]*stalking*. 'Severe sufferers' of CWS will typically feel that they have a special connection with the celebrity and won't listen to voices of reason. Their actions can turn violent when these feelings are inevitably not reciprocated.

But for most of us, our fascination with celebrities is nothing more than a harmless interest in people who lead very different lives. And what could possibly be wrong with that?

TRAIN TO THiNK

Making logical conclusions (syllogisms)

A syllogism is a system of logic where a conclusion is drawn from two propositions that are assumed to be true. It is often attributed to the Greek philosopher Aristotle, who used the following example:

All men are mortal. (proposition 1)
Socrates is a man. (proposition 2)
Therefore, Socrates is mortal. (conclusion)

Syllogisms can only work if both propositions are true, so before we accept any conclusion, we should consider whether each of the propositions on which it is based is indeed true.

1 **Look carefully at these two syllogisms. Find the flaws in the logic of each conclusion.**

   1 A lot of famous people love attention.
     Meryl Streep is famous.
     Therefore, she loves being followed by the paparazzi.
   2 People who have CWS obsess over celebrities.
     Liam has CWS.
     Therefore, Liam is obsessed with Neymar.

2 **WRITING** Work in pairs. Write a valid conclusion and an invalid conclusion for this syllogism.

   Absolution is an album by Muse.
   Lucy has all of Muse's albums.
   Therefore, …

GRAMMAR

Modals 1: *may, might, can, could, will, won't*

1 Underline the modal verbs in these sentences from the article on page 57 and then match each modal with the meanings they give to the sentences in the rule box.

1 You might forgive a casual visitor to Earth for thinking that the leaders here all wear beautiful clothes … [when of course that isn't the case].
2 For these people, the obsession is out of control and can even lead to illegal practices such as stalking.
3 The popularity of the traditional white wedding dress can be traced back to the one worn by Queen Victoria.
4 Our modern-day obsession with celebrities could simply be an extension of a basic instinct.
5 Many of us believe that we'll be famous one day.
6 'Severe sufferers' of CWS will typically feel that they have a special connection with the celebrity.
7 [They] won't listen to voices of reason.
8 Their obsession might even be considered no bad thing if they're taking on the healthy habits of a positive role model.

RULE:
a hypothesising: example ____
b talking about possibility: example ____
c talking about habitual behaviour: example ____
d refusing: example ____
e making a concession: example ____ and ____
f a belief about the future: example ____
g theoretical possibility: example ____

2 **SPEAKING** Work in pairs. Discuss the difference in meaning of the modal verb in a and b in each pair of sentences. Pay attention to any time references.

1 a I may watch the film tonight – I'll see how I feel.
  b They may be rich and famous, but are they happy?
2 a It might rain later. I think I heard that on the weather forecast this morning.
  b They might be French. I think they said something about her parents living in Paris.
3 a Learning a new language can be difficult.
  b He can speak three languages.
4 a We could have a problem.
  b My grandfather could solve most problems.
5 a We'll be a bit late if we don't hurry.
  b Children will get restless if they've got nothing to do.
6 a He won't tell me. It's so annoying. I really want to know!
  b I really don't want to go to the party. I won't know anyone there.

➡ Workbook page 54

Pronunciation
Modal stress and meaning
Go to page 120.

VOCABULARY

Admiration

1 Match the words in italics (1–8) in the article on page 57 with the meanings.

1 someone or something that everyone is focused on
2 very strong habits that are hard to break
3 extreme interest in
4 someone that someone else likes very much
5 someone adored by lots of people
6 the act of following someone around and becoming a nuisance in their lives
7 obsession with
8 to adore

2 Complete the text with words and phrases from the list.

centre of attention | object of affection | addicted
idols | fascination | worshipped | fixated | stalker

When I was growing up, the TV was very much the ¹_____ in our house. Mum, Dad, me, my baby sister, we were all ²_____ on that little box in the living room. It caused a lot of arguments too.

Take Saturday mornings, for example. Lola wanted to watch her pop ³_____ performing on children's TV. Dad wanted to watch the football preview programme to get the latest news on his football team. He ⁴_____ Chelsea! Mum and I were ⁵_____ to the cookery programmes. We couldn't get enough of them. There was one chef who mum absolutely loved. She even wrote him a letter once. I think she might have been a secret ⁶_____!

The problem is these programmes were all on at the same time and we only had one TV. These days, people's ⁷_____ with the TV seems to be much less pronounced. There's a new ⁸_____ in most people's lives: their smartphone.

➡ Workbook page 56

MANCHESTER UNITED

6 FOLLOWERS

LISTENING

1 Work in pairs. Make a list of reasons why people support a particular sports team.

2 🔊 1.31 Listen to a radio programme about Manchester United fans around the world. Which of the reasons you listed in Exercise 1 did you hear? Which other reasons were mentioned?

3 🔊 1.31 Listen again and match the speaker (Yoonsu, Carla or Sammy) with the sentences, which paraphrase the ideas expressed. There are three sentences that don't correspond to any of the speakers.

1 In my heart I know it's wrong to support them.
2 They can never be my number one team.
3 My family say I shouldn't support them.
4 I have mixed feelings about supporting them.
5 A team like Manchester United can help football in our country.
6 I think the history of the club is what appeals to me.
7 It was great to see someone from my country playing at the highest level.
8 It's all about money.
9 I'm not sure how I can feel this way about a foreign team but I do.
10 I was attracted to them because of the way they played the game.
11 They donate a lot of money to help young players from my country.
12 I started supporting them because they were a very successful team.

SPEAKING

Discuss in small groups.

1 What sports teams do you follow?
2 How do you feel when they lose?
3 How do you feel when they win?
4 What do these teams mean to you?
5 Are there any famous players from your country who play in foreign teams?
6 How do people in your country feel about this?

THiNK VALUES

Teamwork

1 Rank the following qualities in order of how important they are to be a good team player (1 = least important; 5 = most important).

☐ being a good listener
☐ possessing strong leadership skills
☐ having a small ego
☐ liking your teammates
☐ respecting your teammates

2 Think of and note down other important qualities and decide on your final top five.

3 **SPEAKING** Work in groups of four. Compare your ranking and agree on a new list of five.

4 **SPEAKING** Discuss in pairs.

1 How easy was it to come up with a group list?
2 Did your group work well as a team? Why (not)?
3 What sports teams can you think of that are an example of
 a good teamwork?
 b bad teamwork?
4 What makes them good/bad?

READING

1 **SPEAKING** Work in pairs. Imagine you're the agent of a famous person. What advice would you give them to help them increase their popularity?

2 Read the article quickly. Which of your ideas are mentioned? What's the purpose of the article?

How to avoid the limelight

It might be hard to believe in today's celebrity-obsessed world, but not everyone who's famous wants to be in the limelight. While it seems the likes of the Kardashians and the Hiltons will do all they can to remain in the public eye (though arguably they're famous for little more than being famous), there are still some publicity-shy celebrities who choose to stay out of the limelight and keep their private lives private.

Global film star Johnny Depp, for example, does his best to avoid fans when not shooting a film by staying at home. As he once said, 'If the choice is between being constantly gawked at and sitting in a chair in a dark room, I prefer the dark room.' Fellow actor Jennifer Lawrence has complained about feeling the pressure from Hollywood to look a certain way. As a result, she tends to keep her head down and not make eye contact with people when she's out.

But the truth is that in a world where there's always someone looking for a story to sell, it's almost impossible to be invisible if you're famous. If you're not happy being the centre of attention, perhaps you should think carefully before stepping into the limelight. But shouldn't it be possible to be known for what you do and not for who you are? Here are a few tips to keep you out of the latest celebrity gossip columns.

★ Stay away from social media. Tweeting or posting updates is an absolute no-no for anyone who doesn't want to increase their media presence. If you're at all serious about keeping a low profile, then you must avoid the likes of Twitter and Facebook.

★ Be on your best behaviour at all times. When you're famous, you can't expect to be able to make a scene in a restaurant without reading all about it in the papers the next day. Your life belongs to the public, unfortunately. But if you don't give them anything to write about, then clearly they can't write anything about you.

★ Decline all invitations to appear on TV. There's no better way to get your face recognised by the masses than by making a TV appearance or two. Even if it's to talk about your latest film or book, TV is something you should avoid.

★ Stick to what you know. If you're an author, write books. If you're an actor, make films. Don't be tempted to try something new. You'll only draw more attention to yourself. And if you do it badly, people will be more than happy to point it out.

★ Don't attend awards ceremonies. Remember, there are hardly any that aren't televised these days. Even if you don't win, the cameras will still be there to zoom in on your reaction as the winner's name is announced. And if you do win, then there's that acceptance speech to make.

★ Have ordinary people as friends. Most celebrities tend to hang out with other celebs forming ever-increasing circles of famous friends. These are always a magnet for drawing attention. Stick with your friends from before you were famous. Hopefully, they'll be good enough friends not to sell your stories to the press.

Of course, the public have short memories and if you don't do anything to remind them who you are, you mustn't be surprised if you soon find yourself on the list of has-beens. It's the price you pay for not playing the celebrity game. But if that happens, you can't really complain, can you?

3 Read the article again and answer the questions.
1 What do the Kardashians and the Hiltons have in common?
2 What do Johnny Depp and Jennifer Lawrence have in common?
3 Why is it really difficult to keep a low profile if you're famous?
4 Why should you be careful how you act in public if you're famous?
5 Why should awards ceremonies be avoided?
6 What is the danger of trying to keep a low profile?

4 **SPEAKING** For each piece of advice given in the article, give it a score from 3 (great) to 0 (rubbish). Then compare with a partner. How different were your scores? What other advice would you give?

6 FOLLOWERS

GRAMMAR
Modals 2: should, shouldn't, must, mustn't, can't

1 Complete the example sentences and check them in the article on page 60. Then match each modal with its function.

1 But _____ it be possible to be known for what you do and not for who you are?
2 If you're at all serious about keeping a low profile, then you _____ avoid the likes of Twitter and Facebook.
3 TV is something you _____ avoid.
4 If you don't do anything to remind them who you are, you _____ be surprised if you soon find yourself on the list of has-beens.

RULE:
a what you'd expect (under normal circumstances): example ___
b strong advice: example ___
c it's reasonable: example ___
d advice: example ___

2 Read the sentences. In each one, who do you think is talking to whom? What do you think they are talking about?

1 a You should think carefully about the offer.
  b You should arrive on time if you leave now.
2 a You shouldn't stay up too late.
  b You shouldn't be surprised if she says no.
3 a They must be really happy about the news.
  b You must watch this film.
4 a You mustn't tell anyone.
  b You mustn't be too hopeful.
5 a You can't go to the party.
  b She can't be very popular.

3 SPEAKING Work in pairs. Look at the sentences in Exercise 2 and discuss the difference in meaning of the modal verb in a and b. Pay attention to time reference in each case.

4 WRITING Choose two of the sentences in Exercise 2 and use them to write mini dialogues of 4–6 lines.

A *You should think carefully about the offer.*
B *Really? I wasn't very impressed with it.*
A *You won't get a better one, I promise.*
B *That's where I disagree. I think I will.*
A *Well, I hope you don't end up regretting it.*
B *I won't.*

Workbook page 55

VOCABULARY
Fame

1 Match the sentence halves.

1 She's enjoyed *being in the*
2 He's an *up-and-*
3 He hasn't made a film for years. He's a *has-*
4 She doesn't like attention and tries
5 I used to really like that band but
6 I really like this new band and they're
7 She *follows* all of her idols
8 The party was amazing. All the *A-list*

a *coming* comedian. He's going to be huge!
b *celebrities* were there.
c *on* Twitter.
d *certainly one to watch out for.*
e *been.* I wonder what happened to him?
f they just *disappeared without a trace.*
g to *keep a low profile.*
h *limelight* since she was in the school play aged six.

2 SPEAKING Complete the sentences with the missing words. Then work in pairs and discuss the questions.

1 What famous people can you think of who like to keep _____?
2 Who are the A-_____ celebrities in your country?
3 Do you enjoy being in the _____? Why (not)?
4 How many bands can you think of that have _____ a _____ in the last year?
5 Do you _____ anyone on social media? Who?

Workbook page 56

WRITING
An essay

1 Read these essay titles.
• Famous people have a right to privacy. Discuss.
• Some people will do anything for fame. Discuss.
• The media is too focused on celebrities. Discuss.

2 Your class had a discussion on the third title. You made the notes below. How could you organise them into an essay structure?
• Famous people sell newspapers.
• They're a distraction from all of the horrible things happening in the world right now.
• Our children are growing up wanting to be famous. There needs to be a balance.

3 Your teacher has asked you to write one of the essays from Exercise 1. Write your essay in 220–260 words.

PHOTOSTORY: episode 2

A new interest

1 Look at the photos and answer the questions.
   1 Where is Jack going?
   2 What is his mum doing and why?

2 🔊 1.32 Now read and listen to the photostory. Check your ideas.

MUM Where are you off to, Jack?
JACK Sorry, Mum. I can't stop. The match starts in an hour.
MUM The match?
JACK Yes, Mum. The match. We're playing City in the cup. I've got to be at Matt's house in 15 minutes, otherwise I'll miss my lift. His dad's taking us.
MUM You might have told me. I'm half way through making lunch for us.
JACK I told you last week, Mum. You probably weren't listening.
MUM Last week? That's no good. I need reminding, Jack. I've got other things to think about than just your social life.
JACK OK, Mum. Do you mind if I go to the football match with Matt? Please?
MUM Well it's a bit late now, isn't it? Just out of curiosity – didn't you go to a match last Saturday?
JACK Yes, Mum. But that was in the league. This is a cup game.
MUM Football, football. It's always football. Haven't you got anything else to do with your time?
JACK Give me a break, Mum. I really haven't got time for this now.
MUM But seriously, Jack. I mean if you're not watching it, you're playing it. It's all you ever talk about. And then there are those awful football PC games you play. I hate to think how much time you waste playing those. There must be other things that you could take an interest in.
JACK Come on, Mum. I really don't need this now.
MUM How about making some new friends? You can't spend your whole life hanging out with just Matt. Haven't you met anyone new at school this year?
JACK Well, yeah, I guess, but…
MUM And what about your homework? I don't suppose you've done that yet, by any chance?
JACK It doesn't have to be in until Thursday.
MUM Well, why don't you do it now? Be one step ahead for a change.
JACK I'll do it after the match when I get back.
MUM Fat chance of that happening. You'll be too tired. You'll just want to watch the football highlights on TV.
JACK Well, I'll do it after that. I promise.
MUM It's just that I worry, Jack. I do. You need more than just football. It's taking over your life.
JACK No it isn't, Mum. I'm interested in loads of other things.
MUM Like what?
JACK Like um …
MUM You see, Jack. You need to go out and find some new interests. Go and make some new friends.
JACK Sorry, Mum, I've got to go.

6 FOLLOWERS

DEVELOPING SPEAKING

3 Work in pairs. Discuss what you think happens next. Write down your ideas.

He's too late and misses his lift to the game.

4 **EP2** Watch the video to find out how the story continues. Did you guess correctly?

5 Answer the questions.
  1 How do Jack and his friend Matt feel after the game? Why?
  2 How does Jack say he deals with his mum's 'strange' concerns?
  3 What do Jack and his mum talk about when he gets home?
  4 What is Jack looking for in the shop?
  5 What does he find out he has in common with the shop assistant, Isabelle?
  6 Where does Jack tell his mum he's going the next day?
  7 Why is she shocked at what he's wearing?

PHRASES FOR FLUENCY

1 Find these expressions in the story. Who says them? How do you say them in your language?
  1 Just out of curiosity
  2 You might have told me
  3 Come on
  4 for a change
  5 …, by any chance?
  6 Fat chance

2 Use the expressions in Exercise 1 to complete the dialogues.
  1 A Have you tidied your bedroom? I want that done before you go out.
    B _____, Dad, I haven't got time. I'll do it later.
  2 A We always eat Chinese. Why don't we try something different _____?
    B OK, let's go to the Italian.
  3 A Do you think we're going to win today?
    B _____. They're way better than we are.
  4 A _____, can I ask you why you're wearing that hat?
    B Yeah, I'm going to a hat party. Everyone has to wear a funny hat.
  5 A _____ you were a vegetarian. I'd have cooked something different.
    B I'm really sorry. I forgot.
  6 A Can you lend me ten pounds, _____?
    B Sorry, I haven't got ten pounds.

WordWise
Expressions with *take*

1 Look at these sentences from the unit so far. Complete them with the phrases from the list.

take my word for it | take his mind off
taken an interest in | take it (that)
take it personally | take over their lives

  1 Finally, something to _____ football!
  2 I _____ they didn't win.
  3 Don't _____. She just thinks that if I had other friends I might find some new interests.
  4 Most people with an interest in celebrities don't let it _____.
  5 Yeah, _____, that will be the end of our dream for a championship win for another year.
  6 Throughout history people have _____ the rich and famous.

2 Choose the correct options.
  1 I told her I wasn't meaning to criticise. Why does she always take everything so *over / personally*?
  2 It's always nice when someone else takes *my word / an interest* in you and your life.
  3 I'm going for a walk to take *my word / my mind* off the problem.
  4 You don't believe me? Well, don't take *my word for it / it personally*. Ask Mr Jones.
  5 What a big smile! I *take it / take your word for it* you've had some good news!

Workbook page 57

FUNCTIONS
Complaining

1 Write the phrases in the correct column.

~~It's always football~~ | Haven't you got anything else to do with your time? | But seriously, … it's all you ever talk about. | ~~Give me a break …~~ | I really haven't got time for this now. | I really don't need this now.

Making a complaint	Responding to a complaint
It's always (football)	Give me a break …

2 **ROLE PLAY** Work in pairs. Role play the conversation between Olivia and her parent. Student A: Go to page 127. Student B: Go to page 128.

Olivia is mad about horses. She's about to go horse-riding. Her dad thinks she spends too much time on her hobby.

63

CAMBRIDGE ENGLISH: ADVANCED

THiNK EXAMS

READING AND USE OF ENGLISH
Part 7: Gapped text

Workbook page 61

You are going to read an extract from a magazine article. Six paragraphs have been removed from the extract. Choose from the paragraphs A–G the one which fits each gap (1–6). There is one extra paragraph that you do not need to use.

FAN BEHAVIOUR

While it may seem understandable that an athlete becomes attached to teammates and to being part of a team, it's clear that sports spectators can also become extremely passionate about their team, to the point that it becomes part of their identity and can affect their well-being.

1 [ ]

Team identification 'is the extent to which a fan feels a psychological connection to a team, and the team's performances are viewed as self-relevant', says Daniel Wann, Professor of Psychology at Murray State University.

2 [ ]

'People are tying up a lot of who they are in their identity as a fan of X-team,' says Professor Wann. 'A huge part of who they are, where they derive a lot of their positive and negative feelings, is from what their team is doing.' Perhaps the most basic question is why people follow sports so ardently. What is it about watching sports that makes people scream, obsess over statistics, and paint their faces, particularly when they know that there's a very good chance that their team will lose?

3 [ ]

'It's a voluntary activity where half of the people aren't going to like the product when they've finished consuming it,' says Wann. 'You wouldn't go see a movie if you thought there was a 50/50 chance you wouldn't like it.'

4 [ ]

Perhaps no fans understand loyalty to a team better than followers of the Chicago Cubs. The Cubs haven't won the World Series for nearly 100 years, yet the team has a legendary community. Ask a Cubs fan why they like the team and they won't say because of the championships.

5 [ ]

The senior vice president of Marketing for the Cubs agrees. 'We're marketing the experience more than other teams,' he says. 'Here, it's about the unique mystique of the Chicago Cubs. What resonates the loudest with the fanbase is the experience.'

6 [ ]

'When we look at motivation for following a sports team, group affiliation is one of the top ones,' says Wann. 'Identifying strongly with a local team where other fans are around – that's a benefit to social-psychological well-being.'

A 'They'll say, "I love Wrigley Field – I love the community here,"' says Wann. So it's evident that identification is not simply a matter of results; it has far more to do with an experience.

B Fans who watched their team win, reported significantly higher estimates of the team's future performance, their own task performance and personal self-esteem than those who watched their team lose.

C When they're watching the action, people do identify with their teams, and for some fans, this is important for their sense of self.

D People report many reasons for following a favourite team, but social connectedness is one of the most frequently mentioned aspects of the experience, as Wann finds in his research on college and professional sports fans.

E Sports fan researchers acknowledge this point: sporting events are competitions in which it's guaranteed that one team must lose, which means that half the fans will be upset with the result. In other activities, those odds might not seem like a worthwhile investment of one's time.

F The professor's research has shown similarities between a fan's identification with a sports team and how people identify with their nationality, ethnicity, even gender.

G So being a fan can't be all about a team's winning performance. 'Everyone is eventually going to lose,' says Wann. 'It's clear there have to be other benefits.'

TEST YOURSELF

UNITS 5 & 6

VOCABULARY

1 **Complete the sentences with the words in the list. There are four extra words.**

worshipped | stunt | A-list | on | daredevil | has-been
for | risk | in | with | kick | crying | noisy | loud

1 He's fixated _____ getting into the football team. He talks about nothing else.
2 I really get a _____ out of travelling. I find going to new places so exciting.
3 For _____ out loud, will you please turn that TV down!
4 My sister's a bit of a _____. She's not scared to try any kind of extreme sport.
5 He doesn't really like being _____ the limelight and tries to keep away from the cameras.
6 My mum _____ a group called ABBA when she was young. She still has all their albums.
7 My two-year-old has got a fascination _____ wheels. He loves anything that moves.
8 There's no need to keep asking. I heard you _____ and clear the first time.
9 I think we should assess the _____ before we attempt the jump.
10 He's a bit of a _____. He hasn't had any real success for years now.

/10

GRAMMAR

2 **Complete the sentences with the words in the list. There are two extra words.**

should | inspiring | might | having | taking | take | inspired | can't

1 He's lying about the chocolates. I saw him _____ the last one.
2 You _____ take your children to see this film. They'll love it.
3 It _____ be warm now, but it'll get cold later, so make sure you take a coat.
4 _____ by the concert, I decided to start piano lessons.
5 His team haven't won all year. They _____ be very good.
6 _____ lived in a cold climate most of my life, I found Brazil extremely hot.

3 **Find and correct the mistake in each sentence.**

1 Walking all morning, we were extremely hungry when we arrived home.
2 I heard the telephone ringing three times before it stopped.
3 She's just had a baby. She can be very tired.
4 They must be very famous – I've never heard of them.
5 Leaving my office, the telephone rang.
6 I looked up and saw the bus crashing into the car.

/12

FUNCTIONAL LANGUAGE

4 **Choose the correct options.**

1 A The way I *understand / see* it, we'll never get anywhere if we keep on disagreeing.
   B OK. *Point / Idea* taken. Let's make some decisions.
2 A To my *opinion / mind*, we should spend less money on defence and more money on hospitals.
   B I *suppose / agree* you're right, but defence is also very important.
3 A You're *always / only* watching TV. If you're not watching it, you're talking about it.
   B Give me a *rest / break*, Mum. I'm trying to watch my show.
4 A I don't *accept / admit* that young people are responsible for most of our crime.
   B That's not how I *see / observe* things either. It's too easy to just blame them.

/8

MY SCORE /30

22 – 30
10 – 21
0 – 9

65

7 BEAUTY IS IN THE EYE OF THE BEHOLDER

OBJECTIVES

FUNCTIONS: language of persuasion
GRAMMAR: substitution (*the ones / so / that / do*); ellipsis
VOCABULARY: fads; emotional responses

READING

1 Work in pairs. Why might people do the activities in the photos? Write down as many reasons as you can.

to increase their energy levels
to feel good about themselves when they look in a mirror

2 Quickly scan the article on the next page. What do these figures refer to?

a 3,000
b 2
c 90
d 100
e 82.69 million

3 ◎ 2.02 Read the article again and listen. Answer the questions below.

1 How did early humans keep fit?
2 Why did they not think about exercise?
3 What is it that the author finds 'infuriating' about the situation today?
4 What similarities and differences are there between exercise now and exercise in Ancient Greece?
5 What is the author's opinion of exergames?
6 According to the author, what do people today generally look for in an exercise programme?

4 **SPEAKING** Work in pairs and discuss the following questions.

1 Which of the fitness activities mentioned in the article have you tried? Which would you like to try?
2 How important is exercise for you? What are your reasons for (not) exercising?
3 Can you think of four more fitness crazes? Rank them from 1–4 according to how appealing they are (1 = least appealing; 4 = most appealing). Compare your ranking with your partner's. How similar are they?

TRAIN TO THiNK

Understanding irony

Irony is a technique used in speaking and writing to create a contradiction between what people say and what they mean. Ironic remarks can sound humorous, but can also sound sarcastic or unkind.

Here's an example from the article: Look out! It's that big, toothy, stripey thing we don't have a word for yet!

Explanation: This is an ironic remark. Early humans would never have said anything like that – they'd probably just have given a warning cry.

1 Match the situations with the ironic remarks below.

1 Mr Brown is in a hurry and has been patiently queuing up in a bank. Just as it's his turn, the assistant asks if he'd mind if she made a phone call before serving him. He says:
2 It's Monday morning. Joanne leaves the house and gets her bike out of the shed to ride it to school, but then notices it's got a flat tyre. She says:
3 Ken drives a brand new sports car. He notices a little stain on the front window and complains about it. His friend Carol drives an old car. She says:

a 'Brilliant. Today couldn't have started any better!'
b 'My goodness! How can you ever think of getting into that filthy car again?'
c 'Sure. Why on earth would you think I'd mind?'

2 Work in pairs. Think of an ironic remark people might make in each of the following situations.

1 It's a beautiful Sunday morning. Sally and her friend have decided to go to the beach. Ten minutes after the girls arrive at the beach, it starts raining heavily. Sally says: …
2 Nick always leaves home early. He hates being late. One day, he arrives at the station half an hour before the train leaves. He sits down on a bench and starts reading a book. He loves the story so much that he completely forgets about the train and misses it. When he notices the train has gone, he says: …
3 Mr Miller has had his new suit cleaned. When he puts it back into the wardrobe, he notices that there are several stains that weren't there before. He says: …

3 Now, in pairs, write down two more situations and think of ironic remarks that you could make about them.

7 BEAUTY IS IN THE EYE OF THE BEHOLDER

A history of fitness fads

Spurious exercise crazes have come and gone for over 3,000 years. Phil Daoust asks, 'How far have we come?'

Life must have been simpler for our ancestors, albeit shorter, nastier and lacking in such basic amenities as the electric toaster. Exercise was something early humans just got, not something they thought about or paid for. It was all 'Quick! Follow that antelope!' or 'Look out! It's that big, toothy, stripey thing that we don't have a word for yet!' and anyone who stood around suggesting, 'Yes, this running's all very well, but you really need to be working on your core stability', ended up inside a tiger.

So how did we arrive at today's infuriating situation, where staying fit seems to involve an expensive bagful of kit and the even more expensive services of at least one personal trainer? Let's start by blaming the Ancient Greeks, since they were the ones that created the unattainable ideal that is the Olympic athlete almost 3,000 years ago.

Enough of the funny stuff. Let's take a serious look at exercise and how it has progressed over the centuries. Many Ancient Greeks believed that developing the body was as important as developing the mind, so athletics was a key part of education. The principles of exercise were much the same as they are today. However, the main aim was not to be healthy and look good. In a society so often at war, men needed to be fit and ready to join the army at all times. Military training was part of their education and exercise was primarily a form of military training. The *palaestra*, or wrestling school, was a popular place for men of all ages. Young men worked with athletic trainers, who worked to balance their physical exercise with their diet, just as we do today. And that's not the only similarity. Even in those days, exercise was done to music. The Ancient Greeks believed that harmonious movement was important, so they often exercised to flute music. So how have things changed?

Nowadays, exercise is big business worth billions of pounds. What was once free, we now have to pay for! And today, living as we do in a digital world, technology inevitably plays a major part in our exercise regimes. Take, for example, the popular *Insanity* workout programme. It's a DVD set that offers a complete body makeover in 90 days and costs just over £100. You get 10 DVDs, a calendar, a pin-up poster and a diet booklet. And apparently, it's 'the world's most insanely tough workout'. If you're not looking for the perfect muscled body and you just want to get a bit fitter, you can dance, bike or kickbox your way to fitness in your own living room with an exergame (short for 'exercise game'). Fantastic! And 82.69 million people also think so. Well, that's how many people had bought WiiSports by March 2015. Although an exergame may not offer as much of a workout as that of real sports, it's got to be better than sitting around on the sofa. Many people still believe that exercise should be done outdoors in the fresh air. Exergames are now offering a solution to this. Games companies have created versions of exergames for smartphones and tablets. For example, they've developed a game in which you can take part in a treasure hunt. This involves a two-hour walk around a town or other location looking for answers to clues provided by the game. As well as getting exercise, you're learning about the geography and environment of a new place, so it's educational too.

The world has changed dramatically since the time of the Ancient Greeks, but the basic concepts remain the same. We want to stay fit and healthy and we look to someone or something to help us do this. What's different then? Today we look for the fastest and easiest way to achieve fitness and as long as we're prepared to pay, we'll also have ever-progressing technology to help us in our mission.

GRAMMAR
Substitution

1 Read the sentences from the article on page 67. Complete them with *that, ones, so, do*. Then choose the correct options in the rule.

1. Let's start by blaming the Ancient Greeks, since they were the _____ that created the unattainable ideal that is the Olympic athlete.
2. Young men worked with athletic trainers, who worked to balance their physical exercise with their diet, just as we _____ today.
3. And 82.69 million people also think _____ .
4. Although an exergame may not offer as much of a workout as _____ of real sports, it's got to be better than sitting around on the sofa.

> **RULE:** We use substitution to avoid repetition.
> *A typical fitness regime today is a lot more expensive than **that of** (people's fitness regimes) 50 years ago.*
> *There are people who take exercise seriously, and there are **those** (people) who **don't** (take it seriously).*
> *That bread is much less healthy than **the other one** (the bread) my mum buys.*
> *Many people say the hula hoop is just a fad, and I **think so** (think it's just a fad) too.*
> *Do you think the fitness club is open on a Sunday? – I certainly **hope so** (hope it is open on a Sunday).*
> *They didn't go swimming and **neither did we** (we didn't go swimming either).*
>
> - The words *that of / those of* tend to be more [1]*formal / informal*.
> - The words *the one / the ones* tend to be more [2]*formal / informal*.
> - The words *so* and *do / did* replace a [3]*word / phrase*.
> - *so / neither / nor* include the meaning 'also'. Here, we invert the subject and [4]*auxiliary / main* verb.

2 Rewrite the sentences, substituting the underlined words. Sometimes more than one correct answer is possible.

1. Today's fitness equipment is a lot more advanced than <u>the fitness equipment of</u> a few years ago.
2. A Are you going to the gym tonight?
   B No, I don't think <u>I'm going to the gym tonight</u>.
3. I don't think the sports facilities in this city are as good as <u>the sports facilities</u> in my previous town.
4. A I really hope we win the match.
   B I hope <u>we win the match</u>, too.
5. My brother doesn't like sports, and <u>I don't like sports either</u>.
6. I'm keen on doing exercise every morning, and <u>my sister is keen on it too</u>.

3 Read the dialogue and underline the repetitive sections. Then rewrite the dialogue using substitution to replace these sections.

A Have you heard of Tough Mudder?
B Yes, I have. It sounds too tough for me though. I wouldn't want to run a mile waist-deep in mud.
A And I wouldn't want to run a mile waist-deep in mud.
B The good thing is there aren't any winners of Tough Mudder and there aren't any losers of Tough Mudder. You have to work as a team and help each other. I think that's a great idea.
A I also think that's a great idea. And the company sounds really cool. I've heard their employees can take as much holiday as they like.
B That's good from a company perspective, too. Apparently, studies have found that high performing employees take more holiday than employees who aren't performing so well.

> Workbook page 64

VOCABULARY
Fads

1 Match the sentence halves.

1. The retro look
2. The latest smartphone quickly
3. We have seen many rather *short-lived*
4. The pilates class was full,
5. Can you remember when
6. Long hair for men was
7. I don't think jeans

a. fitness crazes over the years.
b. ripped jeans became *a thing*?
c. so I'm doing yoga, which is *the next best thing*.
d. will ever *go out of fashion*.
e. *really in* in the '70s.
f. established itself as the new *must-have* device.
g. is *bang on trend* at the moment.

2 Choose the correct words to complete the sentences.

1. Wide-legged trousers are *really in / short-lived*.
2. Everybody's got a selfie stick nowadays. It's a *really in / must-have* device.
3. You can't always take your guitar with you. The Pocket Strings is *a thing / the next best thing*.
4. Cafés with odd chairs and tables were *bang on trend / must-have* in London in 2015.
5. It was *a thing / short-lived* in 2015 to drink out of jam jars.
6. Do you think gyms will ever *be the next best thing / go out of fashion*?

> Workbook page 66

7 BEAUTY IS IN THE EYE OF THE BEHOLDER

LISTENING

1 🔊 2.03 Look at the photos. How do you think these things relate to beauty? Listen and check your answers.

2 🔊 2.03 Listen again. Mark the statements T (true) or F (false) according to what the historian says. Correct the false statements.

1 An American actress is reported to use the venom from a snake to purify her blood.
2 People are prepared to spend money on beauty treatments which lack scientific corroboration.
3 Media stories make us think that we can buy beauty.
4 Japanese women rubbed nuts against their teeth to make them black.
5 Certain ingredients used in facemasks in Ancient Rome and Egypt were difficult to find.
6 Having black teeth in 19th-century Japan signalled that you wanted to get married.

3 Read the list of things people do to improve or change their looks. Check the meaning of the words and phrases. Can you add two more things?

- have plastic surgery, for example a tummy tuck or a face lift
- dye their hair
- buy expensive cosmetics
- have a facial treatment
- cut down on sugar
- have a teeth-whitening treatment
- take steroids
- take up bodybuilding and/or exercise regularly

4 **SPEAKING** Work in pairs. What do you think about each of the things listed in Exercise 3?

It's a safe way to change your looks.
It can be fun.
It poses a serious health threat.
It's ridiculously expensive.
It doesn't have any long-lasting effects.
It may be worth trying.

GRAMMAR
Ellipsis

1 Read these sentences (1–6) from the listening. Match them with the omitted words (a–f). Then complete the rule with *subject*, *informal*, and *verbs*.

1 Not heard that one before.
2 Want to hear another example?
3 Fancy trying any of those yourself?
4 Interesting.
5 Why black teeth?
6 Better to stay single, then.

a That's
b did they want
c Would you
d I think it would be
e I have
f Do you

RULE: We often leave words out, especially in ¹_____ spoken English. This is known as 'ellipsis'. We can omit ²_____ pronouns, articles, auxiliary ³_____ or, in fact, any verb when it's clear from the context what the verb is.

Would you like more ice cream? → *More ice cream?*
I would love some. → *Love some.*

2 🔊 2.04 Read the three dialogues and underline the words that can be omitted. Then listen and check your answers.

1 PETER   Do you fancy another game, Matt?
   MATT   I would love one.
   PETER   What about you, Jamie?
   JAMIE   Sorry, there is not enough time. I have got to be home by five.
   PETER   See you at the same time tomorrow, then?
   JAMIE   That would be great.

2 HELEN   Have you got a minute? I need to talk to you.
   MIKE   No, I'm sorry, I'm busy now. Maybe we can talk later.
   HELEN   That is no problem.

3 EMMA   Do you want a coffee?
   JAKE   I'd love one.

Workbook page 65

69

READING

1 Make a list of five things that you find beautiful.

2 **SPEAKING** Work in pairs. Look at the photos. Where is the 'beauty' in each one? Discuss.

I think this shows the beauty in the power of nature.

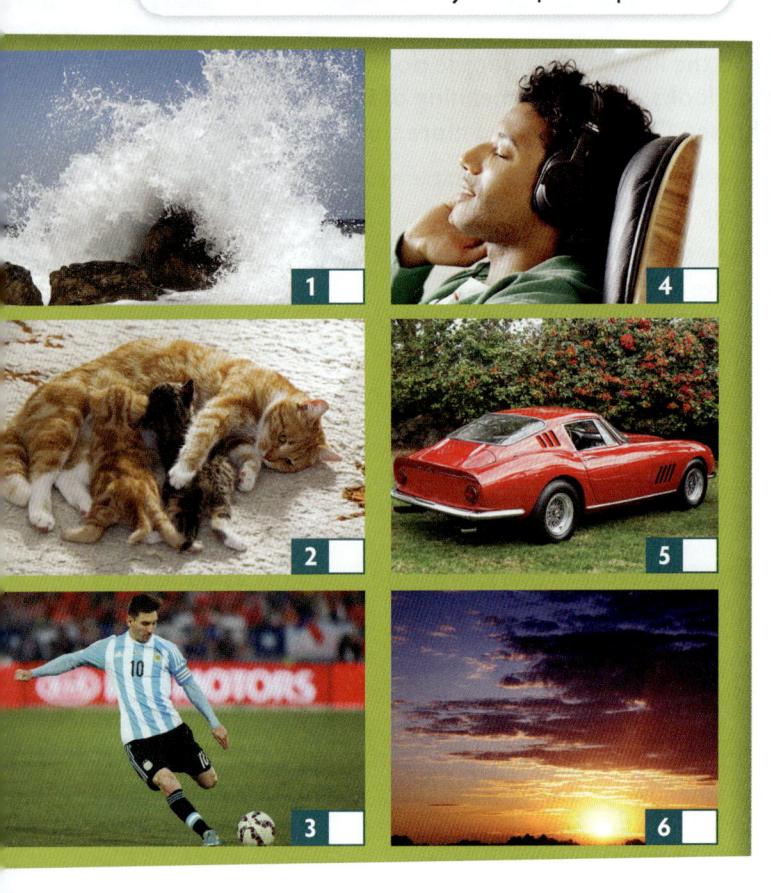

3 Read the blog. Match each photo with a text.

Pronunciation
Connected speech feature: assimilation
Go to page 121.

SPEAKING

Work in pairs and discuss the questions.

1 What did the blog ask readers to do?
2 Which of your ideas in Exercise 1, if any, were mentioned?
3 Underline some of the positive words and expressions used in the texts (that you liked).
4 Read each text again and give it a score from 0–5 according to on how much you liked it. Then discuss your scores in pairs.

I didn't like F. I thought it was pretentious.

My favourite is C. I think it describes beautifully the way Messi plays.

How would you define beauty?

We asked you to define beauty in 50 words or fewer. Once again, you didn't disappoint us. Here are our favourites. Which one do you like the best? Write and let us know.

[A] My uncle has a 1974 Ferrari Dino 308 – 'a thing of beauty, a joy forever', so a poet once said. It's the perfect balance of engineering and design. The noise it makes as it pulls away, it sets my heart racing. A flash of Ferrari red and it's gone.

[B] Fading light. The last gasps of the day. On Earth, colours lose their hold as the sky above drains them. Crimson, rose, blood red. On Earth, I watch in awe. The sun takes its farewell and dips behind the horizon. I leave, wondering what new beauties the day to come will bring.

[C] He turns, he stops, he turns and runs. He stops and turns again.
No two moves are the same.
He looks up, he looks down,
He looks forwards, he looks round.
Will he pass? Will he shoot? Will he turn again?

[D] As I watch my cat feed her hungry kittens, all eight of them, each fighting for a space, I think about the miracle of life – how well it all works, how well it all fits together. It gives me goosebumps down my arm and inside I purr. Does anything get more perfect?

[E] I'm sitting here, head in hand. There is no room left in my head. It's ready to explode. And then the bell sounds, loud and welcome. The sound echoes … echoes through the corridors. Happy children put down their pens and wait for the words, simple but beautiful: 'Off you go.'

[F] I live by the sea. Where else is there to live? The sea fills my heart with joy. A big blue expanse of happiness. The crashing waves, obeying no one, come and then go. I always return to the sea. It knows the answers before I even ask the questions.

[G] Halfway through Pink Floyd's *Wish You Were Here*, there's a guitar solo that sends shivers down my spine. Even though I know it's coming, it gets me every time. It brings a tear to my eye and reminds me what a better place the world is for music.

[H] 'Hello, I'm home.' It brings a smile to my face when I hear my wife's voice. I look up and she's there. Has she walked out of a painting? 'She *is* beauty,' is all I think.

7 BEAUTY IS IN THE EYE OF THE BEHOLDER

VOCABULARY
Emotional responses

1 What does *it* refer to in each of these sentences about the texts on page 70? Complete the sentences with the missing parts of the body. Then read and check.

- ☐ *It* sets my ¹_____ racing when I hear the noise it makes as it pulls away.
- ☐ *It* sends shivers down my ²_____ when I listen to it.
- ☐ *It* brings a tear to my ³_____ and reminds me what a better place the world is with it.
- ☐ *It* brings a smile to my ⁴_____ when I hear her voice.
- ☐ *It* fills my ⁵_____ with joy when I see it.
- ☐ *It* gives me goosebumps down my ⁶_____ and inside I purr.

2 **SPEAKING** Work in pairs. Discuss what gives you the feelings described in each of the sentences in Exercise 1. Then make a list and share your ideas with another pair.

3 **WRITING** Now choose one of the ideas and write your own post for the blog about something you find beautiful.

> Workbook page 66

THiNK VALUES
Valuing the beauty around us

1 **SPEAKING** Work in pairs. Look at the photos and discuss.

1 In what ways are the photos similar?
2 How are they different?
3 Do sights like these bother you? How do they make you feel?

2 Work in groups. Make a list of four things you could do to tackle the environmental problem shown in one of the photos.

3 Work in pairs. Make a list of four 'ugly' sights in the town where you live and complete the table.

Place	Issue	Cause	Solution

4 Choose one of the sights and talk about the advantages and disadvantages of using each of the different media below to raise awareness about the problem. Decide on the best one and, using your notes from Exercise 3, plan a campaign.

- a video
- banners
- social media

FUNCTIONS
Language of persuasion

1 Match 1–8 with a–h to complete the expressions.

1 *I strongly*
2 *Try* our brand
3 *This revolutionary new*
4 *This offer*
5 *Have you always*
6 *Five million people* worldwide
7 *We understand that*
8 *Imagine*

a *is limited.*
b *have already discovered* Nutrawheat.
c *your health is important.*
d *recommend* trying this treatment.
e *having perfect sight again.*
f *new product.*
g *dreamed of* owning a sports car?
h *system is easy to use.*

2 What is the aim of the expressions above?

3 ◆)) 2.06 Now complete the advert with six of the expressions in italics in Exercise 1. Then listen and check your answers.

> **Smile and the world smiles with you – or does it?**
>
> ¹_____ having a perfect smile? Well, now you can. If you want a confident smile, try our brand new, almost invisible tooth-straightening device.
> ²_____ device is easy and comfortable to wear, and it fits perfectly. 'I always tried to hide my teeth when I smiled, but now I show them,' said Karen. 'If you feel the same way, ³_____ trying Smile-Align.'
> ⁴'_____ being able to smile for a photo again,' says Max. 'After using Smile-align, I can do that.' ⁵_____ the price is important, so we have a great offer for you today. The process usually costs £2,000, but we're offering it to you for just £1,500. But hurry – ⁶_____ and must end soon.

4 **WRITING** Now create your own advert for a beauty gadget or piece of exercise equipment. Then present your advert to the class.

71

Literature

1 🔊 2.07 Read and listen to the extracts. Which one:

1. talks about how someone's beauty will never die? ☐
2. talks about remembering beauty and love? ☐
3. talks about seeing someone beautiful for the first time? ☐

2 Look at the first extract. Match these sentences to lines 5–10.

- [8] And when I take her hand, my poor hand will be most fortunate.
- [ ] A white bird looks like this when it walks in the middle of a group of black birds.
- [ ] Have I ever been in love before? My eyes say no!
- [ ] How that woman stands out amongst the other women.
- [ ] Tonight is the first time I've ever seen someone really beautiful.
- [ ] When the dancing finishes, I'll watch where she stands.

3 **VOCABULARY** Look at the second extract. Match the highlighted words with their definitions.

1. walked backwards and forwards while feeling nervous
2. sadness, unhappiness
3. producing a warm light
4. falling asleep
5. someone who makes a long and difficult journey to a special place
6. speak or say something quietly

1 Romeo and Juliet
William Shakespeare

Romeo:
1. O, she doth teach the torches to burn bright!
2. It seems she hangs upon the cheek of night
3. Like a rich jewel in an Ethiope's ear;
4. Beauty too rich for use, for earth too dear!
5. So shows a snowy dove trooping with crows,
6. As yonder lady o'er her fellows shows.
7. The measure done, I'll watch her place of stand,
8. And, touching hers, make blessed my rude hand.
9. Did my heart love till now? forswear it, sight!
10. For I ne'er saw true beauty till this night.

2 When you are old
William Butler Yeats

1. When you are old and grey and full of sleep,
2. And nodding by the fire, take down this book,
3. And slowly read, and dream of the soft look
4. Your eyes had once, and of their shadows deep;
5. How many loved your moments of glad grace,
6. And loved your beauty with love false or true,
7. But one man loved the pilgrim Soul in you,
8. And loved the sorrows of your changing face;
9. And bending down beside the glowing bars,
10. Murmur, a little sadly, how Love fled
11. And paced upon the mountains overhead.

3 Sonnet 18
William Shakespeare

1. Shall I compare thee to a summer's day?
2. Thou art more lovely and more temperate.
3. Rough winds do shake the darling buds of May,
4. And summer's lease hath all too short a date.
5. Sometime too hot the eye of heaven shines,
6. And often is his gold complexion dimmed;
7. And every fair from fair sometime declines,
8. By chance, or nature's changing course, untrimmed;
9. But thy eternal summer shall not fade,
10. Nor lose possession of that fair thou ow'st,
11. Nor shall death brag thou wand'rest in his shade,
12. When in eternal lines to Time thou grow'st.
13. So long as men can breathe, or eyes can see,
14. So long lives this, and this gives life to thee.

7 BEAUTY IS IN THE EYE OF THE BEHOLDER

4 Look at the third extract. Match these phrases to the lines which mean:

- [4] summer does not last very long
- [ ] as long as there are people in the world
- [ ] everything that is beautiful loses its beauty at some time
- [ ] this poem will live on, and will keep you alive
- [ ] you will not die
- [ ] you will not lose the beauty that you have now

5 **SPEAKING** Work in pairs and discuss the questions.

1. Which of the three poems do you like most? Why?
2. Which poem was easiest to understand, and which was the most difficult? Why?
3. Do you know any poems or songs, in English or in your own language, about beauty? Tell the class about it/them.

WRITING
A formal letter

1 Read the letter. What two issues is Clara upset about and how does she hope the newspaper will respond?

2 Complete the letter by choosing the best option for each adverb.

3 Complete the sentences with your own ideas.
1. Although she has made several great films, her latest is arguably …
2. I have to admit I found the book thoroughly …
3. He's a talented singer, but he's an equally …
4. The last chapter of the book is especially …
5. Not being a football fan, I wasn't remotely …

4 Match the paragraphs (1–4) with their functions.
- [ ] This paragraph outlines the issue (what is wrong).
- [ ] This paragraph gives the background information.
- [ ] This paragraph proposes a solution.
- [ ] This paragraph explains why this situation is wrong.

5 While reading a fashion magazine, you noticed that several of the models have been photoshopped to make them look perfect. You decide to write a letter about this. Use the structure of Clara's letter to help you organise your ideas.

6 Write a letter to the magazine complaining about this issue. Use your notes to help you.

Dear Madam,

[1] Being a student in my final year at the London School of Fashion, I was ¹*equally / especially* looking forward to the special fashion edition of your newspaper's weekend magazine. At first glance, I was not disappointed. The clothes that you featured were as original as they were exciting.

[2] However, while I was ²*thoroughly / arguably* enjoying the featured fashion, something did not feel quite right. I was trying to work out what it was when suddenly it dawned on me. Of the 12 different models you used for your shoot, ten were white, one was Asian and one was black – hardly reflective of the multicultural society in which we live. Furthermore, all of the models were what the media like to refer to as size zero. None of them were even ³*remotely / thoroughly* approaching the shape or size of the majority of your female readership.

[3] I have to say that I was particularly disappointed that your paper, which normally prides itself on its forward-thinking articles, should fall into the trap that less progressive magazines are keen to promote; i.e. that women should aspire to unreasonable, and ⁴*arguably / especially* unhealthy, body sizes. I was ⁵*remotely / equally* upset that you did not take the opportunity to portray a fair representation of the women who actually inhabit this world.

[4] I do not imagine that you will consider making amends by offering us another fashion special in the next few weeks which features more diverse models. However, I do hope you will take note of my comments and observations, and make sure that in the future you present us with a fashion edition I know you are capable of producing.

Yours faithfully,

Clara Bowen

8 IT'S ALL GREEK TO ME!

OBJECTIVES

FUNCTIONS: saying that you don't understand or didn't fully hear
GRAMMAR: relative clauses with determiners and prepositions; *however, wherever, whatever,* etc.
VOCABULARY: language and communication; personality (2)

Chester Nez

Chester Nez

READING

1 **SPEAKING** Work in pairs. Look at the photos. Tell your partner what you can see in them.

2 How do you think the turtle might be related to the tank, and the bird to the plane? Read the article quickly to check your ideas.

3 🔊 2.08 Listen to and read the article again. Answer the questions.

1 What are the key characteristics of the Navajo language?
2 Why did the Americans need a new code?
3 What was the potential problem with using Navajo as a code language?
4 How was the problem overcome?
5 In what way was the code unique in the Second World War?
6 Why was a high level of accuracy in using the code important?
7 What two things did the code-talkers have to wait for after the war?
8 What was the reaction to the film that was made about the code-talkers?

4 **SPEAKING** Work in pairs. Discuss your answers to the questions.

1 Some people describe the Navajo code-talkers as 'heroes'. Do you agree? Why (not)?
2 If you could meet one of the code-talkers, what two questions would you ask them?
3 Why do you think the Navajo code-talkers weren't allowed to talk about their work until a long time after the war?

Pronunciation
Stress in multi-syllable words
Go to page 121.

TRAIN TO THINK

Making connections

The article mentions how the creators of the Navajo code needed to come up with new words that the language was missing. Therefore, they decided that 'turtle' could represent 'tank' and 'hummingbird' could represent 'fighter plane'. Of course, while there are obvious similarities between these objects, there are also some differences.

1 Work in pairs. Think of how these objects are similar and how they are different.

turtle – tank
hummingbird – fighter plane
eggs – bombs
whale – battleship

2 What objects could you use to describe these modern items? What are the similarities and differences?

- headphones
- television
- computer
- Facebook
- mobile phones

Headphones could be described as two bowls with a lead between them. The ear pieces are the same shape as bowls but of course they're used for different things.

74

8 IT'S ALL GREEK TO ME!

THE CODE-TALKERS

When Chester Nez died, aged 93, in 2014, he was the last surviving member of the Navajo 'code-talkers', whose work had been fundamental to winning the Second World War in the Pacific from 1941 to 1945.

Nez, a member of the Navajo tribe, was born in 1921 in New Mexico. The Navajo language was, and still is, only a spoken one, with no written alphabet. It is a language spoken almost exclusively by the Navajos themselves and is famous for being difficult for others to learn because of its complex grammar and difficult tones. Indeed, it is a language compared to which most European languages seem easy. All of these factors together resulted in the language, and consequently Nez, being chosen for a wartime mission.

During the Second World War, the American forces were engaged in a campaign against the Japanese in the Pacific. In order to communicate with each other, the Americans had tried using various forms of code, all of which had been broken by the Japanese. American attacks had been anticipated and defeated, with countless lives lost. They needed a new form of code, and they needed it fast.

A former army engineer, Philip Johnston, who had lived on a Navajo reservation as a child and who therefore had a basic knowledge of the language, came up with an idea – to use the Navajo language to communicate.

In 1942, 29 young men, one of whom was Nez, were recruited to develop a form of Navajo that would be incomprehensible to anyone else. For the Navajo men, most of whom had never left their reservation, this was a difficult assignment, but they accepted the challenge and worked hard at it.

One problem was that Navajo did not have words for modern things like tanks or battleships. Johnston was worried that the Navajos might use the English words for these things, in which case they would be easily understood by the Japanese. So what the Navajo recruits did was adapt existing Navajo words. For example, the Navajo word for 'turtle' was used to describe tanks, the word for 'humming bird' was used for fighter planes, and a machine gun was 'a rapid fire gun'. America was 'ne-he-mah', which translates as 'our mother'. In essence, they created a new form of Navajo, and they were so successful that even other Navajo speakers who were not in the programme could not understand the code. It was the only completely unbroken code used during the entire war.

Once the code had been developed, the team of 29 men quickly grew to more than 400, as other Navajo men joined to help. The men, some of whom later became trainers themselves, were trained to an extremely high level of accuracy in the new code language. There was no room for error, since this could cost lives. Once proficient, the team were flown out to the war zone of the Pacific to work on the front line. Not one single mistake was made in all their communications.

After the war was over, the code-talkers were not allowed to talk about their work, not even in job interviews, until 1968. Also, unlike many of their comrades in the Marines, the Navajo code-talkers' contribution to the war effort was not recognised until long after the war ended. Those who were still alive were given medals as recently as 2001. In 2002, a film about the work of the Navajos, called *Windtalkers*, was made. It starred Nicolas Cage and it helped bring the story of the Navajo code-talkers to public awareness, but the film itself was not a critical success. Many people disliked it because they felt that the Navajos were not the main focus of the film. Thus, their enormously important contribution to the US war effort is yet to receive the public recognition it deserves.

GRAMMAR
Relative clauses with determiners and prepositions

1 Complete the sentences from the article on page 75 using the phrases in the list. Then complete the rule by choosing the correct options.

some of whom | compared to which | most of whom
in which case | all of which | one of whom

1 The Americans had tried using various forms of code, _____ had been broken by the Japanese.
2 [Navajo] is a language, _____ most European languages seem easy.
3 In 1942, 29 young men, _____ was Nez, were recruited to develop a form of Navajo.
4 For the Navajo men, _____ had never left their reservation, this was a difficult assignment.
5 The Navajos might use the English words for these things, _____ they would be easily understood by the Japanese.
6 The men, _____ later became trainers themselves, were trained to an extremely high level of accuracy.

> **RULE:** Typically, prepositions go at the ¹*beginning / end* of a clause, e.g. 'Navajo was the language (which) the unbroken code was derived from.'
>
> In writing or in very formal spoken contexts, we can put the preposition at the ²*beginning / end* of a relative clause, e.g. 'Navajo was the language from which the unbroken code was derived.'
>
> In this case, the relative pronoun is always ³*that / whom* for people.
>
> Sometimes the relative clause ⁴*begins / ends* with a determiner e.g. *all, some* or *none*.

2 Rewrite the sentences in more formal language.

0 Navajo is a language that few people are familiar with.

Navajo is a language with which few people are familiar.

1 Grammar is something that I know nothing about.
2 She is a woman that I have never spoken to.
3 Language is something we all give great importance to.
4 Translation is the profession that he has dedicated his life to.
5 He's a friend that I almost never hear from.

→ Workbook page 72

VOCABULARY
Language and communication

1 Read the paragraphs. Which one isn't about spoken language?

A When I'm in France I like to try to practise my language skills. However, my **broken French** is so poor that sometimes I **can't make myself understood** and so it ends in complete **communication breakdown**. I do my best to **pronounce** things clearly but of course I'm not a **native speaker** or anywhere approaching that level, so people often **misunderstand** me.

B The other day, I met someone from another part of the country who had such a **strong accent** that at times I found him virtually **incomprehensible**. It was hard to believe that we shared the same **first language**, to be honest. And it wasn't just the accent – he was actually speaking a different **dialect** and using slang words that meant I just couldn't **follow** him. We had to get someone to **interpret** for us!

C When you travel, there's sometimes **a language barrier** that makes communication difficult. But I've found that **body language**, while obviously not exactly the same around the world, is sufficiently universal to mean that we can 'talk' to other people. **Gestures** and **facial expressions** allow you to show people that you don't understand, that you want a particular thing, or whatever.

2 **SPEAKING** Work in pairs. Discuss the meaning of the words and phrases in bold. Use a dictionary to help you.

3 Use expressions from Exercise 1 to complete the text.

I'll always remember the first time I went to the north-east of England. People there speak with a really ¹_____ and there are some vocabulary differences too, which means it's really a different ²_____ of English. More than once, people said things to me and I just couldn't ³_____ them. And sometimes they ⁴_____ me too. It's strange when there seems to be a ⁵_____ between people who share the same ⁶_____!

→ Workbook page 74

SPEAKING

Work in pairs. Give examples of:

1 a time when you couldn't make yourself understood
2 a slang expression in English
3 a regional accent in your country which you find incomprehensible
4 a dialect that someone in your family speaks
5 mistakes people often make when writing your language
6 someone you know who speaks with a strong accent

8 IT'S ALL GREEK TO ME!

FUNCTIONS
Saying that you don't understand or didn't fully hear

1 **Match the beginnings (1–6) with the correct endings (a–f).**

1 Sorry, there was a bus going past.
2 He was using all sorts of technical jargon,
3 His argument isn't very clear.
4 She hasn't explained it very clearly.
5 That was a bit of a complicated explanation!
6 The teacher said that I needed to 'use some elbow grease',

a so I **didn't quite get** what he said.
b but I wasn't **familiar with** that expression.
c I **didn't catch** what you said with all the noise.
d I'm afraid **you've lost me**. Can you explain it more simply?
e I **don't quite see** what she means.
f I **don't follow** him at all.

2 **How do you say the expressions in bold in your language?**

3 **Answer the questions about the expressions in Exercise 1.**

1 Which one(s) do you like most?
2 Which one(s), if any, do you not like at all?
3 Which one(s), if any, could you see yourself using?
4 Which one(s), if any, would you not feel very comfortable using?

LISTENING
Accents

1 **SPEAKING** Work in pairs. Discuss the question.

How many different varieties of English can you name?

2 ◆2.10 **Listen to the radio programme. Which places in the UK do the speakers come from?**

3 ◆2.10 **Listen again and answer the questions.**

1 What does the news report claim?
2 Why isn't the radio presenter surprised by the report?
3 How does she feel about her own accent?
4 What does the Scottish man say about people in the south?
5 What does the woman say about accents on television?
6 What does the report say about people from Birmingham?
7 How does the man from Birmingham think things might change?

GRAMMAR
however / wherever / whatever, etc.

1 **Match the beginnings and endings of the sentences from the listening. Then choose the correct options to complete the rule.**

1 Wherever I go,
2 Whatever I say,
3 However intelligent you are,

a people won't think I'm clever.
b you'll come across to other people as not very intelligent at all.
c people know immediately that I'm from Liverpool.

RULE: We can add -ever to how and ¹all / some wh-words: however / whatever / whoever / wherever / whenever / whichever.

We use whatever / wherever / however etc. to mean it isn't ²important / necessary what / where / how because the result is always the same.

The word order is -ever word + (adjective) subject + verb.

2 **Rewrite these sentences. Start each one with an -ever word.**

0 It doesn't matter when you arrive – we'll be here.
   Whenever you arrive, we'll be here.

1 It doesn't matter what you say – he won't like it.
2 It doesn't matter when we leave – the roads are always full of traffic.
3 It isn't important which way you say it – it means the same thing.
4 It doesn't matter how strong your accent is – everyone will understand you.

3 **SPEAKING** Complete the sentences, and then compare with a partner.

1 Whatever I decide to do after I leave school, …
2 Whenever I have free time, …
3 Wherever I go to university / on holiday … , …
4 However expensive it … , …

Workbook page 73

77

READING
Multilingual people

1 **SPEAKING** Do you know anyone who is multilingual? Tell your partner about them.

2 Look at the title of the article. What do you think it is going to say about multilingual people? Read it quickly to check your ideas.

3 Put these sentences / phrases into the correct place in the article, A–E. There is one that you won't use.

 1 And their own personas changed, too.
 2 In 1968, Ervin designed another experiment to further explore her hypothesis that the content of bilinguals' speech would change along with the language.
 3 Nearly two-thirds said they did.
 4 while the other session was conducted entirely in English.
 5 She believed that the content of bilinguals' speech would change along with the language.
 6 and asked them to make up a three-minute story to accompany each scene.

4 **SPEAKING** Work in groups. Discuss the questions.

 1 To what extent do you feel 'different' when you speak English (or another language that isn't your first language)?
 2 In what other way(s) could you test the effect that language has on someone's personality?

Multilinguals *have multiple personalities*

Between 2001 and 2003, linguists Jean-Marc Dewaele and Aneta Pavlenko asked over a thousand bilinguals whether they 'feel like a different person' when they speak different languages. **[A]**

Susan Ervin, a sociolinguist at the University of California, Berkeley, set out to explore the differences in how bilinguals represent the same stories in different languages. She recruited 64 French adults who lived in the U.S. and were fluent in both French and English. On average, they had spent 12 years living in the U.S.; 40 were married to an American. On two separate occasions, six weeks apart, Ervin […] showed her subjects a series of illustrations **[B]**. In one session, the volunteer and experimenter spoke only in French, **[C]**.

One of the illustrations Ervin used in her first experiment

Ervin then analysed the stories, [and] she identified some significant topical differences. The English stories more often featured female achievement, physical aggression, verbal aggression towards parents, and attempts to escape blame, while the French stories were more likely to include domination by elders, guilt, and verbal aggression toward peers.

[D] This time, Ervin […] looked at Japanese women living in the San Francisco area […]. Ervin […] had a bilingual interviewer give the women various verbal tasks in both Japanese and in English, and found – as she expected – important differences.

For instance, when the women were asked to complete the following sentences, their answers differed depending on the language in which the question was asked:

1 When my wishes conflict with my family …
 (*Japanese*) it is a time of great unhappiness.
 (*English*) I do what I want.

2 I will probably become …
 (*Japanese*) a housewife.
 (*English*) a teacher.

Scholars have also used more qualitative methods to try to understand language's impact on personality. In 1998, Michele Koven […] spent a year and a half carrying out ethnographic research with bilingual Parisian adults whose parents had immigrated from Portugal. All of her subjects were fluent in both French and Portuguese, and most maintained close ties to Portugal while living in France […]. Koven focused specifically on how her subjects represented themselves in narratives of personal experience, which she elicited by asking them to recount various life events in both languages. Koven […] saw that her subjects emphasised different traits in their characters, depending on which language they were speaking. For instance, the women in the French stories were more likely to stand up for themselves, whereas the female characters in the Portuguese narratives tended to cede to others' demands. **[E]** One girl, Koven writes, sounded like 'an angry, hip suburbanite' when she spoke French, and a 'frustrated, but patient, well-mannered bank customer who does not want attention drawn to the fact that she is an émigré' when she spoke Portuguese. Whether that's due to the different context in which she learned French and Portuguese, an inherent difference between the two languages, or some combination, researchers have yet to figure out.

8 IT'S ALL GREEK TO ME!

VOCABULARY
Personality (2)

1 Look back at the article on page 78 and find two words to describe personality.

2 SPEAKING Here are some people talking about language and personality. Work in pairs. Discuss the meaning of the words in bold. Use the context to help you.

1. I tend to be a bit afraid to say what I think in a foreign language. I can be a lot more **assertive** and **forceful** in my own language.
2. I feel really **self-conscious** if I speak another language, like everyone is listening and thinking I'm not very good at it, so I often don't even try.
3. I love speaking other languages – I feel much more **expressive** than in my own language and my true personality comes out.
4. I'm usually a **modest** person, but when I speak another language I feel like I get a bit **conceited** and start to behave as if I think quite highly of myself!
5. I've got a friend who's more **impulsive** when he isn't speaking his native language – he just says whatever he's thinking!
6. Maybe speaking more than one language helps you become more confident and **self-assured**?

3 Use a word from Exercises 1 or 2 in each space. There may be more than one possibility.

1. He thinks he's wonderful – he's so _____ !
2. She often acts without thinking – she's really quite _____ .
3. It's difficult for me to talk to new people – I always feel a bit _____ .
4. Don't let other people tell you what to do! You have to be a bit more _____ .
5. He's a very well-mannered and _____ child. He never boasts about his achievements.
6. It's captivating watching her tell a story. Her facial expressions are amazing. She's so _____ .

4 Which (if any) of the statements in Exercise 2 do you identify with? Think of examples and make notes. Compare ideas with a partner.

5 SPEAKING Work in pairs and discuss the questions.

1. What's your favourite word in any language other than your own? Why do you like it?
2. What other languages have you heard people speak? How would you describe how they sound? Do you think that they suggest a certain kind of personality?
3. What gestures do native speakers of your language use to help them communicate more expressively? What gestures have you noticed speakers of other languages use?
4. Do you feel different in any way when you speak English compared to when you speak your first language?
5. What do you think are the advantages and disadvantages of being able to speak more than one language?

> Workbook page 74

THiNK VALUES

Learning another language

1 Tick the statements that reflect how you feel. You can tick as many as you like.

A good reason to learn another language is to …
- be able to communicate when travelling;
- learn about another culture;
- improve my job prospects;
- be able to talk to foreigners in my country;
- be able to read books, magazines and newspapers in another language;
- develop myself personally.

2 SPEAKING Work in a group of six to eight. Find out from the other students which statements they ticked. Did anyone tick the same statements as you?

3 Make a graph or chart to show how your group feels.

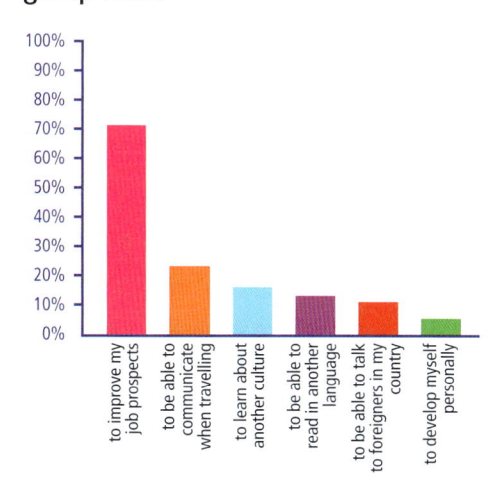

Culture

1 Why might people choose or need to become multilingual? Discuss with a partner and make notes.

2 🔊 2.11 Read and listen to the article and check your ideas.

Multilingual communities around the world

Many countries around the globe have populations who speak multiple languages. Many people can converse fluently in four or five languages, sometimes using multiple languages in the same conversation or even in the same sentence. This linguistic mixture develops for various reasons. It can be caused by a complex colonial history, by strong regional loyalties or by the unavoidable cultural influence of nearby superpowers. Here are a few of the most multilingual places on Earth.

Aruba

Aruba sits in the far Southern Caribbean Sea, near Venezuela. Because it is one of the 'constituent countries' that make up the Kingdom of the Netherlands, Dutch is an official language and is taught in all schools. Both English and Spanish are also compulsory languages in Aruba's education system, and most students reach a reasonable level of fluency by the time they finish school. However, none of these languages is considered the native language of Aruba. On the street and at home, locals communicate with one another in Papiamento, a creole language derived from a mix of Portuguese, Spanish, Dutch and English. Papiamento is an official language alongside Dutch, and it is used regularly in the media and in government.

India

Hindi and English are the official national languages of India, and the majority of educated Indians and urban dwellers have a knowledge of both, though English is preferred over Hindi in southern India. Each state in India has its own official language(s), most of which differ from Hindi. These languages are used in the local media and on the street. This means that a significant number of Indians are at least trilingual, and people who move between states may have a working knowledge of additional languages. So, although they might not be fluent in each one, many Indians are able to communicate in and understand four or more languages.

East Timor (Timor-Leste)

This tiny young nation sits in the far south-eastern corner of the Indonesian Archipelago. It officially gained independence from Indonesia a little more than a decade ago. Once a colony of Portugal, Timor decided to adopt Portuguese as an official language after independence. The local tongue, Tetum, which is heavily influenced by Portuguese, is the most widely spoken language on the street. In addition, English and Indonesian are used throughout the country, and both are officially recognised as 'working languages' in the constitution. Today, an ever-increasing number of Timorese speak both Portuguese and English fluently alongside Tetum.

The 11 languages of South Africa

South Africa has a whopping 11 official languages. In many urban areas, English is the lingua franca. It is also the main language of the government and media, even though less than ten percent of South Africans speak it as a first language. Afrikaans, a Germanic language similar to Dutch, is spoken in the southern and western regions of the country. South Africa has nine official Bantu languages, of which Zulu and Xhosa – the native language of Nelson Mandela – are the most ubiquitous. The most distinguishing trait of some of these languages is their 'clicking' consonant sounds. Many South Africans have a good command of several of the country's languages.

3 Match the statements and the countries according to the information in the text.

1 People speak local languages derived from a European language.
2 Many people here speak three or more languages.
3 The language of government is English.
4 The two official languages consist of a local one and a European one.
5 Schools are multilingual.
6 One of this country's official languages is a mix of different languages.

a Aruba
b South Africa
c India
d East Timor

8 IT'S ALL GREEK TO ME!

4 **VOCABULARY** Match the highlighted words or phrases in the article to the definitions.

1 a language used for communication between groups of people who speak different languages
2 a language that has developed from a mixture of languages
3 city or town inhabitants
4 impossible to prevent
5 quality, characteristic
6 a level of competence that is good enough to be useful
7 huge (informal)
8 based on

5 **SPEAKING** Work in pairs and discuss the questions.

1 How many other multilingual places can you think of? What languages are spoken there?
2 Which of the languages mentioned in the text would you be most interested in learning?
3 What advantages are there to living in a multilingual place?

WRITING
A report from a graph

1 Read the report and complete the empty spaces in the diagram.

Difficulties in learning another language

- No access to native speakers 15%
- Embarrassment when speaking the new language 11%
- 18%
- 24%
- 5%
- 11%
- 16%

1 A lot of people around the world are keen to gain some level of proficiency in another language. Many people start their learning motivated to succeed but then experience numerous difficulties along the way which can hamper their enthusiasm. A recent study was carried out in the USA among adult and teenage learners who were taking a foreign language course outside of their normal school to find out what difficulties they had encountered.

2 By far the most widely cited difficulty was a lack of time, which 24% of respondents reported as their main obstacle – especially (but not exclusively) the adults. 16% of those surveyed stated that an inability to maintain motivation was their main problem, while 15% claimed that it was not being able to meet and converse with native speakers.

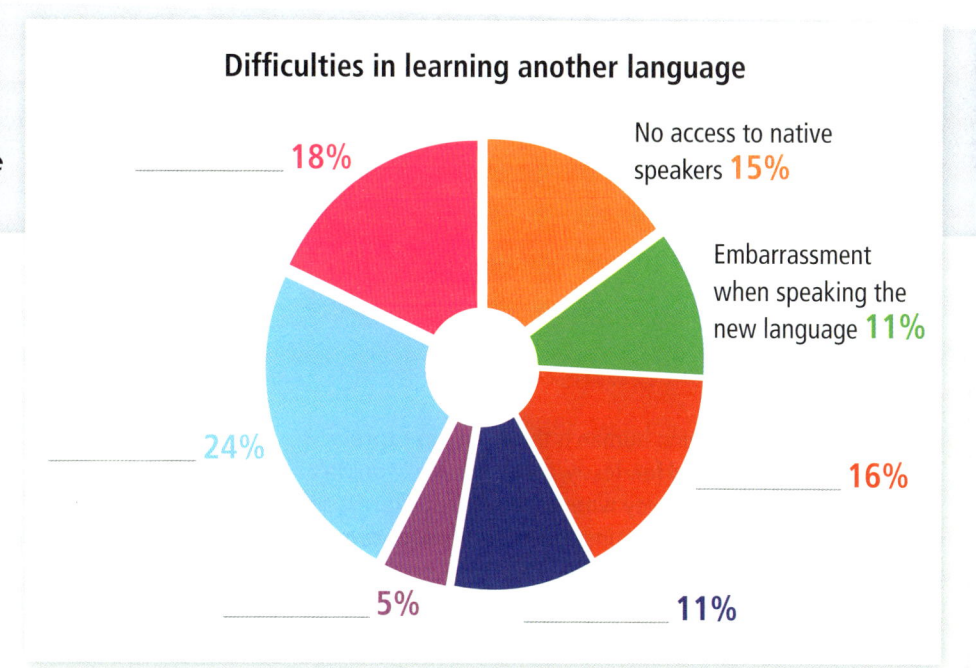

3 Other problems encountered included budgetary constraints impeding their ability to continue their course, which 11% of learners put forward as a reason for giving up. Finally, a meagre 5% of respondents, especially those who were learning less frequently studied languages, such as Bulgarian or Farsi, stated that they had either no access or limited access to good learning materials. 18% of people mentioned various other difficulties.

4 It seems, then, that difficulties are far from rare among language learners. However, of the respondents, only 17% said that the difficulties had made, or might make, them give up, since the benefits of doing a foreign language course far outweighed the drawbacks.

2 Which paragraph of the report:
a starts the presentation of the data?
b introduces the subject of the information in the graph?
c pulls the ideas together and adds a concluding comment?
d adds further data?

3 Read the report again. Find different words which the writer uses to refer to what people said.

said   _claimed_   _____   _____   _____

4 You are going to work with the data you gathered in the Values activity on page 79. Look at it again and:
- remind yourself of the topic and the information you got.
- think about how you can introduce the topic.
- decide in what order to present the main findings.
- decide how you might draw the report to a close and any final comments you might make.

5 Write a report about the graph you drew (180–220 words).

CAMBRIDGE ENGLISH: ADVANCED

THiNK EXAMS

READING AND USE OF ENGLISH
Part 6: Cross-text multiple matching

Workbook page 79

You are going to read four people's opinions on cosmetic surgery. For questions 1–4, choose from the people A–D. The people may be chosen more than once.

Person A
It's clearly the case that cosmetic surgery meets the needs of a certain sector of society in which people are so obsessed with their appearance that this obsession could be considered a form of mental illness. But now that we have available to us both the technology and the expertise to allow people to change their appearance, why should we be concerned if they do this, particularly if it helps to alleviate mental health problems? No one, as far as I'm aware, is forced into having such surgery and as long as the risks are explained to anyone considering it, then I see no need to place legal limitations on it.

Person B
A vital part of being human is the ability to express yourself freely and fearlessly, and I, for one, wouldn't want to live in a society where freedom of expression was limited or legislated against (with the obvious caveat of not using free speech to incite hatred). And is cosmetic surgery not a question of freedom of expression? In what way can its optional use be any different from the freedom to choose things like our hairstyle, the clothes we wear, and so on? If I think my nose is too big or not the shape I'd like it to be, and if I have the financial means, why shouldn't I go to a plastic surgeon and get them to change it? It brings them business and me happiness and satisfaction. Such freedom is at the root of our society's most fundamental values and needs to be protected by law.

Person C
It's all a matter of perception. Some people consider their physical appearance to be truly important, an essential part of their being. But cosmetic surgery does nothing more than alter external circumstances – it doesn't alter the original perception that 'my stomach/nose/mouth (etc.) isn't the way I'd like it to be'. Once the stomach has been operated on, then the patient will very likely turn their attention to something else – the nose, perhaps. No matter what surgery they undertake, they'll most probably find something else that isn't satisfactory soon afterwards. It's not so dissimilar to wanting that really nice car and then, once you've got it, desiring the next model up. Part of our nature is to desire, and that can become an internal illness in itself that cosmetic surgery simply masks.

Person D
It's important to remember that cosmetic surgery has developed over a long period of time in order to help people who have some abnormal physical feature, either congenital or as the result of an accident. In this sense, it's an essential part of modern medicine and needs to be respected as such. However, its existence has, perhaps inevitably, created a situation whereby people who a) have the funds and b) want to look as physically perfect as possible can do so in order to resemble the idealised images of men and women seen daily in magazines and the like. It's hard to view this later development in the application of cosmetic surgery as healthy. Indeed, some people have even been known to use cosmetic surgery in order to make their appearance as abnormal as possible. It might therefore be time for us to introduce legislation to control the abuse of what remains a medical procedure.

Which person believes that …

1. cosmetic surgery doesn't get to the root of the problem that the patient is experiencing?
2. legislation isn't required as long as prospective patients receive relevant information?
3. the way that cosmetic surgery technology and expertise is currently being applied distorts its original objectives?
4. cosmetic surgery should be restricted to dealing with problems that are present at birth or through unavoidable occurrences?

TEST YOURSELF

UNITS 7 & 8

VOCABULARY

1 **Complete the sentences with the words in the list. There are four extra words.**

communication | arms | broken | slang | must-have | short | modest
in | conceited | heart | impulsive | must-get | spine | forceful

1 He's quite _____. He's certainly not shy when it comes to putting himself forward if it means getting what he wants.
2 Loom bands were really _____ a few years ago.
3 That scene at the end of the film sent shivers down my _____.
4 I think we've got a _____ breakdown here. We're really not understanding each other.
5 He's a bit _____ and often acts without really thinking first.
6 Are you cold? You've got goosebumps all down your _____.
7 I make lots of mistakes, but I can just about get by in Brazil with my _____ Portuguese.
8 Are smart watches really going to be the next _____ item?
9 She thinks she's better than everyone else. She's so _____.
10 Nobody knows this band any more – their fame was rather _____-lived.

/10

GRAMMAR

2 **Complete the sentences with the words / phrases in the list. There are two extra words / phrases.**

most of whom | however | whatever | think so | in which case | wherever | hope so | all of which

1 _____ hard I try, I never really understand what he says.
2 I have a lot of friends on social media sites, _____ I rarely see in person.
3 Many people think this film will win an Oscar, but I don't _____.
4 _____ he goes, people recognise him.
5 Do you think it'll be sunny this weekend? I _____ because I'm planning to go to the beach.
6 She has two jobs and three children to bring up on her own, _____ means she never has any time to herself.

3 **Find and correct the mistake in each sentence.**

1 Some people say it's a dangerous sport, but I don't hope so.
2 I have three brothers, one of who lives in Argentina.
3 Whatever do you, don't say anything.
4 She has three phones, both of which are broken.
5 I'll follow you whatever you go.
6 I'm not sure we'll win, but I hope.

/12

FUNCTIONAL LANGUAGE

4 **Choose the correct options.**

A Have you always ¹*dreamed / hoped* of an easier life?
B I'm sorry? I don't quite ²*follow / catch* you.
A An easier life. If you try our ³*brand / known* new product, you'll save hours every week.
B I'm afraid you've ⁴*got / lost* me. What product are you talking about?
A Lush 2.0. It's on offer. But only for a ⁵*narrow / limited* time.
B I'm sorry, but I'm not ⁶*known / familiar* with Lush 2.0. What is it exactly?
A Lush 2.0 – our most advanced washing powder yet. I ⁷*powerfully / strongly* recommend you give it a go.
B Washing powder?! I don't quite ⁸*see / follow* why I'd be interested in washing powder. I'm only 13 years old.

/8

MY SCORE /30

22 – 30
10 – 21
0 – 9

83

9 IS IT FAIR?

OBJECTIVES

FUNCTIONS: talking imprecisely about numbers
GRAMMAR: negative inversion; spoken discourse markers
VOCABULARY: court cases; fairness and honesty

READING

1 **SPEAKING** Work in pairs. Discuss your answers with a partner.
   1 What do you think a *miscarriage of justice* is?
   2 Can you think of any famous miscarriages of justice?

2 Look at the photos, read the headline and introduction on page 85 and check your answers to Exercise 1 question 1.

3 Work in groups of three. Read your text and the questions, and note down your answers.

   Student A: read text 1
   Student B: read text 2
   Student C: read text 3

   1 What was the person / were the people convicted of?
   2 What was the evidence that was used to convict them?
   3 How were they set free, and after how long?
   4 What happened to them after their release from prison?

4 **SPEAKING** 🔊 2.12 Tell your group what you learned. Use your notes to help you. Then listen and read the texts to check.

5 **SPEAKING** Work in pairs and discuss the questions.
   1 Which of the three cases do you think describes the worst miscarriage of justice? Why?
   2 In your country, what kind of punishment is given for:
      - shoplifting?
      - dangerous driving?
      - fraud? (getting money by deceiving people)
      - murder?
   3 Which of the crimes in question 2 do you think a person should go to prison for? Why?
   4 What other crimes should a person go to prison for? Why?

Pronunciation
Unstressed syllables and words: the /l/ phoneme.
Go to page 121.

TRAIN TO THiNK

The *ad hominem* fallacy

'Ad hominem' means 'against the man'. The ad hominem fallacy describes a situation where instead of using logic or evidence to argue against an opinion, claim or point of view, you attack an opponent's character. Often the ad hominem fallacy uses stereotypes and encourages prejudice. For example, a man complains to the police about his noisy neighbours. The neighbours defend themselves saying that they're not surprised about the complaint since he's a really grumpy man and is always complaining about things. Their comments about his personality don't necessarily mean that his complaint isn't valid.

1 Look at the texts again. Which of the victims do these remarks refer to?
   1 They're Irish. They must be guilty.
   2 He's a violent man. He must have done it.
   3 I don't trust lawyers so I'm sure she's guilty.

2 Work in pairs. What examples can you come up with of people (individuals or groups) who often unfairly find themselves victims of the *ad hominem* fallacy?

9 IS IT FAIR?

Miscarriages of justice

Imagine – one day, out of the blue, you are arrested, accused of a crime that you didn't commit, found guilty and sent to prison. Even in the best legal systems, innocent people can find themselves convicted by judge and jury and sentenced to years behind bars.

1 Sally Clark (UK)

Sally Clark was a lawyer and mother of two. Her first son was born healthy in 1996 but died suddenly when he was just three months old. In 1998 she had another son, but he too died aged just two months and in the same circumstances. At this point, social services intervened and Mrs Clark was subsequently put on trial for murder.

The prosecutors based their evidence on the findings of a medical expert who claimed that the chances of two babies from the same family dying a natural death in identical circumstances were virtually nil. Despite protesting her innocence, Clark was found guilty on the basis of that evidence and sentenced to life imprisonment. She appealed the verdict and after three years in jail, she was released when it emerged that evidence proving that one of the children had died from natural causes, had been withheld from her defence lawyers. Furthermore, the statistical evidence on which the prosecution was based was shown to be invalid. One doctor commented that rarely had statistical evidence been so misused in a trial. Sally Clark never fully recovered from her ordeal and she died in 2007, aged only 43.

2 Rubin 'Hurricane' Carter (USA)

Rubin Carter was born in 1937 in New Jersey. He was convicted of several crimes before he became a professional boxer in 1961. Nicknamed 'Hurricane' because of his lightning-fast fists, he was a promising boxer with hopes of fighting for the middleweight world championship. But in 1966, Carter and his friend John Artis were arrested and prosecuted for the murder of three people in a bar. The evidence was weak – two witnesses said they'd seen Carter and Artis running away from the crime but later they changed their story. Not only did Carter and Artis have no motive, but they also had alibis. Moreover, it was never proven that their guns were the ones used in the murders. Nor were any fingerprints taken at the crime scene. Despite all of this, both Carter and Artis were convicted in 1967 and given life sentences. Throughout his incarceration, Carter campaigned for his release, always protesting his innocence. Various people campaigned on his behalf and singer Bob Dylan even wrote a song about his case. Finally, in November 1985, the case was thrown out of court and Rubin Carter was finally released after having spent 18 years behind bars. Artis had already been released four years earlier. Carter died in 2014 at the age of 76. His story was made into an Oscar-nominated film, *Hurricane*, in 1999, starring Denzel Washington.

3 The Guildford Four (UK)

In the 1970s, the Irish Republican Army (IRA) ran a bombing campaign in the UK to protest against British military presence in Northern Ireland. One bomb, in 1974 in a town called Guildford, killed several soldiers and their girlfriends. No sooner had the bombing taken place, than four young people – **Gerry Conlon**, **Patrick Armstrong**, **Carol Richardson** and **Paul Hill** – were arrested and charged. All four of them confessed under police interrogation, but they later retracted their confessions. In 1975 they were sent to prison for life. None of the four had the typical profile of a bomber and furthermore, the prosecution withheld evidence that proved that Conlon had been in London at the time of the bombing. Later, the IRA itself stated clearly that none of the four had been involved in the Guildford bombings. Nevertheless, it took until 1989 for them to be released, fifteen years after their arrest. Conlon went on to become a campaigner against miscarriages of justice both in the UK and abroad. He died in 2014. A film, *In the Name of the Father*, was made about him in 1993, starring Daniel Day-Lewis.

GRAMMAR
Negative inversion

1 **Complete the sentences from the texts on page 85.**

1 One doctor commented that _____ had statistical evidence been so misused in a trial.
2 _____ did Carter and Artis have no motive, but they also had alibis.
3 _____ had the bombing taken place, than four young people […] were arrested and charged.

2 **Here are the same ideas written in a more usual form. What differences do you notice? Think about meaning and form. Then choose the correct options in the rule.**

1 One doctor commented that statistical evidence had never been so misused in a trial.
2 Carter and Artis didn't only not have a motive, but they also had alibis.
3 The bombing took place and immediately afterwards, four young people were arrested and charged.

> **RULE:** We can bring [1]*positive / negative* and limiting adverbs and adverbial phrases, such as *rarely, little, not only … but (also), no sooner … than, never, under no circumstances, on no account*, to the [2]*beginning / end* of a sentence to make it [3]*more / less* emphatic. The rest of the sentence follows the pattern of a [4]*normal statement / question*.
>
> In present and past tense forms of non-modal verbs, we use the auxiliary *do* or *did*, and invert the auxiliary and the subject. With other verb tenses or modals, we use the auxiliary that's already there (e.g. *is / are / have / can / will*).
>
> We use this structure much more often in [5]*written / spoken* English. We can use it in speech when we want to add dramatic effect.

3 **Choose the correct options.**

1 *Never have I / Never I've* read about such disturbing cases.
2 *Not only they were / Not only were they* innocent, but they weren't even at the scene of the crime.
3 *No sooner the case had finished / had the case finished* than the judge set them free.
4 Under no circumstances *could they / they could* be the criminals.

4 **Rewrite the sentences. Use the word(s) in brackets at the start of the new sentence.**

0 The film finished and we immediately left. (No sooner … than)
No sooner had the film finished than we left.
1 We should not discuss this in front of other people. (On no account)
2 I've never read such an appalling story. (Never)
3 He was innocent and so were the others. (Not only … but)
4 Innocent people are not often released from prison following a miscarriage of justice. (Rarely)

> Workbook page 82

VOCABULARY
Court cases

1 **Match the words with the definitions.**

1 to be found guilty / innocent ☐
2 to appeal a verdict ☐
3 a witness ☐
4 to make a confession ☐
5 to retract a confession ☐
6 the defence ☐
7 the prosecution ☐
8 to give evidence ☐
9 to withhold evidence ☐
10 to be sentenced to life imprisonment ☐

a to say that you committed a crime
b to not give information that is important in a trial
c the lawyers who try to prove that someone is guilty
d to have a court say that you did/didn't commit a crime
e to be told that you will spend the rest of your life in prison
f to give information in a court
g someone who says in court what they know or saw
h to ask to go to a higher court for another trial
i to say that the confession you made before wasn't true
j the lawyer(s) who try to prove that someone is innocent

2 **Complete the text using words and phrases from Exercise 1 in the correct form.**

The woman was arrested for murder and she made [1]_____ but three days later, she [2]_____ it. However, the case went to court.
During the trial, about twenty people [3]_____ evidence. A witness for [4]_____ said he had seen the woman at the scene of the crime. But the lawyer for [5]_____ claimed that that wasn't possible. In the end she was [6]_____ and she was [7]_____ to life imprisonment.
The defence [8]_____ the verdict and, in the subsequent retrial, it was shown that the prosecution had withheld [9]_____. The woman was [10]_____ and released.

> Workbook page 84

86

9 IS IT FAIR?

LISTENING

1 **SPEAKING** Look at the photos. Talk about the similarities and differences, and about how a prisoner might feel living in each type of prison.

2 ⏵ 2.14 Listen to the first part of a radio programme. Complete the information about the prison.

3 ⏵ 2.15 Listen to the second part of the programme. Answer the questions.

1 What does Anne, the first caller, think is the most interesting fact, and why?
2 What freedom does she say the prisoners do not have?
3 What does she say about treating prisoners with respect?
4 What does Mark, the second caller, compare the prison to?
5 What does he accept we don't want prisons to be like?
6 How does he feel about the cost of keeping prisoners in Halden?

4 Who do you think might say these things later – Anne, Mark or both? Why? Compare your ideas with a partner.

1 'It's good that prisoners and prison staff are on friendly terms with each other.'
2 'Perhaps we should be more concerned about the victims of crime.'
3 'We need to make sure we're not overspending on criminals.'
4 'If you put bars on windows, then prisoners never forget where they are and that's key.'

THiNK SELF-ESTEEM

Does the punishment fit the crime?

1 What do you think are appropriate punishments for these school 'crimes'? Make notes.

1 talking in class
2 arriving late for lessons
3 not handing in homework on time
4 dropping litter on the floor
5 daydreaming while the teacher is talking
6 showing disrespect to the teacher

2 **SPEAKING** Work in pairs or small groups.

1 Compare your answers to Exercise 1 above.
2 Discuss which of the 'crimes' you think deserves the harshest punishment, and which the least.
3 Of all the ideas you came up with in Exercise 1, which one do you think is the most appropriate? Why?

Halden Prison, Norway

It has been in operation since [1]_____.
Its construction required an investment of about [2]£_____.
It has capacity for approximately [3]_____ inmates.
It is surrounded by a [4]_____ measuring about six metres high.
Each cell is [5]_____ long and ten metres wide and has a [6]_____, a toilet, a shower, a mini-fridge, and unbarred windows.
There is a library with books and DVDs. There is also an area where you can go [7]_____ if you want to be more active.
Prisoners can receive visitors [8]_____ a week for up to two hours. In some cases [9]_____ are permitted to visit prisoners for a whole day.
Interaction between staff and prisoners is designed to create a '[10]_____'.
The cost of housing one prisoner per year is [11]$_____.
In Norway, approximately [12]_____ of prisoners reoffend, while in the UK it can be as high as three times this figure.

WRITING
An essay

1 Note down three arguments in favour of the statement below, and three arguments against it. (You can use your own ideas or any from the unit.)

Prisons should be decent, comfortable places for prisoners.

For	Against
1 _____	1 _____
2 _____	2 _____
3 _____	3 _____

2 Compare your ideas with a partner.

3 Use your notes to write an essay of around 150–200 words.

READING

1 Which of these statements do you agree with?

It's fair that money can buy …
1. a ticket in the front row of a concert.
2. a place in a private school.
3. treatment from the best doctors.

2 Read the book review quickly. Which of these is the best summary of the review? The book …
1. … is about the need to ask ourselves what money should be able to buy.
2. … says that it's wrong for us to have anything we want if we have enough money.
3. … is an important follow-up to a previous book.

3 Read again and answer the questions.
1. What areas of life have market values moved into?
2. What examples does the writer give of things 'up for sale' that we should question?
3. What's the title of Sandel's other book?
4. What are the questions Sandel asks in the book?

4 Now read the comments of four different readers. Which reader gives a different opinion to the other three?

BOOK REVIEW

What Money Can't Buy
by Michael J. Sandel (2012)

We live in a society dominated by the idea of markets. Almost every aspect of modern life revolves around market values; ultimately, money and the idea of buying and selling. Think of, for example, sport, art and education. There seems to be no boundary – everything is up for sale. But should it be? Is it right to pay children to read books or reward them with money for doing well in exams? Is it OK if rich people can pay for a kidney transplant that isn't available to those on a more modest income? And, indeed, is it right that someone gets paid to give one of their kidneys, simply because they need money to live?

This is the central theme of Michael J. Sandel's book *What Money Can't Buy*. In his previous book, *Justice*, Sandel wrote about some of the hard choices that people confront as they go about their normal lives. Here he discusses the choices that a society makes, or should (or should not) make, when it comes to deciding what money can buy. Should we be able to pay in order to not stand in a queue? (Think of no frills airlines!) If someone wants to become a citizen of another country, should they be able to buy citizenship? Sandel's book asks important questions about the nature of our society, about what the role of markets should be, and about how we can defend ourselves against the influence of ideas that are driven solely by money.

Comments

This is an excellent book – I thoroughly recommend it. By the way, did you know that you can pay for permission to shoot a leopard? And one billionaire paid about £25,000 to shoot three. Is that a justifiable thing to do?
Edwin Groves

There are corrupt people everywhere, it seems. Sandel gives lots of really good examples to make us think about what should or should not be for sale. Everyone's views will differ, of course, though personally I find it hard to imagine that anyone really believes it's acceptable to buy an organ from a healthy person.
Annette Gibson

Oscar Wilde once said that there are many people 'who know the price of everything, but the value of nothing'. This book takes that thought a lot further. Go and read it!
Maureen Pollack

We all know that at the end of the day, areas of life like sport are completely dominated by money. The rich football clubs win the championships, and consequently, the game is less interesting than in the past. And to be honest, even if it's unethical, I don't think it's going to change despite books like this. It's a different world from the one I was born into – that said, a lot of people like it, and they're powerful, so there you go. Learn to live with it.
David O'Connor

SPEAKING

Work in small groups. Discuss your responses to the statements. Are there any that you all agree or disagree with?

1. *Why shouldn't I be able to pay to kill a lion or a rhino if I can afford it? I'm sure lions do as much damage to the local area as things like rats and foxes do here.*
2. *People can live perfectly well with only one kidney. What's wrong with people selling one of theirs to give someone else the gift of life (and to make a little extra money of course)?*
3. *The thing is, there will always be some people who have more money than others. And if they want to use it to avoid queues and save time, that's perfectly reasonable.*
4. *Who cares about football? Let's face it, it's a stupid game played by over-paid badly behaved boys and only the richest can ever win. If you want to predict the winner, just look at the club's bank balance.*

9 IS IT FAIR?

VOCABULARY
Fairness and honesty

1 **SPEAKING** Work in pairs. Read the sentences below. Discuss and check the meaning of the words and phrases in bold.

1 Is this really **an acceptable thing to do** or should governments encourage people to stop?
2 Is spending so much on a prison **justifiable** or is it a waste of money?
3 Is it **reasonable** that people can buy a place in a queue or should we all have to wait in line?
4 Using animals to test drugs is **unethical** – it's a form of cruelty.
5 The problem here is that some politicians are **corrupt**. They have no concern for honesty.
6 Referees need to be **unbiased** if they're to make decisions that are fair to both teams.
7 A lot of people here are **prejudiced** against immigrants. They hold really ridiculous views about them that simply aren't true.

2 **SPEAKING** Work in pairs or small groups. Think of examples of:

1 a group of people who are subjected to a lot of prejudiced behaviour
2 an action that some people think is not justifiable
3 a person or an organisation that is/was corrupt
4 a situation where someone in a position of authority has acted in a biased way
5 unethical behaviour by a famous person

3 Complete the noun related to the adjectives in Exercise 1.

0 prejud _i c e_   4 eth _ _ _ _
1 corrupt _ _ _ _   5 bi _ _ _
2 acc _ _ _ _ _ _ _ _ _   6 reas _ _ _
3 justifi _ _ _ _ _ _ _ / justi _ _ _

4 * Write the correct form of the word in brackets in each space.

1 The biggest problem in our country is _____ among politicians. (CORRUPT)
2 I don't think there's any _____ for what they did in that situation. (JUSTIFY)
3 Well I love Britain, so my opinion about the country is a bit _____. (BIAS)
4 She won the award and she gave a wonderful _____ speech. (ACCEPT)
5 I have no problem with your view. It's a very _____ opinion. (REASON)
6 How could they do such a terrible thing? It's completely _____. (ETHICS)

▶ Workbook page 84

GRAMMAR
Spoken discourse markers

1 Complete the sentences from the comments on page 88 and then complete the rule with the correct sentence number.

1 _____, did you know that you can pay for permission to shoot a leopard?
2 The rich football clubs win the championships, and _____, the game is less interesting.
3 It's a different world from the one I was born into – _____, a lot of people seem to like it.
4 And _____, even if it's unethical, I don't think it's going to change.

> **RULE:** We use discourse markers to:
> • talk about a result. Example sentence [a]_____
> • show the writer's opinion. Example sentence [b]_____
> • introduce a change of topic. Example sentence [c]_____
> • introduce a contrast. Example sentence [d]_____

2 Write the discourse markers in the correct column in the table below. Some may go in more than one column.

actually | anyway | as a result of | because of | while | by the way | mind you | however | that said | I mean | nevertheless | on the other hand | to tell you the truth | to be honest | for a start | let's face it | the thing is | at the end of the day | personally | if you ask me

Cause and result	Contrast	Opinion	Topic change	Concession
because of	nevertheless	personally	anyway	while

3 Rewrite each sentence. Remove the word in bold and use a discourse marker from Exercise 3 to replace it. (There are often several possibilities.)

0 I knew it was wrong. **So** I didn't do it.
I knew it was wrong. Consequently, I didn't do it.
1 They all knew it was unethical. **But** they went ahead and did it.
2 I left in the middle of the film. **I thought** it was awful.
3 My brother thinks it's good. **Well**, he always thinks these things are good.
4 The company director resigned. **There were** accusations of corruption.
5 I'll listen to your thoughts. But **finally** it's my decision.
6 He doesn't usually have good arguments. **But** he occasionally has an excellent suggestion.
7 It wasn't at all good. **I think** it was the worst idea ever.

▶ Workbook page 83

89

PHOTOSTORY: episode 3

Saving Ms Hampton

1 Look at the photos and the newspaper headline. How do you think Jack and Matt feel about the news?

2 🔊 2.16 Now read and listen to the photostory. Check your ideas.

JACK Hang on. This can't be right. Matt, have you heard about this?
MATT What's that?
JACK In the newspaper. There's a report here that says there are going to be redundancies at the college. It says here that roughly ten members of the college staff are in line for compulsory redundancy.
MATT Yeah, I actually had heard about it. People were talking about it in biology class yesterday. And it was on the local news last night, if I'm not mistaken.
JACK Well, it's news to me. Why didn't you say anything?
MATT Sorry – I didn't realise you cared so much. Oh, and apparently, Ms Hampton's on the list of possible redundancies.
JACK Ms Hampton? No way! That's totally unfair. She's one of the best teachers here.
MATT Well, you're right about that.
JACK And she's relatively young, as well. 30'ish anyway. Why don't they get rid of some of the older people, the ones who are close to retirement?
MATT Good question. It really does seem unfair when you put it like that. And there aren't that many jobs around these days. I wonder what Ms Hampton's going to do.
JACK More to the point, what are we going to do?
MATT How do you mean, 'what are we going to do?'
JACK About this! It's not fair, and we need to do something about it – help Ms Hampton keep her job.
MATT And just what do you suggest we do? It's the college directors who decide this kind of thing.
JACK Yes, but students have a voice, too, haven't they? I'd have thought our opinions would be worth something.
MATT Yeah, well, they never ask us anything. Why start now?
JACK Well, let's get a petition going or something. I'm sure we're not the only ones who think she should stay. Maybe if we get around a couple of hundred signatures, we can get them to take some notice, maybe even change their minds.
MATT I guess. But first we've got a class to go to.
JACK What? Oh, yeah, you're right. But this afternoon I'm going to see if I can get some support from this lot here at the college.

9 IS IT FAIR?

DEVELOPING SPEAKING

3 Work in pairs. Discuss what you think Jack and Matt are going to do. Write down your ideas.

We think that they decide to organise a demonstration.

4 **EP3** Watch the video to find out how the story continues. Did you guess correctly?

5 Answer the questions.
1 How many signatures have they managed to get between them?
2 What do they think about the idea of a protest?
3 How does Ms Hampton feel about the petition?
4 Is she happy about being made redundant? Why (not)?
5 What is Rachel so excited about? How do Jack and Matt feel about what's happening?

PHRASES FOR FLUENCY

1 Find these expressions in the story. Who says them? How do you say them in your language?
1 …, if I'm not mistaken.
2 It's news to me.
3 Apparently, …
4 … when you put it like that.
5 More to the point, …
6 I'd have thought …

2 Use the expressions in Exercise 1 to complete the dialogues.
1 A This music's horrendous!
   B I'm surprised. _____ you'd like it.
2 A John hasn't turned up yet. Where is he?
   B He's not coming. _____ he's very busy or something.
3 A What time does the match start, Sir?
   B Eight thirty, _____. Or maybe nine?
4 A We've run out of milk, I think.
   B Yes, you're right. But _____ – who left the empty bottle in the fridge?
5 A Paul Graham's taking on the role of Student Representative. Did you know?
   B No. _____.
6 A Let's not go out. It's miserable outside.
   B Well, _____, perhaps a walk really isn't a good idea.

WordWise
Expressions with *on*

1 Look at these sentences from the unit so far. Complete them with the phrases from the list.

on his behalf | on the basis | on trial
on friendly terms | on the way

1 She was put _____ for murder.
2 We're well _____ [to 200], sixty-plus already.
3 The prisoners and prison staff are _____ with each other.
4 Various people campaigned _____ and singer Bob Dylan even wrote a song about his case.
5 She was found guilty _____ of that evidence.

2 Choose the correct options.
1 It must be awful to be put *on the way* / *on trial* for something you didn't do.
2 I'm saving up and I'm well *on the way* / *on the basis* to having enough money for a new tablet.
3 He's not my best friend but I'm on quite good *terms* / *behalf* with him.
4 She couldn't be at the ceremony, so her husband accepted the award on her *behalf* / *basis*.
5 You'll be given marks on *the basis* / *behalf* of the progress you make.

→ Workbook page 85

FUNCTIONS
Talking imprecisely about numbers

1 Complete the sentences from the photostory.
1 _____ ten members of the college staff …
2 And she's … young … 30 _____ anyway.
3 If we can get _____ a couple of hundred signatures …

2 What are the imprecise expressions in these sentences? Do the numbers come before or after each expression?
1 It cost around a hundred and twenty dollars.
2 It took something like three years to build.
3 Fifty people turned up, give or take.
4 I think she's in her mid-60s.
5 In the region of ten thousand people live here.

3 Answer the questions using an imprecise expression.
1 How many people live in your country?
2 How many students are there at your school?
3 How much does a bottle of water cost where you live?
4 How far is it from your house to the town centre?
5 How long does it take you to get to school every day?

91

10 YOU LIVE AND LEARN

OBJECTIVES

FUNCTIONS: reacting to news
GRAMMAR: reported verb patterns (review); passive report structures
VOCABULARY: higher education; life after school

READING

1 **SPEAKING** Work in pairs and look at the photos. What might the people be learning from doing these activities? How might they be feeling? In which of the situations would you most enjoy learning? Why?

2 Think of a memorable teacher you had in primary school. What made him/her memorable? Write down your ideas. Then compare them with a partner.

3 Read the extract from a TV guide below and answer the questions.

   1 What kind of programme is *Face the Questions*?
   2 Is it the kind of programme you'd watch? Why (not)?
   3 What topics might be discussed on a similar programme in your country this week?

4 ◆) 2.17 Read and listen to the review of *Face the Questions* and the comments which follow. What issue was being debated and what question was being answered by the people who commented?

5 Read the comments again. Which of the people who commented on the review do you think might say the following things?

   1 'Future economic growth will be driven by new innovations in computing.'
   2 'The best book I ever read was *Spend or Save?*. I learned so much from it.'
   3 'The most important things children learn at school don't involve academic subjects but rather how to get along with others.'
   4 'More than a third of children in the UK are overweight. We must do all we can to prevent this horrifying statistic growing even further.'
   5 'I hope that none of my children will ever get into debt.'
   6 'We must remember that our planet belongs to all of us.'
   7 'I wish I'd learned computing skills at school. I'm clueless when it comes to doing things online.'
   8 'Remember the saying, "A healthy body, a healthy mind".'

6 **SPEAKING** Work in pairs and discuss the questions.

   1 Should less academic subjects such as food technology, textiles and dance be taught in schools? Why (not)?
   2 List the subjects you study at school. Then put them in order from most to least important. Compare your list with your partner, giving reasons for your choices. Then agree together on a final ranking.
   3 Imagine one of your subjects was going to be cut from the timetable. Agree on which subject that should be.

21.40 – 22.40
Face the Questions
Topical debate as politicians face questions from our studio audience.

10 YOU LIVE AND LEARN

whatwewatched.com – your guide to last night's television

Face the Questions was all a bit boring last night, until a member of the audience asked the panel if the government was right to abolish free music lessons in schools. That got a good debate going. Of course, Kathryn Davies, the education secretary, insisted that they were doing the right thing and accused the opposition of trying to gain votes by making claims that were untrue. And naturally, the spokesman for the opposition, shadow secretary for education, Ian Baker, accused her of always using the same excuse – the sort of thing you hear every week. But then a teacher in the audience suggested that each member of the panel choose one subject, apart from Maths and English, that they felt should never be cut from the school curriculum. Typically, none of the politicians wanted to commit to answering the question.

Ms Davies promised to do everything in her power to protect all subjects. At that moment, a man in a striking red shirt gently reminded her of government proposals to cut music lessons from the curriculum, prompting a mumbled response from Ms Davies. Mr Baker of the opposition boasted that he'd had a wonderful state education and had been given the chance to learn about anything and everything. He recommended going back to a policy of funding all subjects so that future generations would get the same opportunities that he'd enjoyed when he was young.

Well, if the politicians won't give us a straight answer on which subject they'd never cut, it's over to you. Which school subject do you think is the most important and why?

What children most need to learn in school is how to treat other people with kindness and respect. This is something that should be a part of all lessons, but if there's one subject which teaches this more than any other, it's Literature. By reading the great classics, children learn about human relationships and how to empathise with others. There's no greater lesson in life. **Jojo71**

Information Technology (IT) is the single most important subject in schools today. Technology is advancing at such an incredible pace and we need to make sure future generations are able to keep up with it. Whoever controls technology controls the future – we can't afford to be left behind. **AnnieMac**

Economics is a subject that isn't usually taught until later on in one's life, if at all. As money plays such a huge role in all of our lives, I find this rather astonishing. No wonder the country is in such an economic mess. I feel that all children from the age of eight should be taught about money and how to manage their personal finances. **Ballboy12**

I'm not sure there are many people who'd agree with me, but no subject is more fundamental to our understanding of humanity than Geography. Geography opens our eyes to the world out there. Through Geography, children learn that there are different people and cultures in the world and that the life they know isn't the only one. A greater insight into others – that's what Geography teaches. **Ollie55**

I think Physical Education is vital. I also think it's essential that children have the opportunity to play team sports at school. They teach us to work as a team and also that, just as in life, sometimes you win and sometimes you lose. But more than that, we need to increase the amount of exercise our children do in schools if we're to begin to tackle the growing problem of obesity. **Ajay22**

■ TRAIN TO THiNK

Doing something for the 'right' reasons

Before taking a particular course of action, we should make sure that any decision we make is based on valid and logical reasons. We must be careful not to be influenced by reasoning that isn't relevant. For example, Mandy says she wants to study Physics next year because the teacher doesn't give much homework. James wants to study Physics next year because he's interested in studying Medicine at university. Whose reasoning is the most valid?

1 Work in pairs. Read the reasons people give for wanting to go to university. Who has a valid reason? Whose reasoning is flawed? Why?

I want to go to university after leaving school because …
I can't think what else to do. *Kevin*
All my brothers and sisters went. *Susan*
I want to be in the university football team. *James*
I want to be a lawyer. *Diana*

2 Work in pairs. Complete this sentence with two valid and two invalid reasons.

I want to get married before I'm 25 because …

93

GRAMMAR
Reported verb patterns (review)

1 **Read the sentences from the review on page 93 and complete them with the correct form of the verbs in brackets. Then complete the rule with the reporting verbs (in bold in sentences 1–3).**

1 The education secretary **insisted** that they _____ the right thing. (do)
2 [She] **accused** the opposition _____ to gain votes by making claims that were untrue. (try)
3 Ms Davies **promised** _____ everything in her power to protect all subjects. (do)

> **RULE:** Instead of using *say* and *tell*, we can use other verbs to report what someone said more accurately.
>
> | Pattern | Reporting verbs |
> |---|---|
> | + (person) + preposition + gerund | blame / apologise / confess / congratulate / ¹_____
 He **blamed me for** not **helping** him. |
> | + *to* + infinitive / *that* clause | decide / ²_____
 They **decided to build** a gym. |
> | + gerund or *that* clause | recommend / admit (to) / regret / suggest / deny / ³_____
 He **recommended going back** to a policy of funding all subjects. |
> | + (person) + (not) *to* + infinitive | invite / warn
 They **warned us not to take** that route. |

2 **Rewrite the sentences, using the reporting verbs in the list.**

~~apologise~~ | confess | congratulate | deny | suggest

0 'We're sorry that we didn't invite Nick to the party.'
They *apologised for not inviting Nick to the party* .
1 'We broke into the office and stole the computer.'
The men _____ .
2 'I didn't have any idea that the prime minister was planning to reduce the number of English lessons.'
The education minister _____ .
3 'Well done, Andy! You've done a fantastic job!'
The headmaster _____ .
4 'Let's all think carefully before we take any action.'
The project leader _____ .

3 **ROLE PLAY** Work in groups of four (A, B, C, D). Students A & C: Go to page 127. Students B & D: Go to page 128. You have five minutes to reach a decision on what the government should invest in. Then, work in pairs and summarise the discussion using reporting verbs.

> Marcus suggested that ...   Matt convinced Marcus that ...

→ Workbook page 90

VOCABULARY
Higher education

1 **SPEAKING** Match the sentence halves. Then discuss the meaning of the expressions and words in italics with a partner.

1 Anthony *sailed through his* end-of-school
2 He *took a gap year* in Spain before *starting his bachelor's degree*
3 He *did his master's degree*
4 He *wrote his dissertation* on modern
5 After graduating, he *got*
6 He returned to his home country

a *full-time* over the course of a year.
b *a scholarship* to do a postgrad course in New York.
c city architecture.
d *exams* when he was 18.
e as a *fully qualified* architect.
f in Architecture at Cambridge University.

2 **Complete the sentences using the words and phrases in italics in Exercise 1.**

1 She's a _____ doctor now. She starts work at the local surgery next month.
2 He graduates today. He _____ and got a first.
3 She _____ on coastal erosion. It's a tough read!
4 He didn't go straight to university after school. He _____ volunteering in Kenya.
5 She _____ in English Literature this year.
6 After graduating, I _____ to do a postgrad course at Warwick University.
7 He doesn't want to do his M.A. part-time. He wants to do it _____ and finish within a year.
8 After her B.A., she went on to _____ in Medieval History at York University.

→ Workbook page 92

SPEAKING

1 **Choose four of the phrases in italics in Vocabulary Exercise 1 and use them to write three true sentences and one false one about you.**

2 **In small groups, take turns to read out your sentences. Ask follow-up questions to try to work out which sentence isn't true.**

10 YOU LIVE AND LEARN

THiNK SELF-ESTEEM

The relative importance of higher education

1 **SPEAKING** Work in pairs. Choose one of the statements below and try to convince your partner of your opinion. Student A: you agree with the statement. Student B: you disagree with the statement.
   - Being an honest person is more important than being highly-educated.
   - If more people had access to higher education, fewer people would believe everything they heard and read on the news.

2 **SPEAKING** Now discuss your real opinion on the statement with your partner.

LISTENING AND VOCABULARY
Life after school

1 **SPEAKING** Work in pairs and discuss which of these things are typical choices for school-leavers.
   - do voluntary work
   - do military service
   - get a full-time job
   - go to university
   - take a gap year
   - do an apprenticeship

2 🔊 2.18 Listen to Karima, Jessica and Colin talking about life after school and complete the table.

	Karima	Jessica	Colin
1 Did they take a gap year? If yes, how did they spend it?			
2 How did they finance it?			
3 How do they feel now about the decision they made?			

3 🔊 2.18 Listen again. Which of the three people would you most like to talk to? Why?

   It would be interesting to hear about Karima's travels.

   I disagree. She sounds very spoilt. I'd rather talk to Colin. He seems the most normal.

4 🔊 2.19 Listen to a university lecturer giving her opinion. Answer the questions. Use your answers from Exercise 1 to help you.
   1 Which two things does she say her answer depends on?
   2 What would she think about what Karima did?
   3 Do you think she'd approve of Jessica's decision?
   4 What does she say about current trends in gap years?

5 **SPEAKING** Work in pairs and discuss the questions.
   1 Are gap years common in your country at the moment? Have they ever been common?
   2 Which of the lecturer's views do you agree with? Which do you disagree with? Why?
   3 Would you consider taking a gap year? Why (not)?
   4 How would you spend it? How would you finance it?

6 Choose the correct option to complete the sentences.
   1 I'm glad I *took / went* a gap year before starting my degree course.
   2 I've graduated and I now *have / do* a large loan to pay off.
   3 I was very lucky that I *went / got* a scholarship to *do / have* my master's degree.
   4 I'm *going to / doing* university next year, but I'd like to *take / have* a year out first.
   5 I'm *having / doing* a course in French at the moment and I'm really enjoying it.
   6 Lots of young working people live with their parents. This means they *have / afford* a reasonably high disposable income.
   7 I *went / got* a part-time job to help finance my university degree.
   8 I need to *do / have* the right qualifications for the job.

7 Match the verbs in Column A with the words and phrases in Column B.

A	B
1 earn	a gap year
2 get into	straight to university
3 afford	money
4 go	a loan
5 sit	tuition fees
6 pay off	debt
7 pay	an exam

Workbook page 92

Pronunciation
Lexical and non-lexical fillers
Go to page 121.

95

READING

1 **SPEAKING** Work in pairs.

Student A: read the introduction and text 1, and answer the question: What is the Mozart Effect?
Student B: read the introduction and text 2, and answer the question: What statistically significant results have scientists at the University of Leicester discovered?

Tell each other about the article you have read, summarising the key points and including the answer to the question.

~~Music~~ Moosic, and what you probably ~~don't know~~ about it!

We all know that teens love listening to music around the clock – to help them relax, fall asleep more easily, focus better on their schoolwork, or when hanging out with friends. So if a scientist claimed that there was evidence to prove that music does all these wonderful things, you wouldn't question it, right? Because you already know what great effects music can have on you. But recently, psychologists have found out a few new things about music that you might find interesting – the effect it has on babies, for example, and … well, yes, … cows!

[1] None smarter than their peers

In 1993, students at the University of California listened to ten minutes of a Mozart sonata and were then asked to do a puzzle. The scientists conducting the experiment noticed that the students' brains became more active for around ten minutes after listening to Mozart. From their results, they came up with a theory known as the Mozart Effect. According to the Mozart Effect, when young children listen to classical music, they become more intelligent. The idea immediately became popular in the US. For a while, all new mothers in the state of Georgia were given a CD of classical music to play to their babies. The CD, entitled *Build Your Baby's Brain Through the Power of Music*, was thought to significantly boost babies' cognitive capabilities. However, children in Georgia who were listening to these CDs in the early stages of their lives are not known to have become smarter than kids of the same age in other parts of the US, and so it's no surprise the project has long since ceased to exist.

Experts say that there's really no scientific evidence to support the claims. They also say that parents are just too quick to believe in anything that might help their children. However, there is some evidence to show that music can definitely play a very important part in a young child's life. Research has indicated that learning a musical instrument, especially before the age of seven, can help a child's development considerably.

[2] Psychologists' trials find music tempo affects productivity

Dairy cows produce more milk when listening to REM's 'Everybody Hurts' or Beethoven's 'Pastoral Symphony' than when subjected to Wonderstuff's 'Size of a Cow' or the Beatles' 'Back in the USSR', a new study by music research specialists at the University of Leicester has found. Each cow's milk yield was found to rise by 0.73 litres per day when the cattle were exposed to slow rather than fast music.

Psychologists Adrian North and Liam MacKenzie from the Music Research Group at the University of Leicester exposed cattle to fast music, slow music and no music at all over a nine-week period. The trials involved playing music to the cows for 12 hours a day, from 5 am to 5 pm. Dr North claimed: 'These results are statistically significant. They reveal that milk yields could be increased by 3% simply by playing certain types of music to the cows. We have found that cows respond to a pleasant auditory environment by producing more milk. It seems that slow music had the effect of alleviating stress and relaxing the animals, which in turn resulted in greater milk yields.'

So it would seem that it's not just human teenagers that enjoy the relaxing influences of music.

2 Read the texts again and answer the questions.

1 Why were parents given a classical music CD in Georgia, USA?
2 Were the desired results achieved? Why, according to experts, do parents tend to easily believe claims such as the Mozart Effect?
3 What difference did the scientists note between playing fast and slow music to the cows?
4 What reasons might there be for the increase in milk production due to slow music?

FUNCTIONS
Reacting to news

1 **🔊 2.21 Listen to four dialogues of people talking about the news. Number the headlines from 1–4 in the order you hear them.**

☐ Cuts to education budget
☐ Tests for the very young
☐ Pupils get greener learning
☐ Government announces job losses in education

2 **🔊 2.21 Listen again and number the functions in the order you hear them. Then mark the expressions ✓ (= expressing agreement / satisfaction) or ✗ (= expressing disbelief / protest).**

☐ That's outrageous!
☐ I'm glad to hear it.
[1] Finally, someone's taking things seriously. ✓
☐ They've got to be joking.
☐ They can't do that.
☐ What will they think of next?
☐ That's the best news I've heard in ages.
☐ It's about time they did something about it.

3 **ROLE PLAY Work in pairs. Student A: Go to page 127. Student B: Go to page 128.**

GRAMMAR
Passive report structures

1 **Read the sentences from the articles. Then complete the rule.**

1 However, children who were listening to these CDs […] **are not known to have become** smarter.
2 Each cow's milk yield **was found to rise** by 0.73 litres.

RULE: We use passive report structures in more [1]*formal / informal* contexts to report information when the agent is [2]*not important / very important*. We use passive report structures with verbs such as *say*, *think*, *believe*, *know*, *find* and *consider*.

Compare these two pairs of sentences.

A *They say that music has a positive influence on humans, and on animals too.*
B *Music is said to have a positive influence on humans, and on animals too.*
A *They think that people exaggerated the effects of music.*
B *The effects of music are thought to have been exaggerated.*

In the passive reporting structure (B), the underlined words are the [3]*subject / object* of the sentence. The word order is:

Present: subject + *be* + [4]_____ + *to* infinitive
Past: subject + *be* + past participle + *to* + [5]_____ + past participle

2 **Rewrite the following sentences, using passive report structures.**

0 Experts think a lot more research is needed into the effects of music on humans.
A lot more research into the effects of music on humans is thought to be needed.
1 Scientists believe music has beneficial effects on a number of illnesses.
2 Experts have found that some animals react strongly to certain types of music.
3 They say lots of experiments have been done.
4 Scientists think that the experiments were an important breakthrough.

Hedging

1 **Which option in each sentence expresses uncertainty? Choose the correct words to complete the examples of hedging from the article on page 96. Then complete the rule.**

1 Classical music *is believed to have / has* a relaxing effect on most animals too.
2 *It seems that slow music had / Slow music had* the effect of alleviating stress and relaxing animals.
3 They reveal that milk yields *could be / were* increased by 3%.
4 Music, and what you *don't know / probably don't know* about it.

RULE: Hedging refers to cautious or vague language used when a writer [1]*doesn't want / wants* to state something as fact.
We use verb phrases such as: *seems that*, *is thought / believed to be*, *could be*, *might be*, *is said / thought to have been* and adverbs such as: *probably*, *perhaps* and *possibly*.

2 **Replace the underlined verb in each sentence with the hedging expressions in the list.**

is said to have been | is believed to be | seems to
are thought to have been | could help | probably

0 Listening to music <u>makes</u> you learn better.
Listening to music is believed to make you learn better.
1 Playing music in hospital waiting rooms <u>improves</u> patients' moods.
2 My uncle <u>was</u> the best pianist in the country.
3 Early claims about music boosting the brain in babies <u>were</u> exaggerated.
4 Music <u>helps</u> people become better human beings and overcome emotional difficulties.

Workbook page 91 ➔

Literature

1. Would you describe yourself or anyone you know as a daydreamer? Why? What things does a daydreamer typically do?

2. 🔊 2.22 Read and listen to the extract. What does Peter daydream about?

The Daydreamer by Ian McEwan

Peter Fortune is a ten-year-old boy in the UK. The novel follows him as he experiences a life somewhere between dreams and reality, and where he gets transformed into various different things (including the family cat and a grown man). This is an extract about his life at school.

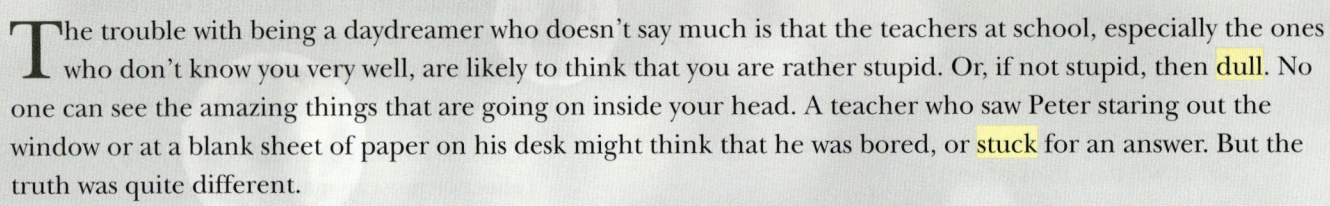

The trouble with being a daydreamer who doesn't say much is that the teachers at school, especially the ones who don't know you very well, are likely to think that you are rather stupid. Or, if not stupid, then dull. No one can see the amazing things that are going on inside your head. A teacher who saw Peter staring out the window or at a blank sheet of paper on his desk might think that he was bored, or stuck for an answer. But the truth was quite different.

For example, one morning the children in Peter's class were set a maths test. They had to add up some very large numbers, and they had twenty minutes to do it. Almost as soon as he had started on the first sum, which involved adding three million five hundred thousand, two hundred and ninety-five to another number almost as large, Peter found himself thinking about the largest number in the world. He had read the week before about a number with the wonderful name of googol. A googol was ten multiplied by ten a hundred times. Ten with a hundred noughts on the end. And there was an even better word, a real beauty – a googolplex. A googolplex was a ten multiplied by ten a googol number of times. What a number!

Peter let his mind wander off into the fantastic size of it. The noughts trailed into space like bubbles. His father had told him that astronomers had worked out that the total number of atoms in all the millions of stars they could see through their giant telescopes was ten with ninety-eight noughts on the end. All the atoms in the world did not even add up to one single googol. And a googol was the tiniest little scrap of a thing compared to a googolplex. If you asked someone for a googol of chocolate-covered toffees, there wouldn't be nearly enough atoms in the universe to make them.

Peter propped his head on his hand and sighed. At that very moment the teacher clapped her hands. Twenty minutes were up. All Peter had done was write out the first number of the first sum. Everyone else had finished. The teacher had been watching Peter staring at his page, writing nothing and sighing.

Not long after that he was put with a group of children who had great difficulty adding up even small numbers like four and six. Soon, Peter became bored and found it even more difficult to pay attention. The teachers began to think he was too bad at maths even for this special group. What were they to do with him?

Of course, Peter's parents and his sister Kate knew that Peter wasn't stupid, or lazy or bored, and there were teachers at his school who came to realise that all sorts of interesting things were happening in his mind. And Peter himself learned as he grew older that since people can't see what's going on in your head, the best thing to do, if you want them to understand you, is to tell them. So he began to write down some of the things that happened to him when he was staring out of the window or lying on his back looking up at the sky.

3. Read the extract again. What evidence is there that Peter …

    1. likes numbers?
    2. isn't stupid?
    3. has an understanding family?
    4. is amazed by some things about the universe?
    5. isn't understood by some teachers at his school?
    6. gradually understood more about relating to other people?

10 YOU LIVE AND LEARN

4 VOCABULARY Match the highlighted words in the extract with the definitions.

1 a small piece
2 looking at something for a long time
3 not able to do something because it's too difficult
4 not very interesting
5 nothing (as a number) [pl. form]
6 supported
7 to move off into another direction
8 let out a long breath of weariness or sadness

5 SPEAKING Work in pairs and discuss the questions.

1 What do you think Peter's teacher should have done at the end of the test?
2 When is daydreaming a good thing, and when is it not so good?
3 Which feelings or actions that Peter describes can you relate to?

WRITING
An essay

1 Read the essay and tick the correct option.

The writer …
- [ ] strongly agrees with the assertion.
- [ ] slightly agrees with the assertion.
- [ ] is undecided.
- [ ] slightly disagrees with the assertion.
- [ ] strongly disagrees with the assertion.

2 Find expressions in the essay which have the same meanings as the underlined ones below.

1 … <u>the most important of which is</u> …
2 <u>For example</u>, it is expensive.
3 <u>Although it's true that education is expensive</u>, it is also a fundamental right …
4 <u>With reference to the argument</u> about salaries …
5 <u>As I see it</u>, there are too many people going to university …
6 <u>Apart from</u> my personal interest …

3 Read the essay again. Give a short summary of what the writer does in paragraph …

A _____
B _____
C _____
D _____

4 Read the essay title and note down your ideas for and against the statement.

No one should go to university before they are 25.

Write your essay in 200–250 words giving both sides of the argument before presenting your position.

Further education should be provided free to all who want it

[A] When my parents went to university in the early 1990s, neither of them had to pay their tuition fees. Sadly this is no longer the case. In a few years I will probably choose to do a degree knowing that I am likely to leave with debts of around £30,000. It has made deciding to go to university a huge responsibility.

[B] My own personal interest aside, I can think of a number of reasons why further education should be free for all and none more persuasive than it means that it really is open to all, irrespective of family wealth. Obviously, the government will argue that there are schemes to help those from poorer backgrounds with funding, but clearly those from rich families will never have to take financial factors into consideration when deciding whether to go to university or not.

[C] Of course there are arguments that refute the assertion that further education should be free for all, namely that it is costly and that those who go on to graduate are likely to earn higher salaries than those who start working at 18. Each of these will be discussed in turn. While education may be expensive, it is also a fundamental right for citizens of any society. It is an important investment in our country's future and without it our ability to compete on the world stage would diminish. As for the idea that having a degree enhances your earning prospects, this is unfortunately no longer always the case. A rise in the number of people going to university means that competition for high paid jobs is fierce and many graduates are struggling to secure the employment they believed having a degree would assure them.

[D] To my mind, too many people are currently going to university, and as a result the value of further education is falling. University entrance should be made harder for all and those who are successful should not have to pay tuition fees. But of course, to make things fair, the government should also be looking at how to provide those who leave school at 18 with opportunities to get ahead in the working world.

CAMBRIDGE ENGLISH: ADVANCED

THiNK EXAMS

LISTENING
Part 4: Multiple Matching

Workbook page 97

1 🔊 2.23 You will hear five short extracts in which people are talking about an evening class that they attended.

   Task One
   For questions 1–5, choose from the list (A–H) each speaker's main reason for choosing the class.

   A to learn to be better at something they'd always enjoyed
   B to meet new people
   C a love of languages
   D to learn the basics of how to make things out of wood
   E to fulfil a long-standing desire to learn something
   F to improve an existing skill
   G the desire to travel
   H to be able to better enjoy something else

   Speaker 1 [ ] 1
   Speaker 2 [ ] 2
   Speaker 3 [ ] 3
   Speaker 4 [ ] 4
   Speaker 5 [ ] 5

   Task Two
   For questions 6–10, choose from the list (A–H) what each speaker disliked about the class they chose.

   A insufficient time to practise
   B there were too many students in the class
   C some students asked really difficult questions
   D the poor language level of the teacher
   E the teacher had a tendency to talk too much
   F the teaching method
   G the discovery that they had no ability in the subject
   H some students were not quick learners

   Speaker 1 [ ] 6
   Speaker 2 [ ] 7
   Speaker 3 [ ] 8
   Speaker 4 [ ] 9
   Speaker 5 [ ] 10

SPEAKING
Part 3: Collaborative task

2 Work in pairs or groups of three. Here are some choices that young people have to make.

   Talk together for about two minutes (three minutes for groups of three) about what people might have to think about when making these decisions. Now you have about a minute to decide **which of these is the most difficult choice to have to make**.

   1 choosing a career
   2 choosing a subject to study at college or university
   3 choosing a college or university to study at
   4 choosing a country to go to in order to improve your English
   5 choosing a language (other than English) to learn

TEST YOURSELF   UNITS 9 & 10

VOCABULARY

1 **Complete the sentences with the words in the list. There are four extra words.**

bachelor's | prejudice | jury | wrote | made | judge | fees
gap | witness | sailed | fare | justifiable | unbiased | evidence

1 He did a _____ degree at Liverpool University.
2 I wanted to go to university, but I couldn't afford the tuition _____.
3 The _____ sentenced the thief to six months in prison. We were surprised by the harshness of his sentence.
4 The _____ took two days to find him guilty.
5 A good referee has to be _____ and fair.
6 He _____ his dissertation on nineteenth-century American poetry.
7 I really wish I'd taken a _____ year before I went to university.
8 It's never _____ to keep a bird in a cage, is it?
9 No witnesses were found to give _____, so the police had to drop the case.
10 He _____ through his exams. They were no problem at all.

/10

GRAMMAR

2 **Complete the sentences with the words / phrases in the list. There are two extra words / phrases.**

meeting | never have | rarely | leave | have never | on passing | rarely does | have left

1 The criminals are thought to _____ the country.
2 _____ I heard such a terrible story.
3 She congratulated me _____ the exam.
4 He recommended _____ a few hours earlier so that we'd have plenty of time to get to the airport.
5 I _____ actually met him.
6 _____ he give an interview.

3 **Find and correct the mistake in each sentence.**

1 Consequently I really like football, my brother prefers rugby.
2 The thieves are thought to steal more than $2 million.
3 No sooner had I got home the phone rang.
4 He's considered to being the finest guitarist ever.
5 He insisted about paying for dinner.
6 Because of it raining, we stayed in all day.

/12

FUNCTIONAL LANGUAGE

4 **Choose the correct options.**

1 A It took *something / anything* like 500 men more than ten years to build it.
  B And *around / area* how much did it cost to build?
2 A We've got half an hour give or *get / take* to get to the station.
  B That's fine. I reckon it'll take us *around / least* ten minutes to walk there.
3 A Finally, someone is *taking / doing* things seriously.
  B Yes, it's the best *news / report* I've heard in ages.
4 A A flying car?! What will they think of *soon / next*?
  B Really? You've got to be *serious / joking*.

/8

MY SCORE /30

22 – 30
10 – 21
0 – 9

101

11 | 21st CENTURY LIVING

OBJECTIVES

FUNCTIONS: telling someone to keep calm
GRAMMAR: more on the passive; causative *have* (review); modal passives (review)
VOCABULARY: (not) getting angry; verbs with prefixes *up* and *down*

READING

1 In the cartoon, find:
   - a motorist
   - a pedestrian
   - a pavement
   - a cyclist
   - a cycle lane
   - a pedestrian crossing

2 **SPEAKING** Work in pairs. What do you think may have happened here? Is this a scene which you might see in your country? Discuss with your partner.

3 Read the article quickly. Who's the *pedestrian*, *cyclist* and *motorist*? Write your answers in the correct spaces next to the names in the text.

4 ◯ 2.24 Read the article again and listen. For each statement 1–6, write A, B or C in the box.

A Sami Patel B Marina Tomlinson C Stefan Markowski

Who believes that some road users …

1 have the capacity to kill people?
2 don't always stay in the areas demarcated for them?
3 act in a suicidal way?
4 should make it clear what they intend to do?
5 should keep their eyes open more?
6 act as if the rules of the road do not apply to them?

5 **SPEAKING** Work in pairs. Discuss the questions.

1 Who do you think is most to blame?
2 Whose arguments do you find the most compelling?

TRAIN TO THiNK

Do as I say, not as I do

When someone says or does something which contradicts what they say they believe, we often find this hypocritical and we can dismiss their advice all too easily as a result. It's important to consider people's advice as separate from their actions. For example, a father who tells his children not to be late for school, even though he himself is sometimes late for work, is still passing on very valid advice.

1 **SPEAKING** Work in pairs. Consider these situations. Why is the advice given still valid?

1 My brother says I should never ride on the pavement, but I've seen him do that.
2 My dad says I should always wear a helmet when I ride a bike, even though he often cycles without one.

2 **SPEAKING** Think of two situations in which you've been given hypocritical advice, but then on reflection, that advice has proven to be very valid. These could be real or imaginary. Tell your partner about them.

Road rage? Pavement rage?
Who's to blame, then?

Road rage has been around since the moment there was more than one car on the road. Pedestrians, cyclists, motorists … everyone's getting worked up and having a go at each other. A symptom of twenty-first century city living, it seems. But who's to blame for the hassle and stress? We asked three people: a cyclist, a pedestrian and a motorist. And guess what? Everyone is ready to blame someone else and so everyone gets criticised!

Sami Patel – _____

Frankly, it's pedestrians who cause the most trouble. And I know what you're going to say – pedestrians are the ones who don't use machines or cause pollution and all that. But these days, pedestrians generally don't seem to have any awareness at all, or pay any attention to what's going on around them. It's bad enough when you're a pedestrian yourself: people suddenly stopping in front of you for no reason; people looking at their phones instead of looking where they're going; groups who walk along side by side and take up the whole pavement. But when you're driving, it's even worse – you're faced with pedestrians who don't look where they're going or think they can just run across the street in front of you. Sometimes I think they actually have a death wish and want to get run over.

Marina Tomlinson – _____

It's motorists who are the worst. Put someone behind the wheel and they act like they own the road and don't have to think about anyone else. Let's face it, cars are lethal weapons, but too many motorists tend to forget that. As far as they're concerned, everyone else is of secondary importance. They beep their horn if they think you're going too slowly; they get far too close to you when they overtake; they don't even indicate when they're about to turn, so you're constantly trying to work out what they're about to do. And for me, the worst thing is when they overtake me and then almost immediately turn, so I have to brake hard. OK, we're not perfect either, but in general, people in cars think they rule the road.

Stefan Markowski – _____

I can handle car drivers – some of them are pretty bad but you can usually hear a car coming and at least they stay off the pavement. It's cyclists I can't stand. They think they don't have to obey the Highway Code – they think they're above that! They sometimes don't stop at red lights, for example, or they cycle the wrong way up a one-way street. I've lost count of the number of times I've seen them cycling on pavements – sometimes mothers with their shopping at the front and their children at the back. There are cycle lanes on the roads where I live, but lots of cyclists don't stick to them. I almost got hit by a cyclist the other day, I didn't hear her coming, and then (I promise I'm not making this up) she shouted at me for not getting out of her way! I really had to bite my tongue, I can tell you. The trouble is, cyclists think they're so environmentally friendly and virtuous that they can do whatever they want.

GRAMMAR
More on the passive

1 **Complete each sentence from the article on page 103 with one word. Then complete the rule by choosing the correct options.**

   1 Everyone is ready to blame someone else and so everyone _____ criticised!
   2 Sometimes I think they actually […] want to _____ run over.
   3 I almost _____ hit by a cyclist the other day.

   RULE:
   - We can use the verb *get* instead of *be* in passive constructions. This is more common in [1]*formal / informal* English.
   - We only use *get* with [2]*state / dynamic* verbs. We don't say *he got believed to be guilty* or *he got loved by his parents*.
   - We often use *get* when there is a clear good or bad effect or when something happens unexpectedly or accidentally, e.g. *he got mugged* or *several things got lost when we moved house*.
   - Sometimes *get* is used rather than *be* to make it clear that [3]*a state / an action* is involved, e.g. *the window was broken* could be a state or an action, but *the window got broken* has to be an action.

2 **Use the prompts to write sentences, using the correct past form of the passive with *get*.**

   0 While / we / be / on holiday / we / rob
   While we were on holiday, we got robbed.
   1 While / she / cross / the road / she / hit / by a car
   2 The man / take / hospital / by ambulance
   3 My bike / damage / when / I / hit / by a car
   4 I / shout at / for cycling / on the pavement
   5 My jeans / ruin / when / I / fall off / my bike
   6 We / not hurt / in the accident

   ➤ Workbook page 100

VOCABULARY
(not) getting angry

1 **Read the three passages. Which expressions in bold are about getting angry? Which are about *not* getting angry? Which involve someone *saying* something?**

   A Yesterday I was late for work and my boss really **had a go at** me. She **shouted at** me really loudly. I wasn't surprised – she's someone who **loses her temper** quite easily and she **gets** really **worked up** if things don't go her way.
   B My mum is great at **keeping her cool**. She always **stays calm**, even when someone else is **letting off steam**. If someone criticises her, she manages to **keep the peace** and not argue back.
   C Alex is having a bad day. I asked him to lend me something and he just **bit my head off**, saying I always borrow things and never give them back! I didn't say anything – I just **bit my tongue**.

2 **Complete each space with one word from the expressions in Exercise 1, in the correct form.**

   0 If I say something she doesn't like, she *bites* my head *off*.
   1 When he shouted at me, I _____ my _____ and smiled at him!
   2 My aunt's so calm – she never _____ her _____.
   3 He's really good at _____ _____ peace when an argument starts.
   4 It's fine – don't _____ _____ up over it!
   5 When you're angry, it's good to bite your _____ and say nothing.
   6 When I'm stressed, I run – it's how I _____ _____ steam.

3 **SPEAKING** Work in pairs. Answer the questions.

   1 Who do you know who always manages to keep the peace when tensions rise in your family?
   2 When was the last time you lost your temper and shouted at someone? What was it that made you cross?
   3 What do you think is the best way to let off steam, apart from shouting at the person who's upset you?
   4 Who was the last person to have a go at you about something? How did you react? How did you feel?

   ➤ Workbook page 102

FUNCTIONS
Telling someone to keep calm

1 🔊 2.25 **Listen to two conversations. Why is the boy angry in situation one? Why is the girl angry in situation two?**

2 🔊 2.25 **Match 1–6 with a–f to make expressions for helping someone who's stressed. Then listen again and check.**

   1 Calm   a easy.
   2 Chill   b getting worked up about.
   3 Take it   c down.
   4 Don't let it   d get under your skin.
   5 He's not worth e out.
   6 Don't let him   f get to you.

3 **ROLE PLAY** Work in pairs. Student A: Go to page 127. Student B: Go to page 128.

11 21st CENTURY LIVING

LISTENING
Stresses and strains of modern life

1 **SPEAKING** Work in pairs. What's happening in each of the pictures? How are the people feeling? Discuss with your partner.

2 🔊 2.26 Listen to the radio phone-in. Number the pictures in the order you hear about them.

3 🔊 2.26 Listen again. Mark the statements T (true) or F (false).
   1 Julian's bike was damaged.
   2 Julian was riding his bike on the pavement.
   3 Alice tries to read on the bus on her way to school.
   4 Alice thinks listening to music could be the answer to her problem.
   5 The party was for Debbie's sister.
   6 The people Debbie told about the problem before the phone-in weren't sympathetic.

SPEAKING

1 The radio host talks about '21st century problems'. i.e. things that your grandparents, for example, would not have had to face. Make a list of these.

2 Work in pairs. Compare lists and agree together on a ranking from most to least serious problems.

Pronunciation
Intonation: mean what you say
Go to page 121. 🔊

GRAMMAR
Causative *have* (review)

1 Read the three sentences from the listening. Which sentences talk about something the person wanted another person to do? Then complete the rule.
   1 I had to have my bike repaired.
   2 I've had my journey ruined so many times by people talking on their phone.
   3 One of the windows got broken, so we had to have it fixed.

> **RULE:** This structure is formed with the verb ¹_____ + object + the ²_____ of the main verb.
> We can use it:
> • when we ask or pay someone to do something for us (example sentences 1 and 3).
> • when someone (often not known) does something unpleasant to us (example sentences 2 and 3).
> We can also use *get* instead of *have*. This is more informal but doesn't change the meaning: *We got the window fixed last week.*

2 Complete each sentence using causative *have*.
   0 Last week, I *had my phone stolen* on the bus. (phone / steal)
   1 This afternoon at 3.00, I'll be in town _____. (hair / cut)
   2 They didn't like the colour of the house, so they _____. (it / repaint)
   3 Next week, I _____. (motorbike / fix) I can take the bus until then.
   4 _____ you ever _____ ? (something valuable / steal)
   5 Tomorrow I'm going to the clinic _____. (blood pressure / check)

3 Which sentences in Exercise 2 talk about unwanted events?

4 Work in pairs. Make a list of as many examples as you can of:
   • something you / someone in your family often have done (intentionally)
   • something you / someone in your family once had done to you

5 **SPEAKING** Work in groups. Compare lists and ask each other follow-up questions.

Workbook page 100

105

READING

1 Look at the photos. These are examples of things that have been 'upcycled'.
   1 What can you see in the photos? What do you think these things are made from?
   2 What do you think 'upcycling' means?

2 Read the blog quickly and check your ideas.

A modern trend: upcycling

What is upcycling?
Upcycling is the process of converting old or discarded materials into something useful and often beautiful.

So, is it the same as recycling?
No. Recycling takes consumer materials – plastic, paper, metal and glass – and breaks them down so their base materials can be remade into a new consumer product, often of inferior quality. When you upcycle an item, you aren't breaking down the material, you're simply refashioning it. For example, you might make flip-flops out of old tyres. Also, the upcycled item is typically of the same, or even better, quality than the original.

Grandma was an upcycler
Upcycling isn't a new concept. Some of the best examples of modern-day upcycling come from the 1930s to 1940s when families had very little economic or material resources. In those days, things were repurposed over and over until they were no longer useful: sacks would be turned into dresses, and an old door transformed into a new dining room table. Indeed, all sorts of interesting ideas must have been tried out. Economising is still a trend today and a major reason why some people upcycle. But an even bigger reason for the rebirth of upcycling is its positive impact on the environment. Things shouldn't just be thrown away when they can be rescued and turned into something useful. Upcycling is also a way of life for people in developing countries. Raw materials are expensive, so people use what they can to create bowls, baskets, jewellery and other useful or decorative items.

Upcycling is green
The plain and simple fact of the matter is that upcycling is much better for the planet than throwing things away. When you upcycle, that's one item less that ends up on the global waste heap. Upcycling is also considerably more environmentally friendly than recycling, which requires energy or water to break down materials. Upcycling just requires your own creativity and effort.

A great example of upcycling
Grace Robinson, from the UK, takes used tea bags and turns them into dresses, shoes and even hats. Every day she drinks some tea, then dries out the tea bags with the tea still in them. When they're dry, she takes the tea out and sews the bags together to make an item of clothing. The colour of the clothes varies depending on the kind of tea in the bag and how long the tea was brewed for. This can take a long time – maybe months for a single dress – so Grace gets friends to help her by drinking tea too and passing their tea bags on to her.

And another!
Meanwhile, over in Denmark, Annemette Magnus uses scraps of old jeans to make denim cushion covers. She gets old pairs of jeans from people she knows, washes them and then tears them into strips. Then she sews the strips together to transform them into cushion covers. Annemette likes the look of different colours of denim within the one cushion, and because denim is a tough and resistant material, she finds that her covers last for ages. She's also started working with old bicycle tyres to make pencil cases, purses and flower pots.

Get started today
There are two ways to support the upcycling movement. Sort through your wardrobe or recycling bin and create items yourself, or purchase ready-made items from upcycled materials. Both approaches benefit the environment and can reward you with something that's both attractive and practical.

3 Read the blog again. Mark the statements T (true) or F (false).
   1 People found new purposes for old things in the past.
   2 One reason to upcycle is to save money.
   3 In wealthy countries, upcycling is a central part of people's lives.
   4 Upcycling incurs fewer costs than recycling.
   5 Grace relies on others for her raw materials.
   6 Annemette's upcycling efforts only involve denim.

4 **SPEAKING** Work in pairs. Think of an everyday object and three ways in which you could upcycle it. Tell others in the class what you came up with.

We could use old CDs and DVDs to make coasters to put glasses on.

106

11 21st CENTURY LIVING

GRAMMAR
Modal passives (review)

1 Read the sentences from the blog on page 106. Complete them with the words in the list.

rescued | remade | tried
thrown | turned

1 Their base materials can be _____ into a new product.
2 Things shouldn't just be _____ away.
3 All sorts of interesting ideas must have been _____ out.
4 They can be _____ and _____ into something useful.

2 Answer the questions about the sentences in Exercise 1 and then complete the rule with *have been* and *be*.

1 Which sentence refers to a past situation?
2 Which sentences refer to the present?
3 Who performed each of the actions?

RULE: We can use modals in the passive voice by using these structures:

Present: modal verb + ¹_____ (infinitive) + past participle

Past: modal verb + ²_____ + past participle

3 Write sentences using the passive. Do not include the agent.

0 Someone must know the answer.
   The answer must be known.
1 People can find more information on our website.
2 Someone might think up new ideas.
3 People should re-use these things.
4 Someone could have hurt you.
5 Someone must have stolen your bike.
6 Someone may have put it here on purpose.

→ Workbook page 101

VOCABULARY
Verbs with prefixes *up* and *down*

1 **SPEAKING** Work in pairs. Read sentences 1–8. Who is talking to whom about what? What is the meaning of the underlined verbs?

1 We can <u>upcycle</u> this tyre and make shoes from it.
2 I've <u>downloaded</u> a new program.
3 Can you <u>upload</u> your photos, please?
4 We got <u>upgraded</u> to a better hotel room.
5 The company <u>downsized</u>, making 20 people redundant.
6 This version of the software is old, so you should <u>update</u> it.
7 The flood alert has been <u>downgraded</u> from severe to medium risk.
8 The government is trying to <u>downplay</u> the problem.

2 Complete the sentences with the correct form of the verbs from Exercise 1.

1 My dad hired a really small car, but he got _____ to a nice big saloon car.
2 I never go to the cinema – I _____ films and watch them on my tablet.
3 Let's go and have coffee so that I can _____ you on what's been going on.
4 These cushion covers were _____ from old bits of cloth.
5 The bank _____ and so my sister lost her job.
6 If you _____ those photos onto Facebook, then I can see them.
7 I never know if she's really OK. She says she's fine but she does tend to _____ things.
8 It's easier to get through the airport now that they've _____ the security alert.

3 **SPEAKING** Work in pairs. Do you agree or disagree with each of these statements? Why? Make notes and then compare your ideas with a partner.

1 These days people focus too much on having up-to-date things.
2 Upcycling is something that we should all try to do.
3 Problems can often be solved by downplaying them.

→ Workbook page 102

THiNK VALUES
Modern life

1 Read the questions and tick (✓) your answer: a or b.

1 When something I own breaks I …
   A ☐ throw it away and get another one.   B ☐ get it fixed.
2 When a new model of my phone comes out, I …
   A ☐ buy it immediately.   B ☐ wait until I need a new one.
3 I think that the Internet …
   A ☐ makes us lazy.   B ☐ is the most useful resource ever.

2 **SPEAKING** Work in pairs. Compare your answers with a partner.

3 **SPEAKING** How do you think your grandparents would answer the questions in Exercise 1? Would they answer them in the same way as you or differently?

107

Culture

1 Work in pairs. Why might people want to make contact with tribes who live in isolation and have never had any contact with the outside world? Write down as many reasons as possible.

2 Why do you think it might be better for the tribes not to have contact with the outside world?

3 ⏵2.28 Read and listen to the article. Which of your ideas are mentioned?

The world's last uncontacted tribes

Skin painted bright red, heads partially shaved, arrows drawn back in longbows and aimed squarely at the aircraft buzzing overhead – the gesture is unmistakable: stay away. Behind the two men stands another figure, possibly a woman, her stance seemingly defiant. Her skin is painted dark, nearly black.

The apparent aggression shown by these people is quite understandable. They are members of one of Earth's last uncontacted tribes, who live in the Envira region in the thick rainforest along the Brazilian-Peruvian frontier. Thought never to have had any contact with the outside world, everything about these people is, and hopefully will remain, a mystery.

Their extraordinary body paint, precisely what they eat, how they construct their tent-like camp, their language, how their society operates, is unknown.

It is extraordinary to think that, in today's modern world, there are about a hundred groups of people, scattered over the Earth, who, apart from a few brief encounters, know nothing of our world and we nothing of theirs.

The uncontacted tribes, which are located in the jungles of South America, New Guinea and the beautiful and remote North Sentinel island in the Indian Ocean, whose inhabitants have also responded to attempts at contact with extreme aggression, all share one desire – to be left alone. And for good reason. The history of contact between indigenous tribes and the outside world has consistently been an unhappy one.

Almost all of these tribes are threatened by powerful outsiders eager to get hold of their land. Some of these outsiders – loggers, miners, cattle ranchers – are even prepared to kill the tribespeople to get what they want. Even in the absence of violence, the tribes can be wiped out by diseases like the common cold to which they have no resistance.

According to Miriam Ross of Survival International, an NGO which campaigns to protect the world's remaining indigenous peoples, 'These tribes represent the incredible diversity of humankind. Unless we want to condemn yet more of the Earth's peoples to extinction, we must respect their choice. Any contact they have with outsiders must happen in their own time and on their own terms.'

When anthropologists first flew over the area, they saw women and children in the open and no one appeared to be painted. It was only when the plane returned a few hours later that they saw these individuals covered head to toe in red. 'Tribes in the Amazon paint themselves for all kinds of different reasons – one of which includes when they feel threatened or are aggressive,' Ms Ross says.

'And they are almost certain to feel threatened by or aggressive towards a plane, which was where the photos were taken from. They are almost certain not to understand what the plane is – perhaps a spirit or a large bird. The jungle is fundamental to their lives and survival. It's their home, their source of food, the source of their culture, etc. Without it, they could not exist as a people.' Ms Ross adds: 'These pictures are further evidence that uncontacted tribes really do exist. The world needs to wake up to this, and ensure that their territory is protected in accordance with international law. Otherwise, they will soon be made extinct.'

11 21st CENTURY LIVING

4 According to the article:
1. what do all of the uncontacted tribes have in common?
2. in what ways could contact with the outside world be dangerous for the tribes?
3. when the researchers flew over the tribespeople's area a second time, what change did they notice in their appearance? What might explain this change?
4. how might the tribespeople perceive a plane?
5. what needs to be done to make sure the tribes do not disappear?

5 VOCABULARY Match the highlighted words in the article to the definitions.
1. a way of standing
2. when a species no longer exists
3. spread out randomly (over a wide area)
4. people who cut down trees for wood
5. naturally existing in a place or country rather than arriving from another place
6. showing a refusal to be intimidated by someone or something
7. pointed directly
8. destroyed completely

6 SPEAKING Work in pairs. Discuss the questions.
1. What would you be most interested in finding out about these people?
2. Which of the modern world's achievements, if any, could improve these people's lives, do you think?
3. In your opinion, should we attempt to make contact with these people or leave them alone?

WRITING
A blog post

1 Sam has a blog and in her latest post, she imagines life in 1966, when her grandparents were teenagers. Read the blog post and look at the photos. Tick the things she mentions.

2 What other differences do you think Sam might notice in 1966?

3 Which of the underlined adverbs means:
1. intently, without moving?
2. in a way that requires a lot of effort?
3. without really wanting to?
4. in an unpleasantly loud way?
5. quickly and willingly?
6. in an extremely worried way?

4 None of the underlined adverbs is completely necessary in the blog. Why do you think Sam uses them?

5 You're going to write a blog post, imagining that you're in the year 2036. Make notes on the following:
1. What different technology exists?
2. What everyday things have been replaced by technology?
3. How do you feel about all of this technology? Is there any technology from your normal life that you miss?

6 Use your ideas to write a blog post (200–250 words). Use adverbs to make it as interesting and involving as possible.

Sam's blog: imagine 1966!!

Here I am. It's 1966, and I'm spending a day hanging out here just to see what things are like and how different everyday life is.

First of all, I wake up to a bell ringing shrilly – it's an alarm clock, not my smartphone. After my shower, I head off for breakfast. I'd like to find out what's been happening in the world, and hunt around a bit desperately for my tablet. No, I have to get my news from a newspaper.

I need to get in touch with my friend Alex, so I pick up the phone and dial his number – and I mean – I have to laboriously dial his number, using my index finger in those holes on the front of the telephone. Since it's the weekend, Alex suggests we go into Manchester for the day and I readily agree. He says to meet him at the corner of Argyle Street. OK, so all I have to do is buy a train ticket online – whoops, no, I'll have to do that at the station. I'd use my credit card, but I haven't got one and neither have my parents. Anyway, Dad reluctantly gives me five pounds and off I go to the station.

On the train I'm thinking: 'Argyle Street? Where's that?' I'd normally check it on the GPS on my phone, but naturally I can't, so when I get off the train I ask someone where it is. It's quite nice, actually – talking to someone rather than just staring fixedly at my screen. [more – click for page 2]

A ☐
B ☐
C ☐

12 UNSUNG HEROES

OBJECTIVES

FUNCTIONS: expressing anticipation
GRAMMAR: future perfect; future continuous (review); future in the past
VOCABULARY: awards; success and failure

READING

1 Look at the photos. Who are they? Why might they be considered heroes?

2 Work in pairs. Make a list of five people who you think are heroes from people you know locally or at school, people from history, the news, music or sport.

3 Work with another pair and compare lists. Categorise your heroes according to their achievements, e.g. *peace, courage, inspiration, fighting poverty, education*. Some may go in more than one category.

4 ◻2.29 Read and listen to the online posts. Which of your categories would each of the three people fall into?

5 Match the title to each post (A–C).

Kicking off for a better future   Learning for change   Street hopes

6 Who or what does *they* refer to in each sentence (1–6)?
1 *They*'d been forced to leave their country. [Text A]
2 Through this initiative *they* found hope for a new start. [Text A]
3 *They*'re home to some of the poorest people in the city. [Text B]
4 Through her initiative, *they*'ve been saved from a life on the streets. [Text B]
5 *They* hadn't had a chance to learn how to read and write before. [Text C]

7 **SPEAKING** Work in pairs. Discuss the questions. Which of the three heroes in the online posts do you admire most? Why? If you could do something heroic to make a difference to other people's lives, what would it be?

▮ TRAIN TO THiNK

Appropriate sampling

In order to reach a relevant and informed conclusion, it's important to conduct research. However, this research should always be done responsibly. One danger is that the research sample is not entirely representative. For example, research might claim that 90% of people believe that the government should give a lifetime achievement award to the manager of their country's national football team. If the survey was based on the views of the readers of a footballing magazine, we cannot claim that this result represents all people.

1 Would these people agree or disagree with this statement?

'We need to protect the habitats of our wildlife.'

Farmer | Building developer | Member of the national bird society

2 **WRITING** Work in pairs. You have been asked to find a *Hero of Our Times*. To do your research responsibly, who would you ask to choose the hero? Choose five people who are representative of the population and make a list of questions to ask them.

3 **SPEAKING** Work in pairs. How would the answers differ across the different people in your list? Discuss with your partner.

Pronunciation

Shifting word stress

Go to page 121.

12 UNSUNG HEROES

WANTED: Real-Life Heroes

We're looking for ordinary people who have made a difference – people who aren't in the public eye but who have changed the world around them for the better. Who do you think deserves to win our real-life hero trophy and £10,000 prize? Read about the first three nominees, and then let us know your views.

A

My candidate for the Real-Life Heroes competition is the Iraqi, **Nabeel Yasin**, who has made an enormous difference to the lives of young people in Iraq and elsewhere. Originally a poet and journalist, Yasin worked as the editor of a daily newspaper in Iraq. He was forced to leave his job by Saddam Hussein in 1976, though he continued to write in spite of the danger that this posed to his own life. After 1979, the lives of all opposition journalists in Iraq were in danger, and Nabeel Yasin helped many of them to escape to safety in neighbouring countries. He was the last to leave in 1980. Nabeel Yasin lived in exile for 27 years, but he continued to raise awareness of the plight of the Iraqi people through his poems and articles, which he published in international newspapers. In 2006, he returned to war-torn Iraq in what he called the 'Hope Tour'. The idea was simple – he wanted to unite communities again by bringing young people from diverse backgrounds together. He wanted to empower them by giving them the confidence and skills to become the leaders of the future. He chose to do this through a team sport, football. And soon, by playing football, young Iraqis from different social, religious and ethnic backgrounds were united and enjoyed a renewed sense of hope that their lives might return to normal. Nabeel Yasin and his son, Yamam Nabeel, set up a charity called FC Unity, which still operates today. The charity promotes the values of unity and tolerance, and since its foundation in London, it has created football-based education and development programmes in several countries around the world, among them Iraq, Sudan, Somalia and Ghana. It calls itself the biggest football team in the world.

keenongoodstories_X11

B

I'd like to nominate **Yvonne Bezerra** from my hometown, Rio de Janeiro. Rio is known for its beauty, vibrant street culture, sandy white beaches, deep-blue water and breath taking mountains. Unfortunately, there are also the *favelas*, or shanty-towns, that cover the steep hillsides on both sides of the city. Many of the inhabitants of these *favelas* are poor, with little opportunity to break the cycle of poverty within which they're caught. In the seventies, Yvonne Bezerra devoted her life to rescuing and changing the lives of children living in the shanty-towns of several countries, including Ethiopia, Sudan, Kenya, Tanzania and Angola. In the 1980s, she moved back to Rio de Janeiro and continued her work with children there. Then, in 1998, she founded the UERE Project, a school for street children living in the Mare, one of the biggest *favelas* in Rio. With a team of dedicated teachers and very little money or funding, she offers education, food, medical care and shelter to children who have been exposed to trauma and violence and some of whom have learning difficulties. She helps them overcome their trauma and integrates them back into the education system so that they'll have a better chance in life. At the school, the children have lessons in Portuguese, Maths, History, Geography, Science and Languages. Workshops in music, Brazilian dance, singing, violin and IT are also held there. By the time these children are 14, they'll have benefited from several years of good education. They'll even have started learning a foreign language, which will also serve them in their future careers. And they'll be receiving nutritious meals and free healthcare. Yvonne is my hero – I think she's doing a fantastic job!

adriana1279

C

My hero is **Saur Marlina Manurung**, an anthropologist who was born in Jakarta, Indonesia, in 1972. I've never met her, but I've read about her amazing work; online. Indonesia is an archipelago (a group of islands), with many tribal people living in remote forest areas. Manurung had a dream of bringing education to the Orang Rimba (Forest People) who lived in a national park in Central Sumatra, one of the main islands. Illiteracy was a huge problem for the Orang Rimba. They didn't understand the contracts they were signing, which resulted in the sale of their land. Nor could they participate in national debates about their future. So, after working as a lecturer at the University of Jakarta for several years, Manurung decided to move to the jungle and teach the forest people how to read and write. Since then, she's expanded her organisation into a network of 14 schools across ten provinces. The young people she taught in the past are now able to liaise between their community and the government, enabling the Orang Rimba to influence policies that affect them. She's given them a voice and changed their lives. And for women in particular, I believe she has a very important message: be yourselves and believe what your heart says.

a_rimba_sunshine

GRAMMAR
Future perfect; future continuous (review)

1. Read through the sentences from text B. Which are examples of the future continuous, and which are examples of the future perfect? Then complete the rule with *present participle* and *past participle*.

   1. By the time these children are 14, they**'ll have benefited from** several years of good education.
   2. They**'ll** even **have started** learning a foreign language, which will also serve them in their future careers.
   3. And they**'ll be receiving** nutritious meals and free healthcare.

   > **RULE:**
   > We use *will be* + ¹_____ to talk about actions that will be in progress at or around a time in the future.
   > We use *will have* + ²_____ to talk about actions that will be finished by a certain time in the future.

2. Complete the sentences using the future continuous or future perfect of the verbs in brackets.

   1. The project will help students who want to study abroad. By the time those students return to their home countries, they _____ important insights into other cultures. (gain)
   2. By the end of next year, 2,000 young people from all over the world _____ the chance to live abroad and they _____ new friends. (have / make)
   3. A week from today, we _____ our exams and we _____ for the results. (do / wait)
   4. **A** Do you think he _____ his new car by the time he comes to see you?
      B No, I think he _____ still _____ his old car. (buy / drive)

   Workbook page 108

VOCABULARY
Awards

1. Choose the correct options to complete the definitions.

   1. **nominate someone:** *show a preference for / officially suggest* someone for an honour, a position, a job or an election
   2. **put oneself/someone forward for something:** *suggest / search for* oneself/someone for other people to consider
   3. **vote for someone:** make your *choice / recommendation*, typically by marking a paper or by raising your hand in a meeting
   4. **elect someone:** *choose / reject* someone for an official position
   5. **campaign for something / someone:** organise a series of activities to try to *help / convince* people to do something or support someone
   6. **be in the running for something:** *have a chance of winning / be likely to lose* a competition
   7. **shortlist people:** select a(n) *increased / reduced* number of candidates for final consideration for something

2. Complete the sentences with the correct form of the words from Exercise 1.

   1. She's decided to *shortlist herself / put herself forward* for the position.
   2. Eric *is in the running / voted* for the award. He's one of three people with a chance of winning.
   3. My class are *nominating / campaigning* for Mr Silver to win the Teacher of the Year prize by handing out fliers.
   4. Claire's video has been *nominated / campaigned* for best animated film. I hope she wins!
   5. He's among the three people that have been *in the running / shortlisted*. He now stands a good chance of winning the prize.
   6. Who are you *voting for / electing* in the elections?
   7. Rebecca's class *elected / shortlisted* her as their spokesperson and she's done a great job so far.

   Workbook page 110

SPEAKING

1. Imagine your class is planning to give awards to the teachers at your school. What three awards do you think should be given? Make notes.

   most inspiring teacher
   best public speaker
   funniest teacher etc.

2. Work in pairs. Compare ideas and agree on just one award category together.

3. Share your idea for an award with the class. Hold a class vote and choose a winner for each award category.

12 UNSUNG HEROES

VOCABULARY
Success and failure

1 Match the sentence halves. Then write the expressions in italics in the table. Use the infinitive form of the verbs.

1 When it was announced that John would play the lead role in *Hamlet*,
2 Readers often feel inspired by people
3 Dede *is recognised as* one of the
4 They had great hopes for the project, but *their plans*
5 When he learnt about his illness, he wasn't
6 If you really want *to pursue your dreams*, you
7 It's ironic that he believed he was the best and
8 My team wasn't playing well, but they still

a his lifelong *ambition* of performing on stage *had been fulfilled*.
b then *failed* so *spectacularly*.
c mustn't waste any time and you have to study hard.
d *fell through* at the last minute.
e managed to *pull off* a last-minute *victory*.
f most talented singers in our country.
g prepared to *give up on his dreams*.
h who manage to *overcome adversity*.

Succeed	Fail	Neither
fulfil an ambition		

2 **SPEAKING** Work in groups. Think about these questions and note down your answers. Then compare your ideas with your classmates.

1 Would you rather pursue big dreams and risk failing spectacularly, or not dare to 'think big' at all?
2 Think of someone who has managed to overcome adversity. What adversity did they overcome? What did they achieve? What personal qualities helped them to succeed?
3 If you could pursue only one dream for your future, what would it be?

3 **WRITING** You've decided to pursue one of your dreams. Write a diary entry detailing your plans and how you feel. Include at least three expressions from Exercise 1.

Workbook page 110

LISTENING

1 ◻)) 2.31 You're going to listen to a presentation about the man in the photos. What do you think he's famous for? Listen and check.

2 ◻)) 2.31 Listen again. Complete each sentence with one or two words.

1 Stephen did very well at school and had wanted to study _____ at Cambridge University.
2 Stephen's father feared that he'd passed the _____ on to his son.
3 Stephen was shocked and saddened by his diagnosis, but decided not to _____ for himself.
4 Stephen came up with a _____ of 46 things to do while he still could.
5 Stephen wanted to write a book, have a go at _____ in front of lots of people, break a world record and see a football match live at Wembley.
6 Lots of people from all over the world supported Stephen's cause, including well known actors, sports people and _____.
7 Stephen's mother keeps his _____ updated.
8 A local band recorded a song, for which the inspiration was Stephen's _____ life.

113

READING

1 Read the article quickly. One of the writers says they aren't sure whether they thanked the person for what they had done for them. In which text? Who did they want to thank? Why?

I just wrote to say... THANK YOU!

In our special Saturday column we give our readers an opportunity to thank someone who's done something special for them. Someone who they never managed to say thank you to at the time. Send us your stories. If we choose yours, we'll send you a £30 book voucher.

I want to say thank you to my English teacher. I was 16, and I was going through a bit of a difficult phase in my life, so I hadn't been working very hard at school. I was convinced I'd failed my GCSE exams and that I wouldn't go back to school to do A-levels or go to university. I remember walking out of the school building on the last day of the summer term. I was sure I'd never ever set foot in there again. Then I turned around for the last time and I saw my English teacher. She asked me if I had a moment to talk to her. We talked for an hour. I told her everything – how I was feeling about life, and why I saw no point in coming back to school to do A-levels or go on to university. By the time we finished our conversation, I'd decided to go back to school and work harder. And that's what I did. I wouldn't be where I am now if it hadn't been for my English teacher. It was thanks to her that I changed my mind, and I'm eternally grateful for that.

This happened on my way home from school the other day. I got on the number 49 bus. It was full of people, and among them were two boys from Year 12. They kept laughing, and I was convinced it was me they were laughing at. And then it happened. I saw the ticket inspector getting onto the bus and I knew there was going to be trouble. But I didn't think that the person who was going to get into trouble was me. I couldn't find my ticket. The inspector told me to either pay the fare or get off the bus. What was worse was that I couldn't find my purse either. I went bright red. I was sure the two guys were going to make fun of me the next day. Then one of them took out a fiver from the pocket of his jeans and paid my fare. They got off the bus before I had time to thank them, so I'm doing it now.

I want to thank a woman I met on the train from Southampton to London a few years ago. I was travelling with my son and daughter. My son was only two years old, and my daughter had just turned four. She wasn't feeling too well – she had a bit of a cold and she was grumpy. I tried to calm her by reading to her. Suddenly, I noticed that my son, James, was having problems breathing, and then he started to choke on something. I panicked. I was sure he was going to die. I started screaming hysterically while slapping his back with one hand. 'You must have eaten something. What did you eat?' I screamed. 'Spit it out!' Then this young woman appeared. She told me later she was a nurse. She was very calm. She took James, and she did what she later called a 'Heimlich' manoeuvre. He choked again, and then a miracle happened – he spat out a sweet. I was so relieved. I don't know if I thanked that woman, but I want to thank her now. You saved my son's life! Thank you!

2 Read the stories again and answer the questions.

1 Why did the boy expect the school year to end badly for him?
2 How did his perspective on his future change after talking to his English teacher?
3 What was wrong with the daughter of the woman on the train?
4 What had her son eaten that caused him to choke?
5 What did the girl on the bus expect would happen the next day at school?
6 How and why did her feelings change in the end?

3 **ROLE PLAY** Work in pairs. Choose one of the stories. Role play a conversation between the writer and the person they want to thank.

12 UNSUNG HEROES

GRAMMAR
Future in the past

1 **Read the sentences from the article and then complete the rule.**

1 I was convinced that […] I **wouldn't** go back to school to do A-levels or go to university.
2 I panicked. I was sure he **was going to** die.
3 I was sure the two guys **were going to** make fun of me the next day.

> **RULE:** When we want to talk about the future as seen from the past, we use was/were ¹_____ or ²_____.
>
> When we talk about actions that were planned for the future but then our plans changed, we often use ³_____ / were or ⁴_____ / weren't going to …
> For example: *I was going to go out last night but I was too tired in the end.* We use was/were(n't) going to when a plan was definite.
>
> We use ⁵_____ or wouldn't when a plan was less likely to happen or when it was just a possibility or idea.

2 **Complete the sentences with the correct form of the verb in brackets. Use was / were going to or would to talk about the future in the past. Sometimes there's more than one correct answer.**

1 Last Friday, our teacher announced that the grammar test _____ probably _____ on Tuesday but that she hadn't decided yet. (be)
2 There _____ a match on Saturday. Then it rained and the match was cancelled. (be)
3 Mike just texted to say he thought he _____ to come to your party, unfortunately. (not be able)
4 You _____ Mark. Why didn't you? (meet)
5 I knew it was going to be cold, but I didn't think it _____. (snow)
6 I didn't expect any problems with the test, but I didn't realise it _____ so easy. (be)

3 **Rewrite the sentences using was/were going to or would.**

0 Martin planned to get home early, but then he had to stay late at work.
Martin was going to get home early, but then he had to stay late at work.

1 She didn't intend to leave the country, but then it became too dangerous to stay.
2 He had an idea to teach the children to read and write, but he hadn't really thought it through.
3 Their plan was to use football to give the boys more confidence, but then they decided to set up basketball teams instead.
4 She intended to set up a charity to promote the values of tolerance and unity, but so far she hasn't been able to do so.
5 They talked about offering free healthcare to children, but then it became clear that the government had other priorities.

> Workbook page 109

SPEAKING

1 **Work in pairs. Think about the last two weeks. What things were you going to do that you didn't do? Ask and answer questions and say why you didn't do them.**

I was going to study for the maths test.

Why didn't you?

I had too much work to do for English so I didn't have time. What about you?

I was going to have my hair cut.

Why didn't you?

I missed my appointment.

THiNK SELF-ESTEEM
Helping others

1 **Read the questions and note down your responses.**

1 Think of the people in the three situations on page 114. How did their helpers notice that they needed help?
2 Think of situations you've experienced in which someone needed help. How did you realise that help was needed and what did you do?
3 Have you ever witnessed a situation in which someone needed help but didn't get any? What happened?
4 Do you find it easy or difficult to ask other people for help? Why?

2 **SPEAKING** Work in small groups. Compare your answers. Who has the most interesting story? Who's witnessed the most heroic act? Has anyone in your group been a hero?

115

PHOTOSTORY: episode 4

Lost and found

1 Look at the photos and answer the questions.
  1 Where are Jack and Isabelle?
  2 What is Jack holding?
  3 What's inside it?

2 ◀)) 2.32 Now read and listen to the photostory. Check your ideas.

JACK I'm starving. Can we eat first? If the show's at eight, we've got about an hour. What do you fancy eating? Have you got anywhere in mind?

ISABELLE No, let's just get off near the venue. There are loads of good restaurants near there. There's a really good Thai restaurant and there's an Indian one just up the road. Or if you're not really into spicy food, there's a pretty decent Italian restaurant on the high street. The food's really good, the people who work there are really friendly too and it's cheap! What's not to like?

JACK OK, let's go there! I'm really looking forward to tonight.

ISABELLE Me too. It's going to be amazing. I haven't been to a good concert for ages, and I think this one … Hey Jack! Are you even listening to me? What are you doing?

JACK That's weird.

ISABELLE What's weird?

JACK There's something down the side of that seat. Look. It's an envelope.

ISABELLE There's something inside. Open it.

JACK I don't believe it. Look. It's full of money!

ISABELLE How much is there? Here, let me count it.

JACK It's OK. I've got it. Let's see. 160 … 180 … 200. There's two hundred pounds here.

ISABELLE How weird is that? There must be a name somewhere. Have a look.

JACK I already have. There isn't. Nothing inside and nothing written on the outside either.

ISABELLE So who do you think it belongs to?

JACK How should I know? Maybe it's someone's pay for the week and it just dropped out of their pocket.

ISABELLE But why was it pushed down the seat then?

JACK Your guess is as good as mine. Maybe it's been here for a few days and just got pushed further down.

ISABELLE But someone would have found it when they cleaned the bus, surely?

JACK Well, I've got no idea. It's a mystery. The question is, what are we going to do with it? I mean, we can't keep it, can we?

ISABELLE Of course not. It's not ours.

JACK But just think of the meal we could have.

ISABELLE What?

JACK I'm only joking. It is tempting, though.

ISABELLE Come on, Jack, we'd feel awful if we spent it. There's someone out there desperately looking for this and we've got to get it back to them.

JACK Yeah, but how?

12 UNSUNG HEROES

DEVELOPING SPEAKING

3 Work in pairs. Discuss what you think happens next in the story. Write down your ideas.
They lose the envelope.

4 ▶ EP4 Watch the video to find out how the story continues. Did you guess correctly?

5 Answer the questions.
1 Where do they take the money first?
2 What are they told to do with the money?
3 Why are they so delayed at the bus station?
4 What do they decide to do?
5 What does Jack discover at the end?

PHRASES FOR FLUENCY

1 Find these expressions in the story. Who says them? How do you say them in your language?

1 … do you fancy …?   4 How should I know?
2 What's not to like?   5 How [weird] is that?
3 … for ages.   6 The question is, …?

2 Use the expressions in Exercise 1 to complete the dialogues.

1 A Do you know where Steve is?
   B Sorry I haven't seen him _____ .
2 A Let's watch a film tonight.
   B OK. What _____ watching?
3 A I love those shoes.
   B Me too. They're comfortable and such a great colour! _____ ?
4 A *Bring Me the Horizon* is on TV tonight.
   B I know! _____ fantastic _____ ?
5 A We've missed the last bus.
   B That's right. So, _____ – how are we going to get home?
6 A Why did he do that?
   B _____ ? You'll have to ask him.

FUNCTIONS
Expressing anticipation

1 Which of these are said by a) Jack, b) Isabelle, c) Neither of them?

1 This time tomorrow, I'll be …
2 It's going to be amazing.
3 I'm so excited!
4 I'm really looking forward to …
5 I'm dying to …
6 It can't happen soon enough.

2 Work in pairs. Talk about some of the things you've got planned for the future that you're eager to do. Use the phrases above.

WordWise
Expressions with *in*

1 Complete these sentences from the unit so far with phrases from the list.

in the circumstances | in the public eye
in spite of | in no time | in particular | in mind

1 We're looking for ordinary people […] who aren't _____ .
2 He was a very active young person with a love of sport, _____ football, and long-distance running.
3 Have you got anywhere _____ ?
4 He continued to write _____ the danger that this posed to his own life.
5 You're right, of course. _____ , we have to take it to the police.
6 Let's get a taxi. Then we'll be there _____ .

2 Choose the correct options.

1 I usually hate standing in a queue, but in *particular / the circumstances*, I just had to be patient.
2 Not all famous people like being in *mind / the public eye*.
3 We got there on time in *spite of / the circumstances* the terrible traffic.
4 I want to go somewhere tonight, but I haven't got anywhere special in *particular / mind*.
5 I really love soft drinks, lemonade in *mind / particular*.
6 I'll have this work finished in *no time / spite of*, and then we can go out.

▶ Workbook page 111

WRITING

Write your own entry (150–200 words) for the newspaper column on page 114. It can be a true story or one you've made up. For example, you could imagine that you're the owner of the money that Isabelle and Jack found. Think about and make notes on who you want to thank and what they did for you.

117

CAMBRIDGE ENGLISH: ADVANCED

THiNK EXAMS

READING AND USE OF ENGLISH
Part 8: Multiple matching

Workbook page 115

You are going to read five people's opinions on modern art. For statements 1–10, choose from the people A–E. Each person may be chosen more than once.

Which person makes the following statements?

I have personal experience of how artists have developed their abilities.	1
There are things that people can do far better than machines can.	2
The value of a work of art is not only a question of the work itself but also of one's personal taste.	3
True art does not need to be explained.	4
Art will always reflect how people, in any period in history, live their lives.	5
The ordinary things that we see every day do not deserve to be called art.	6
There is no requirement for people to hold the same views about a work of art.	7
Art now is not as good as it was in the past.	8
The move towards less representational art is not difficult to explain.	9
If you look at a work of art and have neither positive nor negative feelings, then it is not art.	10

Person A
People have different ideas when it comes to defining 'art'. My personal opinion is that if something evokes a reaction in the person who sees or hears it, then it can be called 'art'. That said, there's the question of whether the viewer or listener likes it or not, and that's essentially subjective. Beauty is in the eye of the beholder, after all, and that's why I don't have the right to say that what they choose to like isn't 'art'. If you like it and I don't (or vice versa), then we simply disagree.

Person B
Most contemporary art is abstract, and I believe there's a simple reason for that. Since the invention of the camera, people are less and less inclined to devote hours of their time and talent to producing a realistic image, which can be done in a second at the push of a button. So art has evolved, necessarily, into something different from what it once was. To me, this is a positive thing – technology, after all, isn't so good at producing abstract images, whereas humans excel at it. Art today is a matter of interpretation, whether you like it or not.

Person C
Most of what is on display in galleries these days is simply not art. Art should reflect beauty and as such, represent the very best of human endeavour. Thus, it should strive to improve our lives and also to improve itself – to develop and become better. These days, what we are seeing is a progressive reduction in the quality of life and also of art. Art is something that should always provoke positive reactions in the human soul, and nowadays, the stresses and strains of life require more than ever that art should provide an enrichment of our experience, and be something remarkable and admirable. A pile of bricks does not do this.

Person D
Art changes with the times and that is necessarily a good thing. The things that people experience in their lives in the 21st century are distinctly different from what our ancestors experienced. Artists are people too and so the changing human experience will inevitably be reflected in art. Many critics of modern art state that it does not require technique to produce but I would dispute that. As an artist myself, I know that all my contemporaries have studied drawing, colour and so on. Now, whether or not they choose to apply those techniques in what they produce is a matter entirely for them.

Person E
I firmly believe that art has to represent something of value to human beings. Something cannot be called art unless it fulfils a number of criteria, and it is not art if it does not require talent and technique on the part of the artist, if it is merely intended to shock an audience, or if it needs some art critic or other to engage in lengthy justifications of its existence. When I look at the products of self-proclaimed artists such as Hirst or Emin, and hold those criteria in mind, then I, for one, am unable to term them art.

TEST YOURSELF

UNITS 11 & 12

VOCABULARY

1 **Complete the sentences with the words in the list. There are four extra words.**

nominate | failed | upgraded | through | vote | temper | put
head | uploaded | shortlist | out | steam | update | tongue

1 Don't take him too seriously. He's just letting off a bit of _____ .
2 I'd like to _____ my dad for the 'local hero' award.
3 You need to _____ your antivirus software to the latest version.
4 He likes to take the opposite view, but I just bite my _____ and ignore him.
5 His attempts to learn the guitar _____ spectacularly and he gave up after two lessons.
6 Be careful what you say. She loses her _____ very quickly.
7 Can you believe it? I got _____ to first class on the flight home.
8 I'd like to _____ myself forward for class president.
9 Do you think people over 16 should be able to _____ in the elections?
10 We wanted to go camping for the weekend, but our plans fell _____ at the last minute.

/10

GRAMMAR

2 **Complete the sentences with the words in the list. There are two extra words.**

can | were going to | will | has | must | have | had | would

1 We've _____ our house broken into three times now.
2 She normally _____ her hair cut by her mum. Her mum's a great hairdresser.
3 Most phones _____ be used as cameras too.
4 I think your cake _____ have been eaten by the dog. He's not looking too well now.
5 I've got the worst memory. By the next time we meet, I _____ have forgotten your name.
6 The ship set sail from England six weeks before it _____ finally arrive in Australia.

3 **Find and correct the mistake in each sentence.**

1 My dad dyes his hair at the barber's.
2 Police say the fire may caused deliberately.
3 The song got written by all of the members of the band.
4 They will be together 20 years in August.
5 They've just won the cup. Fans would be singing and dancing in the streets all night.
6 For a few scary moments, I thought I am going to die.

/12

FUNCTIONAL LANGUAGE

4 **Choose the correct options.**

1 A This *moment / time* tomorrow, we'll be on our way to France.
   B I *can't / must* wait.
2 A Take it *easy / simple*. It's not the end of the world.
   B Don't tell me to *cool / calm* down. I'm really angry about this.
3 A I'm *dying / living* to meet Anne's new boyfriend.
   B Me too. I'm really looking *ahead / forward* to it.
4 A Don't let him get under your *skin / head*. He's just not worth it.
   B I know – you're right. I don't know why I let him *bother / get* to me.

/8

MY SCORE /30

22 – 30
10 – 21
0 – 9

119

PRONUNCIATION

UNIT 1
Intonation: showing emotions

1 🔊 1.07 Listen to the speakers and decide if they are feeling angry (A), cheerful (C), disappointed (D), enthusiastic (E), puzzled (P) or sympathetic (S).

0 She can be mean to me, but she's still my sister. *C*
1 But you haven't got a ticket – how did you get in? ___
2 The homework was difficult, so I'll give you an extra week. ___
3 My cousin was going to phone but I still haven't heard from her. ___
4 I need to move out, Mum. I want to be independent! ___
5 I'm your best friend, Clara. Why didn't you tell me? ___

2 🔊 1.07 Listen, repeat and practise.

UNIT 2
Different ways of pronouncing c and g

1 Look at the sentences, paying attention to the pronunciation of the letters c and g in blue. Write the correct phoneme /k/, /s/, /ʃ/, /g/ or /dʒ/ after each word.

0 There is concern (/k/, /s/) that teenagers (/dʒ/) are not getting (/g/) sufficient (/ʃ/) sleep.
1 Girls (/___/) are especially (/___/) in danger (/___/) of not getting (/___/) the necessary (/___/) hours of sleep.
2 Experts agree (/___/) that sleep and exercise (/___/) are beneficial (/___/) for your health.
3 The causes /___/ of their anti-social /___/ sleeping habits are biological /___/, /___/.

2 🔊 1.10 Listen, check and repeat.

UNIT 3
Unstressed words in connected speech

1 🔊 1.15 Read and listen to the dialogue. What do you notice about the pronunciation of the words in blue?

JANE How did you meet your wife, Rob?
ROB It's a funny story. My sister crashed into her car.
JANE Really? If someone had crashed into my car, I don't think we'd be friends now.
ROB Well, my sister wanted to apologise; she asked me to go with her.
JANE And when you met Petra it was love at first sight!
ROB That's right. If it hadn't been for the accident, we wouldn't be married now!

2 What types of word are unstressed?

3 🔊 1.15 Listen, repeat and practise.

UNIT 4
Telling jokes: pacing, pausing and punchlines

1 🔊 1.21 Read and listen to the ending of Joke 1 from the listening on page 41. What does P indicate?

… After about 20 minutes, he returned from the kitchen and handed her a plate of scrambled eggs.
P She stared at the plate for a moment and said,
P 'I knew it. P You forgot my toast.'

2 🔊 1.21 Listen, repeat and practise. Can you tell a joke in English?

UNIT 5
Connected speech feature: elision

1 🔊 1.25 Read and listen to the sentences.
1 Cheered by thousands, he landed safely in an area full of cardboard boxes.
2 Gary has leapt from many tall buildings.
3 After the jump he said, 'I am just so relieved it's all over!'

2 Practise saying the linked words in blue.

UNIT 6
Modal stress and meaning

1 🔊 1.30 Read and listen to the sentences. One of the modal verbs in each pair of sentences is stressed and the other is not. Write S (stressed) and U (unstressed) in the boxes.

1 a I may watch the film tonight – I'll see how I feel. *S*
   b They may be rich and famous, but are they happy? ___
2 a I might go to the beach – but it looks like it could rain. ___
   b Kate might want to get a lift with us – it's a long walk to the beach. ___
3 a We could have a problem. We need to look into it. ___
   b My dad could solve most problems. ___

2 Circle the correct option to complete the rule.
We stress the modal verb (rather than the main verb which follows it) when we want to emphasise *certainty* / *uncertainty*.

3 🔊 1.30 Listen, repeat and practise.

PRONUNCIATION

UNIT 7
Connected speech feature: assimilation

1　🔊 2.05　Read and listen to the sentences closely. In the pairs of words highlighted in blue, the final sound of the first word changes. How does this sound change in each sentence?
  1　'London Bridge' is a really good book – everyone's reading it.
  2　The meditation class was full, so I'm doing yoga instead.
  3　Listen to this all-woman band – they're brilliant!
  4　We had sunshine on the day of our garden party.
  5　After the robbery she saw a green car speeding away from the bank.

2　Practise saying the linked words in blue.

UNIT 8
Stress in multi-syllable words

1　🔊 2.09　Read and listen to the sentences. Underline all of the words with four or more syllables and draw a circle above the stressed syllable in each word.
  0　The work of Chester Nez was fundamental to winning the Second World War.
  1　Navajo is spoken almost exclusively by the Navajos and it is difficult for others to learn.
  2　The men developed a form of Navajo that would be incomprehensible to anyone else.
  3　Their accuracy was such that not one single mistake was made in all their communications.
  4　Their enormously important contribution is yet to receive the public recognition it deserves.

2　🔊 2.09　Listen, repeat and practise.

UNIT 9
Unstressed syllables and words: the /ɪ/ phoneme

1　🔊 2.13　Read and listen to the sentences, paying attention to the words in blue. Can you hear the /ɪ/ phoneme? This is often used in unstressed syllables and words.
  0　Alex was sitting in the kitchen when he heard that his mother had been arrested.
  1　Of the three cases I think the worst miscarriage of justice is the first one.
  2　Imagine – she was convicted because of a bullet the police found in her pocket!
  3　Since they had no motive, they must have been sent to prison because of prejudice.

2　🔊 2.13　Underline the unstressed /ɪ/ phonemes in the words in blue. Then listen and check.

UNIT 10
Lexical and non-lexical fillers

1　🔊 2.20　Read and listen to the extracts from the listening on page 95, paying attention to the fillers, shown in blue.

It turns out he was right – huh … We spent time in eight different countries and saw, like, so many amazing things. Of course, it was expensive and uh … I had to like beg my dad to lend me the money.
Hmm … I never even considered going to university. I mean, I was always going to go straight out into the world and earn some money. My dad, uh … um … disapproved of my plans.

2　How can fillers help you when speaking?

3　🔊 2.20　Listen, repeat and practise.

UNIT 11
Intonation: mean what you say

1　🔊 2.27　Read and listen to the same sentence said in two different ways. Tick [✓] the sentence where the tone of voice is appropriate and cross [✗] the sentence where it is inappropriate.
  1　a　It's not a problem – don't worry about it, OK?
　　b　It's not a problem – don't worry about it, OK?
  2　a　Don't let him get under your skin – he didn't mean it.
　　b　Don't let him get under your skin – he didn't mean it.
  3　a　Calm down. Shouting won't do any good.
　　b　Calm down. Shouting won't do any good.

2　🔊 2.27　Listen, repeat and practise.

UNIT 12
Shifting word stress

1　🔊 2.30　Read and listen to the sentences, underlining the stressed syllable in each of the words in blue.
  0　a　In order to reach an informed conclusion about something, it's important to conduct research.
　　b　She planned to research the conduct of teenagers in the classroom.
  1　a　When giving a presentation, you must project your voice so everyone can hear you.
　　b　Jo's really excited about her science project.
  2　a　The author was happy to sign the new contract.
　　b　Children in poorer countries contract illnesses which could be prevented.
  3　a　We had to record our voices to practise our English pronunciation.
　　b　She broke a world record at the last Olympics.

2　Which syllable is stressed in the nouns? Which syllable is stressed in the verbs?

3　🔊 2.30　Listen, repeat and practise.

121

GET IT RIGHT!

UNIT 1
Habits in the present

> **Learners often incorrectly use *use(d) to* when talking about present habits.**
> ✓ At school, classmates **tend to** discuss the TV programmes which they watched the night before.
> ✓ At school, classmates **will** discuss the TV programmes which they watched the night before.
> ✗ At school, classmates ~~use to~~ discuss the TV programmes which they watched the night before.
> ✓ Kate **is always taking** my pen and not giving it me back!
> ✗ Kate ~~use to~~ take my pen and not giving it me back!

In all of the sentences, *use(d) to* is incorrectly used in order to talk about present habits. Rewrite the sentences using an appropriate form for talking about the present. Try to use a variety of different forms in your answers.

0 Teenagers use to behave quite rebelliously.
Teenagers tend to behave quite rebelliously.

1 People use to form close relationships with friends they have most in common with.

2 My older brother always used to tease me. It's so annoying!

3 My sister often gets on my nerves as she uses to borrow my clothes without asking.

4 Jenny says that her biology teacher always uses to pick on her. It makes her quite upset.

5 Annoyingly, my best friend uses to act rather self-centredly so we sometimes fall out.

6 Elderly people often use to have traditional values.

UNIT 2
would rather

> **Learners often make mistakes with *rather*, failing to use *would/'d* when talking about preferences, and using it unnecessarily in other structures.**
> ✓ They **would rather** watch videos than play football.
> ✗ They ~~rather~~ watch videos than play football.
> ✓ Many boys dream of becoming politicians, whereas girls **would rather** become journalists.
> ✗ Many boys dream of becoming politicians, whereas girls would rather ~~prefer to~~ become journalists.
> ✓ Do you know where I can have a coffee, or perhaps a beer?
> ✗ Do you know where I can have a coffee, or perhaps ~~rather~~ a beer?

All of the sentences contain errors with *rather*. Rewrite the sentences correctly.

0 Can we meet a bit later? I rather have a lie-in tomorrow morning if you don't mind.
Can we meet a bit later? I'd rather have a lie-in tomorrow morning if you don't mind.

1 Would you have a siesta now or go to bed early tonight?

2 Teenagers need more sleep rather than adults.

3 I rather I wasn't such a light sleeper. I tend to wake up several times during the night.

4 Tom's girlfriend has been complaining that Tom's tiredness has made him grumpy and forgetful. Tom would rather prefer not annoy his girlfriend so he's decided to get more sleep.

5 Some dreams have more meaning rather than others.

6 Kate would rather prefer to take a nap now than later.

GET IT RIGHT!

UNIT 3
Conditionals

> **Learners often use *would* in the *if*-clause when it's more accurate to use the past simple or past perfect.**
>
> ✓ *If I'd known*, I wouldn't have said anything.
> ✗ *If I would've known*, I wouldn't have said anything.

Tick the sentences which are correct and rewrite the incorrect ones.

1 If Jo hadn't been too ill to play, I might not have had the chance to get on the team. ☐
   _____

2 The car wouldn't have broken down if you would have had it serviced. ☐
   _____

3 We would be rich now if we would have won the lottery. ☐
   _____

4 If they didn't think I was capable of taking on the role, they wouldn't have asked me to step in. ☐
   _____

5 John really would have been pushing his luck if he would have asked Sam to help him. ☐
   _____

6 If the photographer wouldn't have photographed the heron he would have missed the woodpecker flying past. ☐
   _____

UNIT 4
Cleft sentences

> **Learners at this level often avoid using emphatic structures such as cleft sentences.**
>
> ✓ *It's often the unexpected that makes us laugh.*
> (*The unexpected often makes us laugh.*)
> ✓ *What makes us laugh is often the unexpected.*

Rewrite the sentences using *What ...*, *It's ... that ...* or *All ...* to add emphasis.

0 A sense of humour is simply the ability to see the funny side of things.
   All <u>*a sense of humour is, is the ability to see the funny side of things.*</u>

1 The misfortune of others often makes us laugh.
   What _____

2 The actions of just two members of the team have made us all a laughing stock.
   It's _____

3 Ollie laughed his head off when he saw his teacher playing air guitar to a rock song.
   What _____

4 They don't understand that we will have the last laugh.
   What _____

5 Simon only said that the show was hilarious.
   All _____

6 Many people enjoy watching funny videos on YouTube and it isn't a secret.
   It's _____

UNIT 5
Gerunds and participles

> **Learners often use a gerund when a past participle should be used and vice versa.**
>
> ✓ *Cooked* properly, Brussels sprouts can taste really nice.
> ✗ *Cooking* properly, Brussels sprouts can taste really nice.
> ✓ *Based* on their recent exam results, all the students will probably do well.
> ✗ *Basing* on their recent exam results, all the students will probably do well.
> ✓ *Talking* loudly, the students walked down the corridor.
> ✗ *Talked* loudly, the students walked down the corridor.

Choose the correct option.

1 *Jumping / Jumped* out of her chair, she said, 'Let's go!'
2 *Discovering / Discovered* in time, a lot of serious illnesses can be cured.
3 *Catching / Caught* outside in the thunderstorm, we ran for shelter under some trees.
4 *Seeing / Seen* from far away, the mountain path didn't look that long.
5 All this noise is making me *confusing / confused*.
6 The new stuntman is a real daredevil *comparing / compared* with the last one.

123

UNIT 6
Modals

> **Learners often confuse the different modals –** *may, might, can, could, will, won't.*
> ✓ I hope you **will** like it.
> ✗ I hope you ~~would~~ like it.
> ✓ You **won't** believe it when you see it.
> ✗ You ~~can't~~ believe it when you see it.

Correct the error and rewrite the sentences.

0 I will be grateful if you could help me tomorrow.
   I would be grateful if you could help me tomorrow.

1 If Jenny wears that outfit tonight she would be the centre of attention!

2 Although I am interested in reading about celebrities, I will not describe myself as obsessed.

3 When people suffer from Celebrity Worship Syndrome, they won't function properly in their normal lives.

4 You wouldn't find much difference between those two celebrities. They're both famous for doing very little!

5 I asked if she can help me stay out of the limelight at the party.

6 You will be an up-and-coming child actor, but you still have to do your homework!

UNIT 7
Substitution

> **Learners at this level often avoid using substitution with words such as** *so, neither, either, that, those, ones.* **This can make sentences sound repetitive.**
> ✓ People's idea of beauty is very different to **that of** 100 years ago.
> ✗ People's idea of beauty is very different to their idea of beauty 100 years ago.

Rewrite the sentences using substitution.

0 Fiona is going to buy some new trainers this weekend. She's going to buy the trainers she saw on sale. (ones)
   Fiona is going to buy some new trainers this weekend. She's going to buy the ones she saw on sale.

1 Some people find these kinds of activities fun, but I'm not someone who finds these activities fun. (those)

2 The survey revealed that none of the students exercised more than twice a week and the teachers didn't exercise more than twice a week. (neither)

3 It brings a smile to my face when I see the delight on a baby's face or on a child's face when they eat chocolate for the first time. (that)

4 I get shivers down my spine when I watch a horror film and Becca gets shivers down her spine too. (so)

5 Tom doesn't agree with people having plastic surgery for cosmetic reasons and also Sally doesn't agree with people having plastic surgery. (either)

6 A Do you think I'll lose weight if I take up running?
   B Yes I think you'll lose weight if you taking up running. (so)

UNIT 8
Relative pronouns with determiners

> **Learners often confuse the different relative pronouns;** *who, whom* **and** *which.*
> ✓ I'm the one **who** would be the best person to do that.
> ✗ I'm the one ~~whom~~ would be the best person to do that.

Rewrite the sentences correctly using *who, whom* **or** *which.*

0 There were about 100 people at the conference, many of who came from Russia.
   There were about 100 people at the conference, many of whom came from Russia.

1 He spoke in broken English, most of who I was unable to understand.

2 As well as speech, people communicate with gestures and facial expressions, both of what can greatly aid understanding.

3 My grandad spoke a northern dialect compared to whom standard English might seem like a different language!

4 I met several people at the party, one of which was the most conceited person I've ever met!

5 Mandy might have brought her hairdryer with her, in what case I'll borrow it from her.

6 Oliver has had many jobs, but interpreting for the United Nations was the job to whom he dedicated himself the most.

UNIT 9
Negative inversion

> Learners at this level often avoid using negative inversion or use it incorrectly. Typical learner mistakes relate to word order or the omission of the auxiliary after a negative or restricting adverb.
>
> ✓ *Never have I* heard such rubbish!
> ✗ *Never I have* heard such rubbish!
> ✓ *Little does she* know he's not who he says he is.
> ✗ *Little she knows* he's not who he says he is.

Rewrite the sentences beginning with the negative or restricting adverb given, paying attention to word order and including any necessary auxiliaries.

0 The members of the jury had never heard such a story before.
   Never *before had the jury heard such a story.*

1 The defence lawyer didn't realise that her client would be found guilty.
   Little

2 The witness gave false evidence, but also committed the crime himself!
   Not only

3 People don't often think it's fair to be able to pay to jump a queue.
   Rarely

4 The children are absolutely forbidden to go in there – it's where I'm keeping all their Christmas presents.
   Under

5 The thief made a full confession and then immediately retracted it.
   No

6 The witnesses did not withhold evidence – that did not happen!
   On

UNIT 10
Reporting verbs

> Learners often use the wrong preposition, omit the preposition, or make mistakes with verb patterns after reporting verbs.
>
> ✓ He accused me **of** cheating in the exam.
> ✗ He accused me ~~for~~ cheating in the exam.
> ✓ They decided **to go** to the beach.
> ✗ They decided ~~going~~ to the beach.

Rewrite these incorrect sentences correctly.

0 I need to congratulate Emma for the great presentation she did in class today.
   I need to congratulate Emma on the great presentation she did in class today.

1 The politician denied to have promised a reduction in student fees.

2 In the end, the government agreed for a change in the school curriculum.

3 Chloe invited Georgina for the wedding.

4 The researcher confessed altering the test results in order to show a better outcome.

5 Helen suggested me that we go ice skating.

6 My dad insisted to pick me up after the party.

UNIT 11
Passive with *get*

> **Learners often use *get* in passives, using it with stative verbs or adjectives where *be* should actually be used.**
> ✓ The baby **was** very loved by its parents.
> ✗ The baby ~~got~~ very loved by its parents.

Tick the correct sentences and rewrite the incorrect ones.

0 Tom gets thought to have a bit of a temper, but he's actually quite calm.
   Tom is thought to have a bit of a temper, but he's actually quite calm.

1 Jim got knocked over by a cyclist the other day.

2 The fence got broken by a motorist who crashed his car.

3 Which road user gets more liked – the cyclist or the motorist?

4 After a week at the sports camp, I'm sure we'll get exhausted by all this exercise.

5 Mrs Summers got disappointed with her son. He had promised to give her a lift to the station, but he didn't turn up.

6 The film got enjoyed by all who watched it.

UNIT 12
Future in the past

> **Learners often make errors when referring to the future from a past perspective, using *will* instead of *would* or *is/are going to* instead of *was/were*.**
> ✓ I thought I **would** be sick.
> ✗ I thought I ~~will~~ be sick.
> ✓ Everyone believed he **was** going to leave school, but he didn't.
> ✗ Everyone believed he ~~is~~ going to leave school, but he didn't.

Tick the correct sentences and rewrite the incorrect ones.

1 Jack and Chloe are going to eat at the Italian restaurant, but they changed their minds and went to the Chinese instead.

2 You said there would be plenty of legroom, but there wasn't.

3 He is going to leave school, but not until he's taken his exams.

4 Sally and Jim are going to go on a round-the-world trip, but their plans fell through when Sally's father fell ill.

5 If I'd known I am going to fail so spectacularly, I wouldn't have bothered trying!

6 Did Mike really think that I will invite him to my party?

126

STUDENT A

UNIT 5, PAGE 51

Student A

Think of reasons to agree with the following statements.

Make notes and then discuss in pairs. Finally, talk about your real opinions.

- A doctor who treats a patient suffering from a life-threatening virus is taking a greater risk than the world's most audacious stuntman.
- Before someone engages in any kind of death-defying action, they should have to prove to a panel of experts that they've assessed the risk.

UNIT 5, PAGE 53

Student A

You believe the following …

Base jumpers are irresponsible and their 'sport' should be banned.

Extreme scuba diving looks like the most amazing sport. You'd love to try it.

Tightrope walking isn't fun; it's ridiculously dangerous.

Try to convince your partner.

UNIT 10, PAGE 94

Student A

Which should your government invest in – more teachers, more sports facilities, better-equipped science labs or after-school clubs?

You think that the government should invest in more teachers. Students B, C and D disagree with you. You must try to convince them.

Student C

Which should your government invest in – more teachers, more sports facilities, better-equipped science labs or after-school clubs?

You think the government should invest in better-equipped science labs. Students A, B and D disagree with you. You must try to convince them.

UNIT 10, PAGE 97

Student A

Tell your partner about the following news, item by item. Also react to their news.

School Summer Holidays to be Scrapped

Compulsory One Term Work Experience to be Introduced for all Sixteen Year Olds

New Minister for Education Says 'No More Homework'

A — *The government is going to increase spending on education.*

B — *I'm glad to hear it. That's the best news I've heard in ages. Schools really don't have enough money.*

UNIT 11, PAGE 104

Choose a situation. Imagine you feel extremely angry about it. Think about how you would explain the situation and how you feel to your partner. Make notes.

1. You lent something to a friend three weeks ago and they still haven't given it back.
2. Someone said something unkind about the clothes you're wearing.

Work in pairs. Take turns to tell your partner about your situation. Your partner should try to keep you calm.

STUDENT B

UNIT 5, PAGE 51

Student B

Think of reasons to disagree with the statements.

Make notes and then discuss in pairs. Finally, talk about your real opinions.

- A doctor who treats a patient suffering from a life-threatening virus is taking a greater risk than the world's most audacious stuntman.
- Before someone engages in any kind of death-defying action, they should have to prove to a panel of experts that they've assessed the risk.

UNIT 5, PAGE 53

Student B

You believe the following …

Base jumping looks amazing and you'd love to try it. Base jumpers take risks but they know what they're doing.

Extreme scuba diving looks terrifying. The risk of being trapped underwater or running out of oxygen is very real.

Tightrope walking looks like so much fun; it must be exhilarating to do it.

Try to convince your partner.

UNIT 10, PAGE 94

Student B

Which should your government invest in – more teachers, more sports facilities, better-equipped science labs or after-school clubs?

You think the government should invest in more sports facilities. Students A, C and D disagree with you. You must try to convince them.

Student D

Which should your government invest in – more teachers, more sports facilities, better-equipped science labs or after-school clubs?

You think the government should invest in after-school clubs. Students A, B and C disagree with you. You must try to convince them.

UNIT 10, PAGE 97

Student B

Tell your partner about the following news, item by item. Also react to their news.

School Day to be Extended by Half an Hour
Government to Increase Spending on Education
Government Bans Mobile Phones From School Grounds

A — *I agree. And I've also heard that they plan to extend the school day by an extra hour.*

B — *They've got to be joking! We're already spending too much time at school.*

UNIT 11, PAGE 104

Choose a situation. Imagine you feel extremely angry about it. Think about how you would explain the situation and how you feel to your partner. Make notes.

1. You got a poor mark for some homework and you think it deserved a better grade.
2. Your favourite team lost a very important match because they played really badly.

Work in pairs. Take turns to tell your partner about your situation. Your partner should try to keep you calm.